YOUR

A Weekly

FAMILY TIME

Plan For

WITH GOD

Family Devotions

YOUR
A Weekly
FAMILY TIME
Plan For
WITH GOD
Family Devotions

JOHN MAXWELL
WITH
BRAD LEWIS

Christian Parenting BOOKS

Christian Parenting Books is an imprint of Chariot Family Publishing
Cook Communications Ministries, Elgin, Illinois 60120
Cook Communications Ministries, Paris, Ontario
Kingsway Communications, Eastbourne, England

YOUR FAMILY TIME WITH GOD
© 1995 by INJOY, Inc.

ISBN 0-7814-0240-9

All scripture quotations are taken from *The Living Bible* © 1971, owned by
assignment by the Illinois Regional Bank N.A. (as trustee). Used by permission of Tyndale House
Publishers Inc., Wheaton, IL 60189. All rights reserved.

Cover design by Joe Ragont
First printing, 1995
Printed in the United States of America
99 98 97 96 95   5 4 3 2 1

All Scripture quotations are taken from *The Living Bible* © 1971, owned by assignment by the
Illinois Regional Bank N.A. (as trustee). Used by permission of Tyndale House Publishers Inc.,
Wheaton, IL 60189. All rights reserved.

This book belongs to

_____

*The date we began
our Family Time
with God*

_____

TABLE OF CONTENTS

FOREWORD

John Maxwell is well known for training leaders in the church. Now he is teaming up with Brad Lewis of *Christian Parenting Today* in this book which offers spiritual leadership training in the home.

You probably agree on the importance of spiritual training in the home, but like many others you wonder how to truly carry it out with your own family. This resource may be the answer.

As the host of a nationally syndicated radio program helping parents, I hear from many who want to raise their children with Christian values, but lack the practical tools to make it happen. Training children in the way they should go spiritually is much easier said than done.

That's why I'm glad to recommend such a practical devotional book as *Your Family Time with God.* Few devotional resources offer both the motivation and action-oriented steps that this book does.

There has never been a better time than now for this book. It is filled with fun and helpful exercises to make your family devotions come alive for an entire year. I especially like the "one hour/one-a-week" approach, which liberates busy families to have a meaningful devotional time with ongoing discussions and reinforcement throughout the week.

So, use this book to gather your family together once a week for a rewarding time of Bible study, discussion and time with God. You'll find it's like having John Maxwell himself visiting your home for a unique time of meaningful devotions. Each weekly lesson centers around one of fifty-two spiritual values that lay a solid faith-building foundation for your family, such as holiness, joy, kindness, love, servanthood, and worship.

The wisdom and inspiration John Maxwell gives to Christian leaders throughout the country he now imparts to you as the spiritual leader of your family. After all, the best place to train leaders is in the home, while they are young.

You'll use this book from week to week as you apply the lessons to improve your family time with God. I'm confident your children's character will be given the kind of nourishment you've been searching for.

Randy Carlson, M.A.
Author and host of "PARENT TALK" radio program
President of TODAY'S FAMILY LIFE
Executive Vice President of the FAMILY LIFE RADIO NETWORK

HOW TO USE
YOUR FAMILY TIME WITH GOD

The year 2000 is rapidly approaching, and in spite of all our modern technology and conveniences, families seem to have less time to spend together. Getting families together with the purpose of spending time with God is even more difficult.

This book is meant to help you accomplish that simple but important goal. It is designed to enable you to spend meaningful time each week focusing on a subject that will draw you and your children closer to God and one another. Every week of the year you will be able to focus on an exciting new topic. They're easy to follow, and the discussion can even be led by some of your older children.

Scripture is an important part of each lesson. Each one has a **memory verse** taken from *The Living Bible* so that children can understand it easily. And the discussion always encourages family members to apply the verse to their lives and situations in a practical ways. Each week's **Family Devotion Time** concludes with **a directed prayer time** that further reinforces understanding of the concepts.

Also included in each lesson is a **Family Worship** section which offers a more in-depth learning and prayer time for parents and older children. This section will take you to a new level of understanding, and it can be done individually, with your spouse, or with the older kids.

Finally, each week's lesson concludes with **Family Time Throughout the Week,** suggestions for the following four days of the week. You can do them when the family is together for a meal, or you can save them for one-on-one times like bedtime or while driving your child to practice in the car.

Here are a few tips to help you make the most of the time with your family:

• Doing devotions together as a family won't be easy. You will have to set aside and schedule time for it in your busy schedule. Some of your children may resist the idea, but don't give in or give up. It will require commitment to stick with it each week. But remember, it will pay dividends in the lives of your children.

• The lessons are designed to take place on Mondays, with the **Family Time Throughout the Week** designed for Tuesday through Friday. If you find it easier to start on another day, simply adjust the following day's activities.

• *Your Family Time with God* has been designed to help make devotions easier for you. There are a number of ways you can approach doing them. You can work your way through the book from front to back, you can choose topics according to family need, or you can let family members choose the subject for the following week, In our home, my wife, our teenage children and I take turns choosing and leading the lessons. If your children are old enough, you may want to do this too.

• Although the activities are fairly simple, you will want to review them in advance. Some require a little preparation. Others don't require any.

• The discussion questions are designed to get your family to communicate. For some families, having an open discussion will be a new experience. If family members are reluctant to talk at first, don't give up. Be encouraging to them. Make your family devotion a safe environment, a time when everyone is allowed to speak his mind without fear of ridicule or reprisal.

• Scripture verses have been included from *The Living Bible* paraphrase, but you may want to use your own Bibles instead.

And you may want your children to memorize from a version such as *The New International Version* or *The New American Standard Bible*.

• Memorization of verses can be done many ways. Breaking verses into phrases and memorizing them a phrase at a time is probably the simplest. Another method involves memorizing key words and then filling in the words between them. Whatever you do, don't skip the memorization of verses. You may be tempted to think memorization is too difficult for children, but they will surprise you. Often they are better memorizers than adults.

• Finally, I want to encourage you and your family to write down notes and observations from your family devotion time. Keeping a family notebook can become a wonderful family tradition, and reading notes together from earlier years can be very entertaining. If your children are older, each family member may desire to keep his own journal or notebook. The choice is yours.

My prayer is that God will richly bless you and your family in the coming year, and that this would be the first of many years that you grow and learn about God together.

WEEK 1: ATTITUDE

Family Devotion Time

ACTIVITY: BALONEY GUESSING GAME. Bring a package of bologna to your family's time together. If you have time beforehand, make finger sandwiches from the bologna to eat while you have your discussion. Ask family members what they think bologna is made of. Make a list. Encourage them to eat a sandwich and guess what the mystery meat might contain. Keep a list, and when everyone has finished guessing, summarize how your family would make bologna if they owned a meatpacking plant! Now, take out the real package and read the ingredients from the label. Ask family members if they know where each of the contents are from. This might be easy with turkey and pork, but a bit more difficult when it comes to ingredients like dextrose or sodium erythorbate!

> **Attitude:** *When what you feel inside shows outside too.*

DISCUSSION: While you clean up the bologna sandwiches (if anyone is still hungry), discuss these questions. Remember that you don't have to get or provide all the correct answers. More important, get your family to talk—about baloney, and about how we can all have an improved and godly attitude.

- Now that we know what's in bologna, do you think it's a good thing to eat?
- Is what we eat important? Why?
- Do you think it's just as important that we put good ingredients inside our minds and thoughts?
- What are ways we can put good thoughts in our minds?
- How can bad things in our minds make us feel?
- If we fill our minds with good things, how can that help

how we feel about things? How can it help us to be better people?

Sometimes, people might say we're "full of baloney" about our attitudes and feelings. Have you heard that before? Now that you know what's in bologna, you have a good idea of what "full of baloney" means. God wants our attitude to look like His character. He wants others to see His attitude in us. But we have to choose the things of God, not baloney. We have a choice, just like *this week's memory verse* says:

"Your attitude should be the kind that was shown us by Jesus Christ." —Philippians 2:5

FAMILY BIBLE TIME: Read Luke 15:8-32. As you near the end of this familiar parable, try to listen in a different way. Examine the bad attitudes of the prodigal son's older brother.

This brother seemed to think he could be in the place and privilege of a son while refusing the obligations of a brother. His outward actions were correct—he was conscientious, industrious and dutiful. But what about his attitude? Did his attitude toward his brother affect his relationship with his father (Luke 15:28)?

The older brother was willing to serve his father faithfully, yet he wasn't in fellowship with him. The older brother had no idea why the father would rejoice over his younger son's return.

The brother who had faithfully served his father was heir to all that his father possessed, yet he experienced less joy than those around him who had nothing. The servants were happier than this older son. They ate, laughed and danced while he stood outside demanding his rights.

A wrong attitude kept the older brother away from the heart's desire of the father, the love of his brother, and the joy of the servants. Wrong attitudes in our lives will block the blessings of God and cause us to love below God's potential for our lives.

FAMILY PRAYER TIME: Together as a family pray about your attitudes. Pray about the "baloney" you need to take out of your minds so that your attitudes can be godly. Have family members use short phrases to finish these sentences in prayer to God. Don't be afraid to have a bit of silent time to let family members think through what they want to say out loud:

"God, help me look at my attitude today. I know that this

'baloney' in my mind sometimes makes me have a bad attitude."
(Use words or short phrases to describe what feelings we have
inside that give us a bad attitude. Help your family get started by
listing words like selfishness, thoughts that aren't pure, anger,
hate and so on).

"God, also help me to fill my mind with good things to
replace the baloney. Help me to have a good and godly attitude.
Put in my mind . . ." (Use words or short phrases to describe the
godly attitude we desire. Help your family get started by listing
words like love for others, joy in any situation, peace about
troubling things, patience with others, and so on. The fruits of
the Spirit in Galatians 5:22 are good qualities that describe a
godly attitude.)

Family Worship Time (optional)

Spend some time going through the following steps. If you
don't make it all the way through at one time, that's OK. Come
back and finish when you can. Make it a goal to work all the way
through the steps, in spite of interruptions.

PREPARATION TIME: Think about areas where your attitudes
could use some improvement. You might even list these in a
notebook. Ask God to help you to be honest with yourselves,
and to bring to each of your mind's areas where you might be
"full of baloney."

WAITING TIME: Think about the story of the prodigal son.
Try to imagine how the father could love both the older brother,
who had served him for many years, and the prodigal, who had
foolishly left the father's security.

During your waiting time, let God love you, search you and
show you His desires when it comes to your attitudes. Ask Him
to reveal phrases that complete these simple prayers:

"God, I feel Your love today, especially in the area of . . ."

"God, You have my permission to reveal any rotten attitudes
in my life . . ."

"God, as I enter this day, is there anything about my attitude
that I need to know. . . ?"

CONFESSION TIME: When our attitude begins to erode, we should remember two things that the father explained to the older brother:

1. Our privilege: "My child, you have always been with me."
2. Our possessions: "All that is mine is yours."

Confess your ingratitude to God. Think about what He has provided you in the areas of both privilege and possessions. It's hard to admit that you haven't been thankful, but remember that God isn't surprised at what we think or do. So be honest. List what you have from God, and promise Him now that you will do your best to thank Him—and have a better attitude about what you have!

BIBLE TIME: When we pray God's Word back to Him, we can be certain that we are praying for His will in our lives. Read Philippians 2:3-8 slowly several times. These verses talk about the attitudes we should possess as Christians. After reading, have your family close their eyes and ask God to reveal a main truth to each of you about your attitudes.

Now, pray this Scripture back to God and allow Him to minister to you. Your prayer might go something like this: "God, help me to act selflessly, especially when I'm tempted to be boastful just to impress other people. Make me humble. It's hard to put other people before me—sometimes hardest of all is putting the people closest to me before myself. But I know that's what You want and expect of me. Help me to take on even a part of Christ's attitude. Help me not to be demanding or self-righteous. Help me to put aside my pride and any other negative qualities that make up my 'bad' attitude. Put Your good and godly qualities inside me. While I can never pay the kind of penalty You did for others, and while I can never repay You, I can humble myself every day, and do my best to serve You as I serve and love others around me. In Jesus' name, Amen."

MEDITATION TIME: After praying, write down in a notebook any thoughts that God impressed upon any of you about your attitudes. Think for a while about how a godly attitude and being humble are related. Can you have the kind of attitude God wants you to have if you're not willing to be humble?

INTERCESSION TIME—PRAYING FOR OTHERS: Think about areas where your family struggles with their attitudes. Chances are that the people you want to pray for struggle in many of the same ways. Ask God to bring to mind people who need your prayers concerning their attitudes. Pray that God will reveal to them how their attitudes need to be changed. Pray that they will honestly desire a change of attitude.

PETITION TIME—PRAYING FOR YOURSELVES: Now spend a few minutes talking to God about the areas where your family is struggling concerning your attitudes. Recall the areas you thought of during the preparation time. Be honest with God about why you want to change in these areas. Now invite God to work on those areas of your life. Consider making a list so that during the next week you can see how God is working in your life to change you.

APPLICATION TIME: List in a notebook what steps your family can take toward obeying God more fully this week when it comes to your attitude. Beside each step, note how your obedience can improve your attitude so that you can fully know God's will. Since obedience is an action, use strong action words and "I will" statements. For example, if you answered the first question with a statement like "God wants me to not judge others so quickly," your action steps might include statements like: "I will listen to people more carefully." "I will refuse to 'read between the lines' of what others are saying." "I will hold my tongue and not criticize other people's opinions."

FAITH TIME: Faith is our positive response to what God has said. Spend a few moments praying together, telling God the positive things you see happening because of His goodness. Let God know that you have faith in His power to change your attitudes to ones that will bring honor to Him and that will help you in your service to Him.

PRAISE AND THANKSGIVING TIME: Reread the story of the prodigal son. This parable says a lot about who God is and what He does for us. Now praise God by recognizing who He is—a Father who loves us as we are. And thank God by recognizing what He has done—provided us with many privileges and possessions we don't deserve.

Family Time Throughout the Week

MONDAY—Do the Family Devotion Time. If you can, work together on the Family Worship section.

TUESDAY—Keep plugging away on the Family Worship section. As a family, talk about the kind of attitudes you want to have. Are the attitudes you talk about godly or not? Pray for each other, that you will have attitudes that God can use for His work. Commit to praying for each other through the rest of the week.

WEDNESDAY—Finish the Family Worship section. If possible, talk with family members individually about a problem each one is having right now. Talk about different ways that person might react to the problem. Are the actions negative or positive? Now, here's the challenge: Try to discover at least three possible benefits from this problem. Ask each person to answer these questions: "If I see this problem as a way to learn, how can it help me one year from now? How can it help me next week?" Now, encourage each person to attack the problem with his eyes on the benefits, not the barriers.

THURSDAY—For one week, agree with your other family members to treat the people you talk to as the most important people on earth. This won't be easy. It will take extra time. But you will all notice something different about your own attitude toward others. Another benefit: you'll find that others will begin treating you the same way!

FRIDAY—Our attitude doesn't remain stagnant. Think and talk about these object lessons together (or better yet, use one of them as an object lesson): A balloon half blown up is full of air but is not filled to capacity. A rubber band pulls the object it holds together and is effective only when stretched. Now talk about the troubles you are facing that demand the stretching of your attitude. How are different family members adjusting? Talk about what problem or trouble you might face next. Now, think through how you can avoid a bad attitude regarding that situation.

WEEK 2: BECOMING HOLY

Family Devotion Time

ACTIVITY: PAPER BAG MASKS. Give each family member a paper grocery bag with as little printing on it as possible. Cut out holes for eyes, nose and mouth, helping younger kids if necessary. Using markers or crayons, each person draws a face on the paper bag. Suggest different kinds of "moods" or "emotions" family members might want to draw, such as frightened, frightening,

> ***Becoming Holy****
> *means that when
> others look at us they
> see God too.*

surprised, angry, mean. Complete the following discussion while wearing your masks—if some laughter is mixed in with your "serious" discussion, don't worry. Your goal is for your kids to catch a *glimpse* of what it means to become holy.

DISCUSSION: As a family, discuss these questions. Your goal isn't either to get or to provide all the right answers. More important, get your family to talk about holiness and how we can be holy.

• How is the face on the outside of the mask different from the person inside the bag?

• How is the face on the mask *like* the person in the bag?

• If God is inside you, how do you think other people can see Him when they look at you?

• The goodness inside us is when God is inside us. How can you get rid of the things you don't want people to see, and put in things that you do want them to see?

• What kinds of things inside you would you like to get rid of—what kinds of feelings or thoughts do you think are "bad"?

• What kinds of things that God gives us would you like to

have inside you—what kinds of feelings and thoughts are "good"?

We can't really be holy on our own. But we can choose to allow God to put good things inside us. Only God can make us holy. We just have to choose to let Him. We make that choice when we accept that Jesus Christ died for our sins—to make us holy—and ask Jesus to be our personal Savior. *This week's memory verse* acknowledges that only God makes us holy:

"God . . . decided then to make us holy in his eyes, without a single fault." —Ephesians 1:4

FAMILY BIBLE TIME: Read through 2 Peter 1:2, 3, 5, 6. It's important to remember these facts about holiness:
- Just like salvation, becoming holy is accomplished by faith.
- God gives us holiness, we can't just try to "be" holy.
- Holiness comes as we allow God to paint the picture inside us of who we are: The righteousness of God in Christ.

FAMILY PRAYER TIME: Together as a family pray about letting God be inside us, to make us holy, and to let others around us see that. Have family members finish these sentences in prayer to God:

"God, today I want You to take these bad things out of my life." (Use words or short phrases to describe things in your lives that may not be pleasing to God.)

"God, today I really want You to put Your holiness in my life by putting these good things in my life." (Help your family by listing words like honesty, kindness, love, cheerfulness.)

Family Worship Time (optional)

Holiness is a quality inside us that we can feel when we take a gift that God has promised. He has promised to give each of us a new identity. If we accept that gift, and live by faith, the new identity inside us will change our outward behavior. We will live out what is inside us.

Spend some time going through the following steps together. If you have interruptions, that's OK. It happens in families. Come back and pick up where you left off.

PREPARATION TIME: Read through 2 Peter 1:2, 3, 5, 6 again, and then ask yourselves:

In what areas are we missing out on experiencing God's holiness in our lives?

How can we know God better so that we can know more of His holiness?

Now think about your personal lives, your family life, your church life and your business life. Where are any of you not experiencing holiness?

WAITING TIME: During your waiting time, let God love you, search you and show each of you His desires in your lives in the area of becoming holy. Ask Him to reveal to you phrases that complete these simple prayers:

"God, I feel Your love today, especially in the area of . . ."

"God, You have permission to reveal any unclean, unholy areas in my life . . ."

"God, what truth from Your Word do I need to embrace as I pursue holiness. . . ?"

CONFESSION TIME: "Obey God because you are his children; don't slip back into your old ways—doing evil because you knew no better. But be holy now in everything you do, just as the Lord is holy, who invited you to be his child. He himself has said, 'You must be holy, for I am holy.'" —1 Peter 1:14-16

Together or individually confess to God areas where you've turned away from His holiness because you're not obeying Him.

BIBLE TIME: We can never pray out of God's will when we pray God's Word. Read the passage above slowly a few times, then close your eyes and ask God to allow a main truth to surface in each of your hearts. Now pray the Scripture back to God and allow Him to minister to your family. Your prayer might go something like this: "God, help us to obey You because You are our Father and we are Your children. Help us not to slip back into the ways we used to live before we knew You. We know what is good and bad, and if we don't, please reveal it to us. Help us to be holy in everything we do. Help others to see Your holiness inside of us—without the masks! You are holy, and because we are Your children, we want to live a life of holiness too. Thank You for helping us to live a holy life each and every day. Amen."

MEDITATION TIME: After praying the Scriptures, write down in a notebook the thoughts that God has impressed upon your minds. How are obedience and holiness related? Why do parents want children to obey them? Why do you think God wants us to obey Him?

INTERCESSION TIME—PRAYING FOR OTHERS: Ask God to bring to your mind people who might also need to know and experience God's holiness in their lives. Don't forget about the other members of your family too. Pray that God will reveal His holiness to them, and that they will honestly want to become holy.

PETITION TIME—PRAYING FOR YOURSELVES: Now, pray that God will continue to reveal His holiness to each of you, and pray that you will desire the holy things of God in your life. Ask God to paint a picture inside each of you of what your righteous life in Christ is to look like. Ask Him to bring that about in your life—so much that others begin to see it from the outside.

APPLICATION TIME: List in a notebook what steps your family can take toward obeying God more fully this week. Beside each step, note how being obedient can help you replace unholy things in your life with the holy things of God.

FAITH TIME: Faith is our *positive* response to what God has said. Spend a few moments praying through your eyes of faith. Tell God the positive things you see happening in your family because of His goodness!

PRAISE AND THANKSGIVING TIME: Read 2 Peter 1:4. Then praise God by recognizing who He is—a powerful God. Thank Him by recognizing what He has done—provider of blessings, savior from evil, and giver of character.

Family Time Throughout the Week

MONDAY—Do the Family Devotion Time. If possible, get a start on the Family Worship section.

TUESDAY—Complete the Family Worship section. With the other members of your family, together at a meal or individually at another time like bedtime, follow up on the simple definition of holiness at the beginning of this section. Read 2 Timothy 1:9. Talk about how the definition relates to this verse.

WEDNESDAY—With other members of your family, either individually or together, review this week's memory verse. Read Paul's prayer in 1 Thessalonians 3:12, 13. Pray these verses as a prayer for younger family members, substituting each one's name for the word "your." Older kids and adults may want to pray this for themselves, substituting "my" for the word "your."

THURSDAY—With others in your family, put on your paper bag masks again. While you might feel a bit silly, having the mask on may help others—and you—to talk a bit more openly. Talk through again the things in your lives that you would like to get rid of. Talk about why you think they may be "unholy." Talk about what holy things God might want to replace the unholy things with. End with a time of prayer, asking God to help you accept His gift of holiness.

FRIDAY—After dinner, read Romans 12:1, 2 to your family. Now ask these questions: What kind of behavior "of this world" shouldn't we copy? How do you think we can be "new and different"? Then pray together as a family, asking God to remind you that His holiness is available to us if we just accept it.

WEEK 3: BEING FAITHFUL

Family Devotion Time

ACTIVITY: THE "HAPPY MEAL" UNDEAL. This week's discussion takes place at a McDonald's restaurant. Your kids get Happy Meals. Across North America—probably around the world—a Happy Meal is a Happy Meal. The only thing that changes is the packaging and the surprise inside. But with a Happy Meal, you always

> ***Being Faithful*** *means sticking with something no matter what happens.*

get a burger, fries and a beverage. The discussion focuses on what would happen if you ordered a Happy Meal and didn't get what you expected!

By the way, McDonald's has made inroads into even small communities. However, if you don't have one nearby, this activity might take a bit more creativity. But you can do it! Go to a familiar restaurant and order something you've ordered a number of times before. You may have to adapt the questions, but you can still talk about the difference between what you expect and what you don't expect.

DISCUSSION: While enjoying your Happy Meals and whatever else you've ordered, talk through the questions below. Try to guide the conversation to be as practical as possible so that your family feels free to talk, and so they grasp a bit of what it means to "be faithful."

• When you order a Happy Meal, what do you get?
• How would you feel if the next time we came here, they told you they couldn't put the same things in a Happy Meal anymore because those things cost too much? So now you get liver and onions, broccoli, fruit and no prize.

• McDonald's, in a way, is promising that you can always get the same thing when you get a Happy Meal. Why are the promises we make so important?

• If a friend promises you something, like a new toy, or letting you borrow his camera, and then he says he won't, how does that make you feel?

• How do you think we can stick with the promises we make?

• Do you think God is faithful? Does He keep His promises?

• How does that make you feel?

The way we are faithful is to keep the promises we make. We stick with something, even when things go wrong. God wants us to be faithful to Him as well. Just like He is faithful to us. He wants us to stick with Him, even when things are hard. When things don't go our way, we sometimes try to take control back from God, and try to run things ourselves. But God wants us to stick with Him through everything. *This week's memory verse* tells why we can be faithful to God no matter what happens:

"Many others have faced exactly the same problems before you. . . . You can trust God to keep the temptation from becoming so strong that you can't stand up against it."
—1 Corinthians 10:13

FAMILY BIBLE TIME: Though we've talked about our faithfulness so far, faithfulness is a strong characteristic of God.

"I will proclaim the greatness of the Lord. How glorious he is! He is the Rock, His work is perfect. Everything He does is just and fair. He is faithful, without sin." —Deuteronomy 32:3, 4

God's faithfulness is more than just a characteristic. It is actively carried out in our lives. Look up the following verses to see the different ways God is faithful to us:

2 Peter 3:9—God faithfully fulfills His promises.

1 John 1:9—God faithfully forgives our sins.

1 Corinthians 10:13—God faithfully ministers to us in our temptations.

Psalm 119:90—God always faithfully responds to all ages.

Our faith and our act of being faithful is possible because God is faithful to us. We know that we can trust Him and that He will keep His promises. Though He knows we are not perfect, God desires that we remain actively faithful to Him.

FAMILY PRAYER TIME: Together as a family, pray about being faithful. God wants us to be faithful to each other (1 Peter 4:10) and to him (1 Peter 1:21). Ask your family to pray these simple phrases after you pray them. Ask for a volunteer to close your prayer time.

"God, please help us to be faithful. . . . We trust You. . . . Help us keep our promises to You. . . . Give us Your strength. . . . Help us to be faithful to others too. . . . Help us to keep our promises, no matter what. . . . Remind us how to keep faithful to You and to others every day. . . . In Jesus' name, Amen."

Family Worship Time (optional)

As you do each week, spend some time alone or with another family member going through the following steps. Do your best to complete the steps during the next two or three days.

PREPARATION TIME: Read Proverbs 20:6. Now ask yourselves: Which am I—the person who says I'm loyal and faithful, or the person who is loyal and faithful?

Think about the different areas of your lives—personal life, family life, church, business or school. Ask God to make each of you a faithful person in each area this week.

WAITING TIME: During your waiting time let God love you, search you and show each of you His desires where you need to be more faithful this week. Ask Him to place in your hearts phrases that complete these simple prayers:

"God, I feel Your love today, especially in the area of . . ."

"God, You have permission to reveal any area of unfaithfulness in my life . . ."

"God, is there anything I need to know today about my lack of faith or the demonstration of my faithfulness. . . ?"

CONFESSION TIME: The following verses provide four biblical reasons why we need to be faithful. Read them and confess areas of weakness to God, either silently or together:

1. To be qualified for ministry—1 Timothy 1:12.

2. To guarantee God's blessings on our lives—Proverbs 28:20.
3. To prepare me for our leadership roles—Nehemiah 7:2.
4. To receive God's reward for faithfulness:—Matthew 25:21.

BIBLE TIME: We can never pray out of God's will when we pray God's Word. Read Matthew 25:14-28, and ask yourselves, "Which servant am I?" Now pray a portion of this passage back to God and allow Him to minister to you. Your prayer might go something like this: "God, help each of us to be the servant of Yours who handles well whatever You give us. Help us to be faithful with whatever You provide. We thank You for whatever tasks You give us. We even ask that You would help us to be so faithful that we can be entrusted with even more for You. Thank You that You reward the faithfulness of Your servants, even when You could expect our faithfulness without reward. Help us to joyfully serve You today, this week and throughout our lives. In Jesus' name, Amen."

MEDITATION TIME: After praying the Scriptures, write down in a notebook the thoughts that God has impressed upon each of your minds. Consider how it's not enough just to protect what God has given us. Faithfulness is also moving forward with the things He entrusts to us and investing and using them.

INTERCESSION TIME—PRAYING FOR OTHERS: Ask God to bring to mind those around you who might be struggling with their own faithfulness to God. Also, those who are having difficulty seeing God's faithfulness in their lives. Remember the other members of your family. Pray that God will reveal His faithfulness to them, and that they will see the importance of being faithful in return.

PETITION TIME—PRAYING FOR YOURSELVES: Now pray the same things for yourselves. Pray that God will reveal His faithfulness to you, and that He will give you the strength and power to be faithful in return. Ask God to make each of you such a faithful person that this quality of God inside you will also show on the outside, even as you are faithful to people around you.

APPLICATION TIME: List in a notebook what steps your

family can take toward obeying God in the area of being faithful this week. Beside each step, note how being obedient will lead you to faithfulness.

FAITH TIME: Faith is our positive response to what God has said. Spend a few moments praying through your eyes of faith. Tell God the positive things you see happening because of His goodness!

PRAISE AND THANKSGIVING TIME: Praise God by recognizing who He is—a faithful God. Thank God by recognizing what He has done—kept His promises to us, no matter what.

Family Time Throughout the Week

MONDAY—Do the Family Devotion Time. Also, try to get a start on the Family Worship section.

TUESDAY—Talk as a family about how you each spend your money. This could be a little awkward if you're not used to talking about finances. But bring it down to your kids' level. Talk about allowance, and where it goes. See if your kids can tell you where most of the money went last week. Read Luke 16:11. Ask different family members what this verse means. Ask if God could trust them based on how they spend their money now.

WEDNESDAY—Talk as a family about obeying God and being faithful to God in the area of serving Him. Does anyone in the family teach Sunday school or sing in a choir or serve God in another way? How is serving God being faithful to Him. Read 1 Samuel 2:35 to get your discussion started.

THURSDAY—Today talk together about how you can be faithful to God by caring for others. Does someone in the family mow a lawn or shovel snow for a neighbor who can't? How about taking meals to someone who has been through a hard time? Read Philippians 2:20-22. What do these verses describe as some of the qualities for caring for other people.

FRIDAY—Talk together about what it means to disciple another person. Read 2 Timothy 2:2.

WEEK 4: BROKENNESS

Family Devotion Time

ACTIVITY: OREO COOKIE ICE-CREAM CAKE. This week, do the activity first, then have your discussion while the "cake" refreezes. Assure everyone that you'll eat the treat after your family prayer time.

> ***Brokenness:*** *From something broken comes something even better.*

Before you meet as a family, gather these ingredients: a dozen or so Oreo cookies, a mixing bowl, ¼ cup melted butter, a pint of vanilla ice cream—you want this to be slightly softened.

First, ask all family members to wash their hands. Then give each person two or three Oreo cookies, and break them up into a mixing bowl. Mention that you might be tempted to eat the cookies instead, but that the final result will be even better.

Once the cookies are broken and crushed, have one person measure out 1½ cups. Mix the cookie crumbs with ¼ cup melted butter and press the mixture firmly against the bottom and sides of a pie plate. Bake this crust at 350° F for 10 minutes. Now place the slightly softened ice cream into the cookie pie crust. Sprinkle any remaining cookie crumbs on top of the pie. Put in freezer while you have your discussion time.

(For a healthier treat, substitute Granola snack bars for the Oreo cookies, decreasing the crust's baking time to 6-8 minutes. Use low-fat ice cream.)

DISCUSSION: While your treat freezes, discuss these questions. Again, your goal should be getting your family to talk about brokenness and what it means, not just to answer every question about the topic.

- What do we usually do when something is broken?
- Is there ever a time when something breaks, but we just can't throw it away?
- How much value must something have for us to think it's worth fixing if it breaks?
- Do you think God values you enough to "fix" you when you're broken?
- How does God fix us?
- How can you play with a toy/listen to a stereo/watch a TV if it's broken? Can you do these things after each item is fixed?
- Do you think God wants us to remain broken? Or does He want to use us?
- How can He use us more after we've been broken and He's "fixed" us?

Remember that sometimes—often in the way that God works—good things come out of what we might think is bad. We may feel that something God wants us to do seems impossible. Yet, if we let God use us, it's a chance for His power to be demonstrated to others. That's the theme of *this week's memory verse:*

"[God] said, ' . . . I am with you; that is all you need. My power shows up best in weak people.'" —2 Corinthians 12:9

FAMILY BIBLE TIME: John McEnroe, the championship tennis player, once said, "My greatest strength is that I have no weaknesses." In sports, school, business—sometimes even family and parenting life—we might want to have that same quality: no weaknesses.

But how do the following words sound different?

"Notice among yourselves, dear brothers, that few of you who follow Christ have big names or power or wealth. Instead, God has deliberately chosen to use the ideas the world considers foolish and of little worth in order to shame those people considered by the world as wise and great. He has chosen a plan despised by the world, counted as nothing at all, and used it to bring down to nothing those the world considers great, so that no one anywhere can ever brag in the presence of God."
—1 Corinthians 1:26-29

Which do you think is the way God really wants us to live?

FAMILY PRAYER TIME: Pray together about how God might "fix" you so that He can use you in better ways. Encourage family members to silently complete these thoughts in prayer:

"God, show me areas where You need to fix me . . ."

"Show me how You can use me if I let You fix me in these areas . . ."

"Show me how things will be even better for me because I've let You take over and fix me . . ."

Family Worship Time (optional)

Read these verses, and note the opposites that each one contains. Matthew 5:3; Matthew 19:30; Matthew 20:20-22; Luke 9:24-26; Luke 22:26, 27; John 12:24; Romans 8:13; 2 Corinthians 11:30 and 12:9, 10; James 4:7.

God really wants us to be broken—in all the right places. Think about what that means. What does it look like to be broken in the right places? What's the difference between broken and beaten? Why is it important that we are broken rather than beaten by circumstances that come into our lives?

To help this idea sink in more clearly, spend some time going through the following steps. Again, if you have interruptions, or if you can't do all of this in a single sitting, that's OK. In families, interruptions are inevitable, and God understands and will help you concentrate even if you have to break this into smaller pieces. If you are interrupted, come back and pick up where you left off.

PREPARATION TIME: Think about these things in God's Word that were broken but that became effective after they were broken:

Broken pitchers (Judges 7:18, 19)—the light shone out.

A broken box (Mark 14:3)—the ointment was poured out.

Broken bread (Matthew 14:19, 20)—the hungry were fed.

A broken body (1 Corinthians 11:24)—the world was saved.

WAITING TIME: During your waiting time, let God love you, search you and show each of you His desires in your lives in the area of being broken. Ask Him to reveal to each of you phrases that complete these simple prayers:

"God, I feel Your love today, especially in the area of . . ."

"God, You have permission to reveal any unbroken areas in my life . . ."

"God, as I enter this day, is there anything about being broken that I need to know. . . ?"

CONFESSION TIME: "Then, accompanied by the disciples, [Jesus] left the upstairs room and went as usual to the Mount of Olives. There he told them, 'Pray God that you will not be overcome by temptation.' He walked away, perhaps a stone's throw, and knelt down and prayed this prayer: 'Father, if you are willing, please take away this cup of horror from me. But I want your will, not mine.' Then an angel from heaven appeared and strengthened him, for he was in such agony of spirit that he broke into a sweat of blood, with great drops falling to the ground as he prayed more and more earnestly." — Luke 22:39-44

Confess to God areas where each of you needs to be broken, areas where you need to examine yourselves and allow yourselves to be broken.

BIBLE TIME: We can never pray out of God's will when we pray God's Word. Read the passage above to your family slowly a few times, then close your eyes and ask God to allow a main truth to surface in each of your hearts. Now pray the Scripture back to God and allow Him to minister to you. Family members may pray aloud or silently. Your prayers might go something like this: "Father, we know that we could never face such a horrible situation as Jesus faced. Thank You for sending Him to earth to die for our sins. But as He prayed, we want to live Your will, even in areas where it's hard to ask You for it, areas where we need to be broken. We pray that we will seek Your will by praying earnestly. Though we may never sweat drops of blood, encourage us to pray fervently because of the demonstrations in our lives of Your answered prayers. Amen."

MEDITATION TIME: After praying the Scriptures, write down in a notebook the thoughts that God has impressed upon your minds. Think about how brokenness and our desire to do God's will are related.

INTERCESSION TIME—PRAYING FOR OTHERS: Ask God to bring to your minds people who might also need to know and experience brokenness in the right places in their lives. Don't forget about the other members of your family too. Pray that God will reveal to them areas where they need to be broken.

PETITION TIME—PRAYING FOR YOURSELVES: Now, pray that God will continue to reveal to you exactly where any of you are holding back, and pray that you will desire God's will in the area of brokenness in your lives. Ask Him to change you so that you all will want the best for your lives—God's best.

APPLICATION TIME: List in a notebook what steps your family can take toward obeying God more fully this week in the area of brokenness. Beside each step, note how your obedience can break you in the right places so that you can fully experience God's will.

FAITH TIME: Faith is our positive response to what God has said. Spend a few moments as a family praying through your eyes of faith. Tell God the positive things you see happening because of His goodness!

PRAISE AND THANKSGIVING TIME: Read 2 Corinthians 12:9. Now praise God by recognizing who He is—a powerful God. Thank God by recognizing what He has done—placed His power within me!

Family Time Throughout the Week

MONDAY—Do the Family Devotion Time. If possible, get a start on the Family Worship section.

TUESDAY—Complete the Family Worship section. With the other members of your family, together at a meal or individually at another time like bedtime, follow up on the simple definition of brokenness at the beginning of this section. You may want to memorize it with your kids. Also read the Sermon on the Mount in Matthew 5. Talk about why God chooses people who are broken and hurting to do His work on earth.

WEDNESDAY—With other members of your family, either individually or together, review this week's memory verse. Read through Luke 22:39-44. Talk together as a family about the sacrifice that Jesus made. Discuss why Jesus had to suffer—not just on the cross, but through the agony described in these verses.

THURSDAY—With others in your family, talk about the difference between what being broken meant before and what it means now that you've begun to understand what it means to be broken so God can use you more effectively. Talk about how we might not want to let God be in control. Discuss what we gain if we do let God use us.

FRIDAY—Pray this prayer:

Disturb us, O Lord, when we are too well pleased with ourselves:

When our dreams come true
only because we have dreamed too little.
When we arrive safely
only because we sailed too close to the shore.
When with the abundance of things
we are losing our thirst for more of God.
When in loving time, we have ceased to dream of eternity.
When in our desire to build on this earth
we have lost our vision of a new heaven.

Talk together as a family about what these words might mean. Help younger kids understand the word pictures in this prayer. Talk about taking risks for God, and about giving Him our time and desires.

WEEK 5: COMMITMENT

Family Devotion Time

ACTIVITY: TRIP TO AN ICE-CREAM STORE! (or another place your family enjoys). This week, announce to your family that the activity will take place at a local Dairy Queen or other favorite place. Then, as everyone is getting ready, announce that you've changed your mind, and that you'll do tonight's discussion at home after all.

> **Commitment** *is keeping promises no matter what.*

DISCUSSION: Even though everyone is disappointed, try to get them to talk about these questions. Since you didn't keep your commitment, the discussion could happen easily:

• How did you feel when I changed my mind about going out to have ice cream?

• What does it mean to make a promise?

• How do you think other people feel if you don't keep your promises, if you fail to do what you say you will?

• How do you think God must feel when we don't keep our promises to Him?

• What kinds of commitments and promises should we be making to God?

• How do you think we can keep our promises to God?

Commitment means keeping our promises to each other. That's why we *will* all go our for ice cream after all—right after prayer time. Commitment to God means keeping our promises to Him—serving Him and doing His will. Scripture promises that if we keep our commitments to God, He will help us do anything that is within His will. That's the theme of *this week's memory verse:*

"Commit everything you do to the Lord. Trust him to help you do it and he will." —Psalm 37:5

FAMILY BIBLE TIME: God can do anything and everything through people who are fully committed to Him.

In the Old Testament, Daniel knew the meaning of commitment. When he and his three teenage friends were captured and taken to Babylon, he knew tough times were ahead. But he decided to remain committed to God. He made his stand and God blessed him and his friends. Soon Daniel found himself in a place of leadership. But the king was jealous.

So, the king decreed that everyone could pray only to him. The king's men knew that Daniel prayed three times every day to God. With full knowledge of the consequences—being thrown to the lions—Daniel kept his commitment to God. He knelt and prayed. And the king's men caught him.

Read Daniel 6:16-23. Daniel didn't know beforehand that God would save him from the lions. But he still kept his commitment. He was thrown to the lions. Of course, we know that the lions kept him warm through the night and waited for a morning breakfast of the king's men. But Daniel didn't know that would happen. The choice belonged to God.

FAMILY PRAYER TIME: Pray together about the kinds of commitments you all make, especially to God. Encourage family members to repeat these sentences in prayer to God:

"God, today I want to commit myself to You. I want to give You my time. I want You to have my energy. You can use anything I have to do Your work. I pray that You will remind me of my commitment, and that You will use my commitment. In Jesus' name, Amen."

Family Worship Time (optional)

Read Luke 14:25-30, where Jesus describes the cost of commitment. In this passage, Jesus teaches us about commitment:

1. Count the cost before we commit.

2. Life-changing commitments flow from a life of smaller commitments.

3. We make the commitment, but leave the results to God.

Spend some time going through these steps to help this idea sink in more clearly.

PREPARATION TIME: Read Luke 6:49. Think about how firm your family's commitment is to God. What commitments is He calling each of you to make in your personal life? Your family life? Church life? Business or school life?

WAITING TIME: During your waiting time, let God love you, search you and show you His desires in the area of your commitments. Ask Him to reveal to each of you phrases that complete these simple prayers:

"God, I feel Your love today, especially in the area of . . ."

"God, are there any commitments I have made that I am not fulfilling. . . ?"

"God, is there anything I need to know about my lack of commitment in a certain area as I enter this day. . . ?"

CONFESSION TIME: Read Hebrews 12:1-3. Then confess to God areas where you've become "fainthearted and weary," times when you've not remained committed to Him in spite of the price He paid for you. Allow family members to pray silently or aloud.

BIBLE TIME: We can never pray out of God's will when we pray God's Word. Read the above passage again slowly a few times. Then encourage your family to close their eyes and ask God to reveal a main truth He wants each of you to learn. Now pray the Scripture back to God and allow Him to minister to you. Your prayer might go something like this: "God, I thank You for the people of faith in Scripture who remained committed to You even when they didn't know how things would turn out. We pray that we would be that committed to You. Thank You for Your forgiveness—for taking away our sin. Help us to realize Your forgiveness so that the memories of old sins don't keep us from being fully committed to You. Help us to look to Jesus as an example, for He made the ultimate commitment with His willingness to die for us. Help us to know that because of His death, we can also know joy and know that someday we will be in Your presence. Help us to remain strong and committed to You, and to do Your will no matter what the Enemy puts in our way. Thank You for the blessing that comes as we remain committed. In Jesus' name, Amen."

MEDITATION TIME: After praying the Scriptures, write down in a notebook the thoughts that God has impressed upon your minds. In the passage in Hebrews, how can patience in a race help a runner win it? How can patience help you remain committed to God in the "race" called life?

INTERCESSION TIME—PRAYING FOR OTHERS: Ask God to bring to your minds other people who want to be committed to Him. Pray for people who come to mind who need to be committed, yet maybe don't know how. Don't forget to pray for the other members of your family. Pray that God will demonstrate to each—through other people and through His Word— what it means to be committed.

PETITION TIME—PRAYING FOR YOURSELVES: Now pray that God will also demonstrate to each of you how you can be committed to Him. Pray that you will honestly want to be committed to Him. Ask Him, above all, to reveal His will for your lives—even if you don't know the final outcome—so that you can remain committed to Him.

APPLICATION TIME: In a notebook, list what steps your family can take this week to obey God in the area of commitment. Though this lesson has been mostly about commitment to God, think about the other commitments in your life. What other commitments do you have—to family members and others? How do these often relate to your commitments to God? Beside each step you think of, note how obeying God will lead all of you to deeper commitment.

FAITH TIME: Faith is our positive response to what God has said. Spend a few moments praying as a family through your eyes of faith. Tell God the positive things you see happening because of His goodness!

PRAISE AND THANKSGIVING TIME: Read Hebrews 11:39, 40. Now praise God by recognizing who He is—a God who desires the very best for His children. Thank God by recognizing what He has done—prepared great rewards for those who obey and commit to carrying out His will.

Family Time Throughout the Week

MONDAY—Do the Family Devotion Time. If possible, get a start on the Family Worship section.

TUESDAY—Complete the Family Worship section. With other members of your family, work on this week's memory verse. Take the verse a phrase at a time, and talk about what it means. Ask God to help each of you to apply it to your life so that it becomes more than just words.

WEDNESDAY—Make a list of the commitments in your life. Think about your relationships—to God, to your family, to friends, to work or school. If you had to list which commitment was most important, which one would it be? Look at your list again. Which commitment should be number one? Talk together as a family about your different commitments. How can you hold each other accountable to make God the top priority in each of your lives?

THURSDAY—Read Luke 12:48. Now look at the list of commitments you made yesterday. How does this verse make you feel about everything that you have? Ask God to help you with your responsibilities. With your family, either at a mealtime or bedtime, review the simple definition of commitment at the beginning of this section. Ask how God can help us keep our promises.

FRIDAY—After dinner, review this week's memory verse. Pray together as a family—perhaps for the person on your left around the table—for God's help in trusting Him in *everything* you do.

WEEK 6: COMPASSION

Family Devotion Time

ACTIVITY: MAKING A SNACK TRAY. When the family is gathered, work together to make a snack tray. Use paper plates and arrange fruit, vegetables, meats, cheeses, chips, dips or whatever else can be eaten as a snack on each plate. After your family discussion and prayer time, or sometime the next

> ***Compassion*** *is feeling exactly what someone else is feeling.*

day, deliver the trays to another family from your church or in your neighborhood who has been going though a hard time. The actual act of delivering the trays will help this lesson sink in, so try to have the whole family go along.

DISCUSSION: Talk through these questions. Your goal is for your family to catch a glimpse of what it means to be compassionate:

• Do you think you can ever really feel exactly what someone else is feeling?

• How can you get to know your friends and family members so well that you understand what they feel?

• Do you think being compassionate stops with just feeling what someone else feels, or should you do something about it?

• What are some things you can do if you feel compassion for someone else?

• Can you think of any times when you felt what someone else felt? What did you do about it?

Compassion is feeling what someone else is feeling. Then you should take action to help that person. But you have to know someone well enough to know what he's going through to know how to help him. ***This week's memory verse*** tells us a way we can have compassion for other people:

". . . You should be like one big happy family, . . . loving one another with tender hearts and humble minds." —1 Peter 3:8

FAMILY BIBLE TIME: Can you remember any Bible stories when Jesus showed compassion for other people? Ask one of your children to tell the story of the good Samaritan, or read it in Luke 10:30-37. Ask the other members of your family: What are some ways God shows compassion toward us?

FAMILY PRAYER TIME: Pray together as a family about how we can feel what others are feeling, and ways we can take action to help their hurts. Encourage silent prayers as you read out loud each line. Afterward, you can discuss anyone whom God brings to mind, and whether you can show compassion individually or as a family.

"God, help us to be aware of what others are feeling this week. Bring to our minds people who need our compassion . . ."

"God, as we think of these people we've named, bring to our minds ways we can demonstrate our compassion, things we can do to show them that we care and are praying for them . . ."

Close your prayer time by asking if someone will pray for God to bless your family as you feel and show your compassion for others this week. If no one volunteers, close the prayer yourself.

Family Worship Time (optional)

Have you ever heard the expression, "Don't cry over spilled milk"? Have you ever wondered what it means? After you read the following story, you'll have a new idea about that old expression. But you might want to avoid trying this activity at your dinner table!

A pastor went to dinner at the home of one of his church families. Several other families were there too. As the families sat down and ate dinner, the pastor noticed that the parents were unusually strict with their 5-year-old daughter. Maybe, he thought, they just want her to be on her best behavior for company.

When dinner was almost over, the little girl knocked over her milk. Fearfully, she looked up at her parents. The parents seemed frozen—upset that spilled milk had ruined their dinner party, and maybe more upset that all their lecturing about "best manners" had failed.

After a rather long silence, the pastor purposely knocked over his almost-finished drink. Another couple knocked over their glasses as well. The anger on the faces of the parents slowly melted away and turned to a smile. They both reached out and knocked over their drinks as well! The whole group broke out in hysterical laughter and had a wonderful evening, because of the compassion of the pastor for a 5-year-old girl.

Think again about what compassion means. Try these three expanded definitions on for size. Do they sum up what compassion is?

1. Compassion requires being with people and looking for their needs.

2. Compassion requires identifying with the people's situation and what they feel.

3. True compassion results in action.

Think about how each of you treats others, at school or at work. Would others consider you a compassionate person? Do you identify with what other people are going through and the emotions they are experiencing? Do you have true compassion that would result in action—even spilling your milk at a fancy dinner gathering?

Working through these steps will help you gain an even deeper understanding of compassion.

PREPARATION TIME: Read Psalm 111:1-4. Now think about your own "work"—those actions in your lives where you show compassion (or areas where you fail to act because you lack compassion). Think of three or four family relationships (Mom, Dad, brother, sister, son, daughter). How do you think you could improve your level of compassion for each person? What about your friends and the people you work with? How can each of you demonstrate more compassion in those relationships?

WAITING TIME: During your waiting time, let God love you, search you and show each of you how you can be more compassionate toward those around you. Ask Him to give you phrases that complete these simple prayers:

"God, I feel Your love today, especially in the area of . . ."

"God, reveal to me areas where I need to be more compassionate, and show me how to demonstrate compassion . . ."

"God, what truth from Your Word do I need to embrace as I seek to be more compassionate. . . ?"

CONFESSION TIME: Read Matthew 25:42-46. Then silently confess to God the times when you've failed to show compassion for others. Individually ask His forgiveness for how your failure has hurt Him and His kingdom.

BIBLE TIME: Read through Psalms 78:37, 39; 111:2-4; Mark 1:40, 41; 5:33-37. Ask God to use these verses to reveal His compassion to each of you. Now reread the verses above under the Confession Time. Close your eyes and ask God to bring a main truth to your hearts.

Now pray Matthew 25:42-46 back to God and allow Him to minister to your family. Your prayer might go something like this: "God, open our eyes to the needs of others around us. Help us to see those who are facing problems like hunger, loneliness, financial problems, illnesses. Help us to have compassion for them and to minister to them in Your name. Help us to see that when we serve them, we are serving You. In Jesus' name, Amen."

MEDITATION TIME: After praying the Scriptures, write down in a notebook the thoughts God is impressing upon your family concerning compassion. Think again about how serving God comes through ministering to others because you are compassionate enough to know their needs.

INTERCESSION TIME—PRAYING FOR OTHERS: Think about the relationships that came to mind during the Preparation Time. Ask God to bring others to your minds too. Now ask God to help you show compassion to these people, and to help you know how to show your compassion. Pray for the other members of your family, and that all of you would be known to others as compassionate people who selflessly serve others and God.

PETITION TIME—PRAYING FOR YOURSELVES: Now spend a few minutes talking to God—and listening to Him. Pray that He will help each of you discover small ways to increase your compassion for others. Again, ask God to help you specifically in each of the relationships you've noted. Be honest with God about why you need to change your actions in each relationship.

APPLICATION TIME: List in a notebook what steps you need to take as a family toward obeying God more fully this week in the area of compassion. Next to each step, write how you can show that compassion. For example, if one of your steps is to show compassion to your overworked youth pastor, you could write "We'll write him a note of encouragement for the long hours he puts in, and invite him and his family over for dinner so that our family can minister to his" as how you might show compassion. Don't forget to actually do what you write!

FAITH TIME: Faith is our positive response to what God has said. Spend a few moments praying together, thanking God for the compassion He has demonstrated for you. Acknowledge your faith in His power to make each one of you a more compassionate person. You can list in a notebook any ways that you see yourselves changing in the area of showing compassion.

PRAISE AND THANKSGIVING TIME: Praise God by recognizing who He is—a God who is moved with unlimited compassion for us. Thank God by recognizing what He has done—demonstrated His compassion over and over again by carrying us through times of grief, illness, loneliness, depression.

Family Time Throughout the Week

MONDAY—Do the Family Devotion Time, as well as working on the memory verse. If you have time, get a start on the Family Worship section.

TUESDAY—Complete the Family Worship section. As a family, around the dinner table or at bedtimes, talk about the compassion Jesus showed for us when He went to the cross. Pray together thanking Him for His ultimate, unselfish compassion.

WEDNESDAY—As a family, make a list of hurting people and pray for their needs as you know them. Make a prayer chart to place on your refrigerator and leave room for answers to your requests. If you think you can do anything to help someone on the list, discuss what your family can do together.

THURSDAY—Review the simple definition and the memory verse. Together as a family, talk about what it means to have tender hearts and humble minds.

FRIDAY—Commit to praying for other family members throughout the week. Agree that you will pray for each other without pointing out areas where family members should have shown more compassion, only that you will pray for those areas without judging them.

WEEK 7: CONFRONTATION

Family Devotion Time

ACTIVITY: TEAM COLORS. Encourage family members to take a few minutes to go back to their rooms and change into their favorite team's apparel. Put on your favorite NFL team's sweatshirt, your favorite Major League team's baseball cap, your favorite college team's sweatpants. If you don't have any team apparel, put on your favorite team's colors.

> ## *Confrontation:*
> *Telling others the truth to make them better people.*

When everyone has regathered, encourage them to spend a few minutes telling why the team clothes they are wearing is their favorite team.

DISCUSSION:
- Think about your favorite team. Are they winners or losers?
- Do you like to watch their games? Why?
- You might hear a sportscaster refer to a big game as a "confrontation," or say something like, "In the last confrontation between these two team. . . ." Why would a simple game be called a confrontation?
- What do you think confrontation means?
- Is it possible for confrontation to be bad? How?
- Is it possible for confrontation to be good? How?

Before you work on your memory verse or pray together, read the story from the first part of the Family Bible Time section below. Then ask, "How would the boy have behaved differently if his mom had said something right away? If she had said something, she would have been confronting him in a good way." When we lovingly confront others, we help them be more like Jesus. As *this week's memory verse* says:

"We will lovingly follow the truth at all times . . . [becoming] more and more in every way like Christ." —Ephesians 4:15

FAMILY BIBLE TIME: A sixth grader was a few minutes late getting home from school one spring night. His mom didn't think much about it. The next night, the boy was a half hour late. The mom had been concerned, but didn't say anything. After all, he'd made it home safely, and it was just 30 minutes. The next night, the boy was two hours late.

His mom was livid, worried and exhausted at all once! She called all of his friends' homes, called the school, and was even ready to start calling hospitals or the police to see if something had happened.

When the boy finally got home, his mother managed to keep from shouting, but her son knew by the look on her face and her tone of voice that he was in trouble.

"Where have you been?" she asked.

"I was just at the mall, playing some games at the arcade. I guess I lost track of time," he answered.

"Who were you with? I called all your friends' houses, and they were all already home."

"I just went by myself. It's almost on the way home, and I just wanted to kill some time."

The boy went on to explain that he'd stopped there the last two nights, and that he'd been a little late, so he didn't think his mom would care if he stayed out a little longer. And he didn't know it was two whole hours. He said that he was really sorry, and that it wouldn't happen again.

Later, his mom realized that if she'd just said something one of the previous nights, if she'd just confronted him about his lateness right away, she probably would have saved herself some worry and her son some punishment and guilt. *Next time,* she resolved.

Read Ephesians 4:14-16. From these verses we can see these three biblical thoughts about confrontation:

1. It is a command of God.
2. It is to be done in love (right heart; gentle; sensitive).
3. It brings growth, individually and in the Body of Christ.

FAMILY PRAYER TIME: Spend a few moments together in prayer, asking God to help you live as the memory verse says. Use the phrases of the verse to lead your family in prayer, with them praying sentence prayers to God after you say each phrase. Then close in prayer, especially asking God to help you obey the verse.

Family Worship Time (optional)

Spend some time now going through the following steps. They're probably looking familiar by now, but try not to let that stop you from taking the time, even if it's interrupted, to work through these steps and gain a better idea about confrontation.

PREPARATION TIME: Read Ephesians 4:25-27. Now ask God to bring to your minds anyone with whom you might need to have an honest conversation.

WAITING TIME: During your waiting time, let God love you, search you and show each of you the desires of His heart concerning the topic of confrontation. Ask Him to give you phrases that complete these simple sentence prayers:
"God, I feel Your love today, especially in the area of . . ."
"God, You have permission to reveal any people with whom I might need to speak the truth in love . . ."
"God, is there anything regarding confrontation that I need to know as I enter this day. . . ?"

CONFESSION TIME: Read Matthew 5:23, 24, which deals with making our relationships right before we go before God. Now individually confess any people or situations that you need to deal with as soon as possible.

BIBLE TIME: We can never pray out of God's will when we pray God's Word. Read Galatians 6:1 slowly a few times. Then close your eyes and ask God to bring a main truth to the surface in your hearts. Now pray this Scripture back to God and allow Him to minister to you. Your pray might go something like this: "God, help us to recognize those around us who need help concerning sin in their lives. We don't want to know so that we have something to hold over their heads. We want to help them. Help us to deal with our own sin in ways that keep us close to You, then help us deal with others who are struggling in gentle ways and humble ways. There's an old saying, 'there but for the grace of God go I.' Help us to remember those words when we're trying to help someone, realizing that some other time it might be us who is struggling, and this person or another who is helping us. Thank You for Your forgiveness and grace that enable us to live lives free from sin in Your sight. In Jesus' name, Amen."

MEDITATION TIME: After praying the Scripture, write down the thoughts that God has impressed upon your mind about confrontation. Especially think through the kind of attitude He wants you to have when you must confront someone you love.

INTERCESSION TIME—PRAYING FOR OTHERS: Ask God to now bring to your minds others who need to be confronted in love. Spend a lot of time over the next few weeks praying for those who come to mind. Ask God to help you make sure that this is someone you should speak to. If you still sense that he or she is, spend even more time praying that God would give you a proper attitude and the right words to say and the right timing when you speak to this person.

PETITION TIME—PRAYING FOR YOURSELVES: Pray the following sentence prayers to God. After each one allow a time of silence for God to speak to each of you:

"God, I ask for Your spirit of gentleness, love and truth to be reflected through me as I confront these people."

"I ask, Holy Spirit, that You would go before me and prepare the hearts of these people."

"I ask for the right timing to have these conversations."

"God, do I need wise counsel regarding any of the above?"

Make sure you spend time listening too, waiting for communication from God—possibly through others, about answers to these prayers.

APPLICATION TIME: Now list in a notebook what steps you

think your family might take in order to lovingly confront others. Beside each step, try to note how obedience to God can change your attitude.

FAITH TIME: Faith is our positive response to what God has said. Spend a few moments praying through your eyes of faith. Tell God the positive things you see happening because of His goodness!

PRAISE AND THANKSGIVING TIME: Read Ephesians 4:32. Now praise God by recognizing who He is—a forgiving and loving God. Thank God by recognizing what He has done— imparted His forgiveness to us and given us the privilege to spread it to others.

Family Time Throughout the Week

MONDAY—Do the Family Devotion Time. Get a jumpstart on the Family Worship section.

TUESDAY—Work on your memory verse—Ephesians 4:15. Memorize it, but also talk through it as a family to make sure that everyone understands what it means. Take the verse apart, phrase by phrase, and discuss what each phrase means. You want your family to memorize it, to understand it, and to be able to begin applying it to their lives, no matter how young they are.

WEDNESDAY—Read James 3 together. Although in a later week you'll look at taming the tongue, the principles for controlling the tongue are good ones to examine when you talk about confronting each other in love. Talk together about how small the tongue is, but how much damage James says it can do. Why then is that so important to keep in mind when you must confront someone?

THURSDAY—Read Ephesians 4:25-32 together, perhaps with each family member old enough to read having his own Bible. Ask everyone to pick out words that sound like commands. Have someone write down a list of do's and don'ts. For example, from the first two verses of this passage, you would list:

<u>**DO**</u>	<u>**DON'T**</u>
tell the truth	lie
get over your anger	hurt yourself
	be angry
	hold grudges

FRIDAY—Play a team game or sport together as a family. Afterward, while having something warm or cold to drink (depending on the time of year), talk about how much easier it is to "confront" each other during competitive things than in real life. Discuss how confrontation when we're being competitive is different than the kind of confrontation God wants us to do with individuals.

WEEK 8: CONTENTMENT

Family Devotion Time

ACTIVITY: THE UNFAIR SHARE. Using grapes or something else you can divide easily, pass out a portion to each family member. However, hand out unfair portions. For example, give one family member 10 grapes and give everyone else five. Or give one family member three cookies and give

> **Contentment** *means being happy with what you have.*

everyone else one. Maybe you will want to repeat the activity so that several family members—at least the children—benefit from getting more than the others.

DISCUSSION: Now talk through these questions. This is an important lesson, because as the old saying goes, "life isn't always fair." As Christians, we often look around and see people who deliberately dishonor God, yet who seem to have more than we do. Kids, especially, notice this. Yet God really does desire that we be content with what He provides for us. Help your family grasp even just a bit of the concept of being content.

• How did it feel when one person had more than you did?

• How did it feel when you had more than everyone else?

• How do you think God wants us to feel? Do you think He wants us to feel that way even if we don't get our fair share?

• If we can't have everything we want, but our friends seem to get everything they ask for, how do you think we can feel content?

• One way we can feel content with what we do have is to be thankful for it. What can you think of that you can thank God for today?

Contentment isn't easy to understand. Some people think

we should never be happy with what we have. But God wants us to be happy with what He gives us. And whatever we have, we should be thankful for. We can be content even when others have more than we do, because God provides all our needs. He gives us the ability to do what we need to do. Note what the Bible says in *this week's memory verse:*

"I have learned the secret of contentment in every situation, . . . for I can do everything God asks me to with the help of Christ who gives me the strength and power."
—Philippians 4:12, 13

FAMILY BIBLE TIME: The Old Testament story of Ruth, a young widow, is a great example of someone who modeled contentment. While her mother-in-law, Naomi, was losing sight of God's goodness, focusing on the present distress, Ruth never criticized or complained. Ruth volunteered to provide for her family's support by gathering what the harvesters left behind—this was really the humbling act of accepting charity. It was also hard work, meaning that Ruth labored in the fields all day, determined to be part of the solution.

If you read Ruth 1:12-17, you'll see four things Ruth did that allowed her to experience contentment in the midst of uncertainty and stress:

1. She chose to serve the one true God.
2. She chose to serve others.
3. She chose to obey.
4. She chose a thankful, grateful spirit.

Our goal should be to incorporate those same qualities into our lives that lead to contentment. Again, while God gives us contentment, we can choose to serve, to obey and to be grateful—all qualities that will bring us contentment.

FAMILY PRAYER TIME: Ask your family to pray in short sentence prayers about contentment:

Pray that God will help you feel happy or satisfied with what He has given you.

Ask Him for His "strength and power" for the times you feel angry or jealous when you don't have the things you want.

Tell God about times you've felt mad because you didn't feel content. Ask for His forgiveness and thank Him for forgiving you.

Thank Him for the things you listed during your discussion time for which you can be thankful.

Family Worship Time (optional)

Christian contentment is the God-given ability to be happy—or at least satisfied—with whatever God provides in every situation.

Now spend some time alone or with other members of your family going through the following steps. If you have interruptions or need to take a break, that's OK. But do your best to come back and pick up where you ended.

PREPARATION TIME: Read together what God's Word says about commitment in Philippians 4:11, 12. Now think about areas or situations in your lives—your personal lives, family life, church life, and business or school life—where any of you feel discontent.

WAITING TIME: During your waiting time, let God love you, search you and show each of you areas where He wants you to experience contentment. Ask Him to bring to mind phrases that complete the following prayers:

"God, I feel Your love today, especially in the area of . . ."

"God, You have permission to reveal any area of my life where there is a complaining or grumbling attitude, any place where I am not grateful for what I have . . ."

"God, is there any specific area of my life You want to focus on today regarding contentment. . . ?"

CONFESSION TIME: Together or individually, confess to God any areas where you've been dissatisfied—whether it is in the area of finances, material wealth, notoriety, or even spiritual maturity. Confess areas where you've been ungrateful.

BIBLE TIME: We can never pray out of God's will when we pray God's Word. Read 2 Corinthians 12:9, 10 several times. Close your eyes and allow a main truth to surface in each of your hearts. Now, pray the Scripture back to God and allow Him to minister to your family. Your prayer might go something like this: "God, help us to experience Your amazing, unequaled grace. Help us to understand that it's OK to be weak, because when we are willing to be weak for You, Your power shows through us. Help us to honestly be content with exactly what You provide for us, and help us to remember that the places in our lives where we may feel inadequate, are the places where You may use us the most."

MEDITATION TIME: After praying the Scriptures, write down in a notebook the thoughts that God has impressed upon you about contentment. Especially think about how each of you can be content for what you *don't* have as well as for what you *do* have.

INTERCESSION TIME—PRAYING FOR OTHERS: Ask God to bring contentment into the lives of those around you, including your family members. Pray that God will demonstrate in and through their lives how He will provide everything they need, and will use them in spite of the areas where they feel weak.

PETITION TIME—PRAYING FOR YOURSELVES: Now silently ask God to help each of you to be content with whatever you have. Ask Him to show you His provision for everything you need. Give Him permission to use you in every area—even where you feel most inadequate to be used.

APPLICATION TIME: List in a notebook the steps your family can take to feel more content this week. Again, think about how you should react when others have more than you do— especially people who aren't following God. Think about how you can choose to serve, to obey and to be grateful. How can each of you live out these qualities that bring contentment?

FAITH TIME: Faith is our positive response to what God has said. Spend a few moments praying through your eyes of faith. Tell God the positive things you see happening because of His goodness!

PRAISE AND THANKSGIVING TIME: Reread this week's memory verse. Now praise God by recognizing who He is—a mighty and powerful God. And thank God by recognizing what He has done—He's given us His help through Christ.

Family Time Throughout the Week

MONDAY—Do the Family Devotion Time. If possible, get started on the Family Worship section.

TUESDAY—Complete the Family Worship section. With other members of your family, talk about the kinds of feelings we have when other people around us seem to "have more" than we do. What about the neighbor who gets a new toy/bike/car? What about the person at school who gets picked first for games or the person at work who gets a raise when you don't? Talk about how God wants us to feel in these situations.

WEDNESDAY—Read Philippians 4:4-7. Talk about how these verses relate to receiving contentment from God.

THURSDAY—Review this week's memory verse. Together as a family, talk about why contentment is called a "secret" here. Discuss how we can receive strength and power from God.

FRIDAY—Read 2 Corinthians 12:9, 10 to your family at the dinner table. Talk about the last line of that passage together. How can we be strong when we are weak?

WEEK 9: DECISION MAKING

Family Devotion Time

ACTIVITY: THE MONEY GAME. Place a penny, nickel, dime and a quarter on the table in front of each family member. Now, ask this question, "You can each have just one of the coins I put in front of you. Which do you want?" Unless someone has a favorite coin, most everyone will choose the quarter.

DISCUSSION: These questions are meant to lead your family to discover that when we choose the things God desires for us, we are making the best decisions we

> ### *Decision Making:*
> *Making up my mind the way God wants.*

can possibly make. Again, the questions are meant to stimulate discussion, not necessarily to get all the right answers.

• When I gave you the choice of coins, why did you choose the quarter?

• Why would most of us choose to have the most?

• When we make other choices, God wants us to choose the best. How do you think we can make sure we are choosing God's best for our life?

• What are some places we can look to figure out what God's best is?

• If you had chosen the penny instead of the quarter, what would you have been missing?

• What do you think we miss if we don't choose God's best for us?

God doesn't direct or control our lives unless we invite Him to be in control. He wants what is best for us. But He doesn't barge in and take over even when we make bad choices. But if we want the best, and if God wants the best, we have to let Him work in our lives. Then we can learn what He wants us to do. The Bible says we are wise when we try to choose God's best for us. Read *this week's memory verse:*

"Be wise . . . try to find out and do whatever the Lord wants you to." —Ephesians 5:16, 17

FAMILY BIBLE TIME: Even Jesus prayed to His Father about decisions He had to make. The night before He named His 12 disciples, He climbed up onto a mountainside and talked to His Father through the night. Read Luke 6:12-16. Why do you think He prayed that night?

FAMILY PRAYER TIME: This prayer time can help your family understand ways to seek God's best, and how to be patient as you wait for answers. Have your family repeat these simple words together (broken into short phrases) after you read them:

"God, help me to make choices You want me to make. . . . Help me to want what You want for me. Help me to read Your Word and look to other people who know You . . . so that I can find out the choices You want me to make. . . . As I make decisions that follow Your desires for me, please bless me and protect me. . . . Thank You for Your love and care for me. Amen."

Family Worship Time (optional)

Have you heard the story about the personnel manager who had advertised a job opening? Times were hard in the city, so a large number of people applied, many of them in person. The waiting room at the company was full.

When the first applicant—a young man—was ushered into the personnel manager's office, she explained the job to him: "We need someone in this job who can make fast decisions, someone who can really think on his feet," she said. "Can you show me that you're capable of doing that?"

Without a word, the young man got to his feet, stuck his head out the door, and announced to the waiting applicants, "OK, everyone. You can go home—the job's just been filled!"

Of course, in daily life, the decisions we have to make don't always come so easily. But a look at the way Jesus made decisions may help you develop a game plan for the continued decisions each of us must make. The Lord always dealt with stressful situations in the same way, whether it was temptation in the wilderness or the hour of decision at Gethsemane. He made the right choice and obeyed. But how?

Jesus held to His objectives. It's impossible to make difficult decisions without a sense of personal destiny. Jesus knew His divinely appointed assignment and He wouldn't allow anything to sidetrack or seduce Him. His heart was fixed on the cross. Every decision He made was tested against His calling.

In order to hold to our God-given objectives, we must wear blinders—like a racehorse—that remove potential distractions from our lives.

Jesus heeded God's Word. Jesus made decisions by standing firmly on the Word of God. When we look to His Word for answers, it can help us sort out the other advice that people are giving us.

To put it simply, life can be simpler when we live according to God's Word. Most of the struggles in our lives are the result of not doing what we know is right. If we live by God's Word, He will fight for us, not against us.

Jesus helped others before Himself. Many people feel used at times. But being used is different than letting yourself be used. Serving means choosing—unselfishly—to put others first without harboring bitterness, anger or resentment. When you really are living for others, decisions are much easier to make. You've already decided to put others first.

Jesus honored God's will. He restricted His decisions to the will of God. When He spoke to people, He said to them things that God the Father had already been saying to them.

Life can be simple, but that doesn't mean it's easy. If we resist God's will, then our lives rest solely in our own hands. But if we're obedient to God's will, our future rests with Him.

Jesus humbly prayed. He prayed all the time. That was His custom. His faithful example is a constant reminder that the weapons of warfare at our disposal are heavenly, not worldly.

In Gethsemane, the night before He went to the cross, He wrestled in prayer through the long dark hours, while the disciples slept.

Scripture says, "Don't act thoughtlessly, but try to find out and do whatever the Lord wants you to" (Ephesians 5:17). We begin to understand God's will for our lives simply by coming before Him and saying, "God, I want Your will in this situation, but it's not clear to me what You want me to do."

Now give God the opportunity to teach each of you more about making decisions based on His will. Spend some time going through these steps.

PREPARATION TIME: John Boykin, author of *The Gospel of Coincidence,* wrote:

"Rather than viewing our circumstances as God-caused, we should view them as a point on a continuum. Our vocation as human beings is to make decisions, and God's part in our lives is to work with us. He plants His Holy Spirit in our heart and He begins to change the kind of person we are. When we change, our values change, then our decisions change. Our relationship with God is a process of changing our values to agree with His so that the decisions we make will be godly ones."

Pray this simple prayer together: "God, change me into the person of Your desires. May my heart beat as Yours, so that my thoughts will be Your thoughts. Amen."

WAITING TIME: During your waiting time, let God love you, search you and show each of you His desires in your lives when it comes to making decisions that are of His will. Ask Him to give each of you the words to complete these simple prayers:

"God, I feel Your love today, especially in the area of . . ."

"God, You have permission to reveal any wrong motive in my life when it comes to how I make decisions . . ."

"God, is there anything that I need to know about decisions I might face today as I enter this day. . . ?"

CONFESSION TIME: Read Proverbs 3:1-12. Now, individually confess the areas where you have not trusted God completely, areas where you've relied on your own judgment. Admit to God areas where your own selfishness and conceit didn't allow you to trust Him.

BIBLE TIME: We can never pray out of God's will when we pray God's Word. Read the passage above slowly a few times, then close your eyes and allow a main truth to surface in your hearts.

Now pray the Scripture back to God and allow Him to minister to your family. Your prayer of Scripture might go something like this: "God, we do want long and satisfying lives. We want to follow You and know Your will for our lives. Help us to have—and practice—the virtues of loyalty and kindness. Help us to trust You far more than we trust ourselves. You've given us the ability to make good judgments; You've given us common sense. Help us to use these gifts even more effectively by trusting You and asking Your will for our lives. Remind us to put You and Your ways first. Thank You for promising that when we do, we will know success, health and vitality. What a wonderful promise! In Jesus' name, Amen."

MEDITATION TIME: After praying the Scriptures, write down in a notebook the thoughts that God has impressed upon your minds about making decisions that lead you to live within His will. Think about the way each of you make choices, even in the smallest areas of your lives. Are you completely trusting God?

INTERCESSION TIME—PRAYING FOR OTHERS: Ask God to bring to your minds others who are seeking God's will for their lives. Pray that they will understand and know God's will when He presents it to them. Don't forget the other members of your family. Pray that God will reveal His will in their lives. Pray that they will truly desire to know His will.

PETITION TIME—PRAYING FOR YOURSELVES: Now, pray that God will continue to reveal His will in each of your lives. Ask Him to guide you in every one of your decisions—even in the very "littlest" things of life. As the above Scripture says, ask God to live His will through you so completely that you will gain favor and good reputation with other people and with God.

APPLICATION TIME: List in a notebook what steps your family can take toward obeying God in the area of decision making. Beside each step, write how being obedient to God can help you know His will for your lives.

FAITH TIME: Faith is our positive response to what God has said. Spend a few moments praying through your eyes of faith. Tell God the positive things you see happening because of His goodness!

PRAISE AND THANKSGIVING TIME: "If you humble yourselves under the mighty hand of God, in his good time he will lift you up. Let him have all your worries and cares, for he is always thinking about you and watching everything that concerns you." —1 Peter 5: 6, 7

Praise God by recognizing who He is—a mighty God who works in our lives.

Thank God by recognizing what He has done—provided a way for us to be free from worry, because if we let Him, He watches over us and everything that concerns us!

Family Time Throughout the Week

MONDAY—Do the Family Devotion Time. If possible, get a start on the Family Worship section.

TUESDAY—Review the five decision making principles in the life of Christ. Consider writing them on an index card to put in a place where you'll see it frequently—near the phone, on the bathroom mirror, in a daily calendar you carry. As a family, talk about how we can each know God's will for our life. Where are some places we can turn if we are unsure of what God wants us to do in a certain situation?

WEDNESDAY—Remember the quarter everyone chose during the family activity time? Encourage each member of your family to tape his quarter to an index card and write the words, "Choosing the best—making up my mind the way God wants" on the card (words from this week's definition). Each person can then put the card someplace where he'll see it regularly to remind him that good decision making means choosing God's best for our lives.

THURSDAY—With your family, talk through the memory verse. Notice the don'ts and the do's. On a piece of paper, make a chart listing the do's and don'ts. Pray together that you will each have strength to "do the do's."

FRIDAY—After dinner, talk about any tough decisions anyone has coming up. Then pray together as a family through the prayer you prayed during the Family Prayer Time, this time adding any specific requests based on the decisions you've just discussed. Even if some family members don't have a specific request, take turns praying this prayer for each other.

WEEK 10: DISCIPLESHIP

Family Devotion Time

ACTIVITY: BREAD MAKING. Using frozen bread dough from the grocery store freezer, make some homemade bread. Follow the directions on the package, but during your activity time, notice a couple of things: first, notice how the bread dough needs to rise. Talk a bit about how yeast in the dough makes that happen and why.

> ***Discipleship*** *is helping others to know Jesus better.*

Later, after discussion or prayer time, you can pop the bread in the oven for baking. Then gather the family back together to note how the bread rose more while it was baking.

DISCUSSION: Spend some time talking through these questions together:

• You saw the dough rise. Why do you think that's needed for the bread to taste good?

• What do you think the bread would look like after you baked it if it didn't have yeast in it?

• What do you think we would be like if we didn't grow physically?

• What would we be like if we didn't grow in spiritual areas?

• Is there anything like yeast that makes us "rise" spiritually?

God wants us to grow to be more like Christ. And He wants us to help others to grow closer to Him. It's another one of those privileges He gives us, when He could have accomplished growth in many other ways. But just like parents get to watch and enjoy their children grow up, spiritual "parents" get to watch and enjoy their spiritual "children" grow up too. That's why ***this week's memory verse*** says:

"We were as gentle among you as a mother feeding and caring for her own children." —1 Thessalonians 2:7

FAMILY BIBLE TIME: Read Matthew 28:18-20. In fact, if you have time, read it from several translations. This is called the Great Commission. Why? Perhaps because Jesus is commissioning all believers here. Now consider these biblical truths found in this passage about the privilege we have of discipling people:

1. Jesus has given us His authority to make disciples.

2. "Making Disciples" is the main Greek verb in this passage. The process of making disciples is to "go" (share Christ), "baptize" (help others publicly identify with Christ), and "teach to obey" (teach application of His Word, not just knowledge).

3. Discipleship is the means to reach the world for Christ.

One other interesting thing to note from Matthew 28:18-20. In the last verse, Jesus says, "I am with you always." Jesus is also called *Immanuel,* which means "God with us." It's reassuring to know that we can feel about Jesus' leaving the same warm, sweet feeling we feel about Jesus' coming: *God is with us!*

FAMILY PRAYER TIME: Before you pray together, ask if each person can think of someone who has been a spiritual parent, someone outside of the family who has taught him about God. This could be a Sunday school teacher, a pastor, a family friend, or an adopted grandparent. Then spend a few moments praying for these other people God brings into our lives to help us grow as Christians.

Family Worship Time (optional)

Spend a few minutes going through the following steps together. Don't let their increasing familiarity destroy the communication that can take place between you and God as you go through the steps. The pattern and progression are both intended to help you spend quality time in communion with the Lord.

PREPARATION TIME: Read 2 Timothy 2:2. Now think about two different kinds of people. First, who were and are your spiritual mentors? Talk about how these people helped you. Now think about who the people are who God is calling each of you to disciple, to spiritually mentor.

WAITING TIME: During your waiting time, let God love you, search you and show each of you His desires and will. Pray these prayers openly back to God, asking Him to give you the answers you need to give to these simple sentence prayers:

"God, I feel Your love and presence today, especially in the area of . . ."

"God, what do You want to say to me in the area of discipleship . . ."

"God, is there anything I need to know as I enter into this day. . . ?"

CONFESSION TIME: Think about this question: Is there anything that God has given any of you that you have been unwilling to pass on to others? Confess these areas to Him.

BIBLE TIME: We can never pray out of God's will when we pray God's Word. Read 1 Thessalonians 2:7-12 slowly a couple of times. Then close your eyes and allow a main truth to surface in each of your hearts. Then pray the Scripture back to God and allow Him to minister to you.

MEDITATION TIME: After praying the Scriptures, write down the thoughts that God has impressed upon your mind about discipleship, especially about being a spiritual parent to other baby believers.

INTERCESSION TIME—PRAYING FOR OTHERS: Ask God to bring to your minds someone who served as a spiritual mentor to each of you. Take a few moments to thank God for those people, to ask for blessings upon them, and to pray for peace and reward and continued service for their lives.

PETITION TIME—PRAYING FOR YOURSELVES: Now ask God to bring to your minds the name of someone who you have mentored spiritually in the past. Thank God for allowing each of you to be a part of His great design for the world and for individuals. Pray that you will once again burn with desire to disciple others. Pray that God will grant you proper motives and abilities. Ask Him to give each of you someone who you can mentor—and in discipling this new Christian, a time where your own faith will be challenged and strengthened.

APPLICATION TIME: List in a notebook what steps your family can take toward obeying God in the area of making disciples. Ask yourselves if you see ways how being obedient is itself a step toward having a proper attitude as you disciple others.

FAITH TIME: Faith is our positive response to what God has said. Spend a few moments praying through your eyes of faith. Tell God the positive things you see happening because of His goodness!

PRAISE AND THANKSGIVING TIME: Read 2 Timothy 2:1, 2. Praise God by recognizing who He is—our provider of strength. And thank Him by recognizing what He has done—allowed us to fit into His great spiritual lineage.

Family Time Throughout the Week

MONDAY—Do the Family Devotion Time. Get a start on the Family Worship section.

TUESDAY—For an evening snack, enjoy the homemade bread you made yesterday. How does the "growth" of the bread and the yeast that causes it make the bread taste? Also, talk through the discussion questions you answered yesterday again briefly.

WEDNESDAY—Talk together about the people you thought of during the Family Activity Time who were your spiritual teachers or mentors. Today, spend a few minutes writing notes of encouragement to your mentors. Take time to pray for these people and ask God to prepare their hearts to receive your notes of encouragement. Seal the notes and send them.

THURSDAY—Read Luke 10:1-9 after a family mealtime when everyone is gathered. Read verse 2 several times again after reading the whole passage. Talk together about what "the harvest" means. Who are the "laborers"? What does this verse really mean?

FRIDAY—Work on memorizing 1 Thessalonians 2:7. Also, talk through these questions to help you understand and apply the verse in your own lives. Why do you think the apostle Paul compared himself to a nurturing and caring mother in these verses? List some of the qualities of a mom. Why are these so important in discipleship? Do you think a spiritual mentor is someone who is superior to the person being discipled? Or do you think God wants the mentor to see himself as a servant?

WEEK 11: FAILURE

Family Devotion Time

ACTIVITY: COIN TOSS. Pair off members of your family, and give each pair a quarter, a piece of paper and a pen. Have one person in the pair toss the coin into the air, and have the other person call heads or tails. Repeat this at least 10 times, and keep track of how many times it lands heads, how many times it lands tails, and how many times the person calling heads or tails is correct.

> ***Failure** is when you blow it, blame others, then give up.*

Then have the pair switch roles and do the coin toss 10 more times, keeping track of the same thing.

Then compare notes as a family. Did anyone get the call right every single time? What was the highest number out of 10 that someone got?

DISCUSSION: Now, keep those results in mind as you talk through these questions about failure:

• Take the highest number of correct calls, and subtract from 10. That is the number of failures the best "caller" had. For example, if she had seven out of 10 calls correct, subtract seven from 10 for a total of three that were incorrect.

• Do you think the result is a very good rate of success?

• What if that same rate applied to everything you did? Say the result was failure three out of 10 times. Would you ever want to ride your bike if you knew that you'd have a flat tire every three out of 10 trips?

• Do you think God wants us to succeed or fail?

• Read the "Failure is . . ." box. Do you feel like this describes you? Have you ever felt this way?

• Do you think failing is always bad? Can we fail and learn from our failures?

Failure isn't all bad. It really depends if we let it beat us, or if we choose to win over it. How can we beat it? Learn from our mistakes, and then move on. This allows us to remember what we've learned, but forget about the failure itself. As *this week's memory verse* says:

". . . Forgetting the past and looking forward to what lies ahead, I strain to reach the end of the race and receive the prize for which God is calling us. . . ." —Philippians 3:13, 14

FAMILY BIBLE TIME: Read Luke 15:12-32. Talk for a few minutes on the love the father showed his prodigal son when he returned home after a time of failure.

FAMILY PRAYER TIME: Ask family members to be as honest as they can be this week. You can be the model. Encourage everyone to reveal areas of their lives where they have failed. It could be a lie that one of your children told to stay out of trouble. It could be a teenager who stayed out past his curfew. It could be that your company has a strict policy about how long lunch breaks are, yet you took 10 extra minutes. Make this a safe time, where admissions will not be punished, just prayed for. Then take some time to pray, asking God to turn these failures into successes by helping each of you learn from them.

Family Worship Time (optional)

Failure is not falling down—failure is staying down.

Mary Lou Retton, America's Golden Girl gymnast at the Summer Olympics in 1984, said that success comes from setting a goal and then being willing to pay the price to achieve it. "Achieving that goal is a good feeling, but to get there you have to also get through the failures. You've got to be able to pick yourself up and continue."

Everyone falls, but not everyone fails. It depends on whether you fail backward or you fail forward.

We fail backward when:

• Failure keeps us from trying again.

- We become negative about life.
- We make excuses and blame others.

We fail forward when:

- We learn from our failure.
- We discover our own true self.
- We turn everything over to God.

Look up the following verses together, and be encouraged by what the Bible has to say about failure:

God does not fail—Deuteronomy 31:6

God's Word does not fail—Joshua 23:14

God's love and compassion does not fail—Lamentations 3:22, 23

What we do for God does not fail—Matthew 6:20

Faith does not fail—1 Peter 1:9

The promise of eternal life will not fail—John 10:28

Love does not fail—1 Corinthians 13:8, 13

Now spend some time together going through these increasingly familiar steps. Ask God to show you how the failures in your lives can be turned into successes.

PREPARATION TIME: List the failure issues you are wrestling with in your personal lives, your family life, your church or ministry life, and your business or school or social life.

WAITING TIME: Read Luke 15:12-32 again. Then ask God to love you, search you and show each of you what He wants you to learn about failure and success. Ask Him to give you the appropriate thoughts and words to complete these simple sentence prayers:

"God, I feel Your love today, especially in the area of . . ."

"God, You have permission to reveal any wrong motive in my life . . ."

"God, is there any failure You want to prepare me for as I enter this day, any lesson You want me to learn. . . ?"

CONFESSION TIME: Read John 10:10. Satan's mission is to hurt. Jesus' mission is to heal. Confess areas in your lives that have failed because your focus was on the enemy. Confess your desire today to change your focus to the One who promises a full life.

BIBLE TIME: Reread the story of the prodigal son in Luke 15:12-32. Remembering that we can never pray out of God's will when we pray God's Word back to Him, read this passage slowly a couple of times. Then close your eyes and allow a main truth to surface in each of your hearts. Now pray the Scripture back to God and allow Him to minister to you.

MEDITATION TIME: After praying the Scriptures, write down in a notebook any thoughts God has impressed upon your minds about failure. Especially think about how success and failure are related. Are they really opposites? Or are they two different parts of the same process?

INTERCESSION TIME—PRAYING FOR OTHERS: Ask God to bring to your minds people you know who have failed or feel like a failure. Ask Him to remind each of you of other members of your family who may feel like they are failing. Ask God for two things: that these people will begin to experience more successes, and that they will recognize from their failures what God wants them to learn and how He wants them to grow.

PETITION TIME—PRAYING FOR YOURSELVES: How are you doing in this area? Do you feel like you are failing or have failed? What does the failure do to you? Does it make you give up? Or does it inspire you to learn from your mistakes and move on with life—"forward to what lies ahead," straining toward the goal to "receive the prize for which God is calling us"? Ask God to help each of you recognize your failures for what they are. Of course, you don't want to fail; but ask God to help you see your failures as opportunities to grow closer to Him.

APPLICATION TIME: List in a notebook what steps your family can take toward obeying God even during times when you feel like you failed. Note how being obedient is itself a step toward being a success.

FAITH TIME: Faith is our positive response to what God has said. Spend a few moments praying through your eyes of faith. Tell God the positive things you see happening because of His goodness!

PRAISE AND THANKSGIVING TIME: Read Genesis 1:27, 28. Praise God by recognizing who He is—our Creator and Equipper. And thank Him by recognizing what He has done—given us the desire and means to be successful.

Family Time Throughout the Week

MONDAY—Do the Family Devotion Time together. Also, get started on your own or with your family on the Family Worship section.

TUESDAY—During your family time, read the list from Scripture of things that will not fail under the first part of the Family Worship section. Talk through these and see if anyone has examples from their lives when they've seen these be true? Can anyone think of other things that will not fail?

WEDNESDAY—Read the story of the prodigal son to your family again. Encourage everyone to think about which of the three characters they are most like. Which one of the three was a failure in the end? Could it be that an attitude of failure is worse than a failure in action? What did or could each of the characters learn from their failures? How can we use that in our lives every day?

THURSDAY—Read this "Failure Formula" to your family: "Whenever we make excuses for failing, we will fail even more." Now talk about any areas or times when you are making excuses. If we try to blame our failures onto other things or people, do you think God is able to use our failures to teach us?

FRIDAY—Read what C. S. Lewis calls "Satan's Strategy", from *The Screwtape Letters:* "Get Christians preoccupied with (or worried and upset about) their failures. From there the battle is won."

Commit to God and to the other members of your family that from this moment on, your focus will be upon Him and His goal for your life. Reread Philippians 3:13, 14. Make the promise of these verses be the power of your life.

WEEK 12: FAITH

Family Devotion Time

ACTIVITY: THE ELECTRIC COMPANY. This week's activity is simple, but thought provoking. Take a little tour through your home. Have family members take turns switching lights, televisions, and appliances on and off. This activity might also produce a few giggles from family members who feel silly

> ***Faith*** *is believing in something you can't see or hear.*

walking through the house all together—think of how few times we move through the house with anyone else, let alone our entire family!

DISCUSSION: Through any giggles, you can start the discussion time. As always, you are just trying to help your family catch a glimpse of what this week's subject—faith— means.

• When we took turns turning on different things, how did you know that they would work?
• What makes a lamp work when you turn it on?
• Unless we get a shock or see a spark, we can't really see electricity. How do we know it's there waiting for us to use it?
• Even though we can't see God, how can we know that He's there?

God is! It's funny how the very most powerful "person" that is, is also Someone we can't see. Some people go through their whole lives without *faith* that God exists. They don't feel any of God's power or His love. Like electricity, He's right there waiting to light up people's lives. But they never "flip the switch" and ask Him to work in them. ***This week's memory verse*** sounds a lot like the definition for faith above:

"What is faith? It is [knowing] . . . that what we hope for is waiting for us, even though we cannot see it up ahead."
—Hebrews 11:1

FAMILY BIBLE TIME: Read Hebrews 11:1, 2, 7-12—part of what is referred to as the "faith chapter" in the Bible. Why do you think Noah and Abraham are given to us as examples of men of faith?

FAMILY PRAYER TIME: This prayer time will help you focus on the simple faith of accepting what you can't see—not like a fantasy character your kids might pretend to be, but things that are real and true, yet not right in front of us. Pray this prayer aloud, then close with a time of prayer around your family circle. Encourage each person to pray for the person on his left by name, that this person's faith will be strengthened.
"God, even though we can't see You, we know that You are there. . . . When we think about it, we have "faith" in a lot of things: that electricity will light our lamps, that water will come out of the faucet when we turn it on, that someone will be on the other end of the conversation when the phone rings. Even if we have that simple of faith in You at first, we pray that we would have that faith. And we ask that You take that 'germ' of faith and strengthen it in each of our lives . . . (Encourage people to pray for others in the family by name now.) In Jesus name, Amen."

Family Worship Time (optional)

Years ago, a small town in Maine was chosen for the site of a great hydroelectric plant. A dam was going to be built across the river, and the town would be submerged. When the project was announced, people were given many months to relocate.
An interesting thing happened during the time before the dam was built. All improvements in the town stopped! People stopped making repairs on their homes and business buildings. Roads and sidewalks deteriorated without repair. Day by day the whole town got shabbier and shabbier. A long time before the dam was built and the waters came, the town looked uncared for

and abandoned—even though the people had not yet moved away. One person who lived there explained: "Where there is no faith in the future, there is no power in the present."

Someone has offered this untrue definition of faith: "The ability to believe in something without evidence." Faith is always based upon evidence: God's handiwork in creation, the death and resurrection of Christ, the miracles and growth of the first century church, and the change that is produced in the hearts of people who know Christ—these are all bits of evidence that God does exist and that He intervenes in the lives of people.

Read through all of Hebrews 11. In these verses, have family members look for the following characteristics of true faith:

1. *Faith sees the invisible.* A young man lost both eyes in an explosion during World War II. When a British entertainer attempted to comfort him, the soldier said, "It doesn't really matter. I'm going to be a minister someday, and you don't have to have eyes to please God."

When Russian cosmonaut Gherman Titov returned from space, he said, "I looked for God but I didn't see Him." However, when American astronaut James McDivitt returned, his statement was completely different: "I did not see God looking into my space cabin window . . . but I could recognize His work in the stars." Unlike the Russian cosmonaut, McDivitt possessed an inner eye of faith.

2. *Faith hears the inaudible.* In a single large city, there may be up to 9,000 radio signals. There are also signals for cellular phones and television signals. But without the aid of the right receiving equipment, the words and music go undetected by us. Our faith is like a radio receiver. God is all around us, and faith allows us to sense God's direction and reassurance in our lives.

3. *Faith believes the incredible.* Have you ever heard anyone say, "I just can't believe in miracles or in heaven and eternity; I can't believe the story of creation." Hebrews 11:3 answers, "By faith—by believing God—we know that the world and the stars—in fact, all things—were made at God's command; and that they were all made from things that can't be seen."

4. *Faith thinks the unthinkable.* While people without faith declare, "It's impossible, it can never be done," the person with faith is thinking of ways to accomplish what doubters of faith refuse to consider.

5. *Faith accomplishes the impossible.* After faith thinks the unthinkable, it accomplishes the impossible. According to Charles Haddon Spurgeon, God delights in impossibilities: "One man says, I will do as much as I can. Any fool can do that. He that believes in Christ does what he cannot do, attempts the impossible, and performs it." And of course it was Jesus who said that if we have faith even the size of a mustard seed, we can even do the impossible.

6. *Faith inherits the indestructible.* Only treasures stored in heaven are protected from rust, moths, thieves, inflation and taxes. It is faith, manifested through our acts of service, that inherits eternal and indestructible rewards.

Faith is an inner quality that increases in strength and improves in quality when we exercise it. The greatest faith we can achieve is the ability to believe when God's voice is silent and His hand is still. A victim of the German Holocaust scratched these words into the crumbling wall of his home before his death: "I believe in the sun, even when it does not shine; I believe in love, even when it is not shown; I believe in God, even when He does not speak."

Now take some time to go through the following steps together to help the idea of faith sink into your life personally. As always, make it your goal to work through all the steps in the next few days, even if you have distractions that pull you away.

PREPARATION TIME: George Mueller said, "The beginning of anxiety is the end of faith, and the beginning of faith is the end of anxiety." Ask God in a simple way to give each of you faith, and to remove any anxieties any of you are experiencing right now.

WAITING TIME: Think about the ways that God reveals His faith—through creation and as He works and ministers through other people. During this waiting time, allow God to love you, search you and show each of you His desires for your lives in the area of your faith. Remember that it's OK to be honest with God—He knows what's on your hearts and minds before you do. Ask Him to bring to mind phrases that complete these simple prayers:

"God, I feel Your love today, especially in the area of . . ."

"God, You have permission to reveal any doubts in my life, these areas where my faith doesn't exist or is weak . . ."

"God, what do I need to know which will require more faith as I enter this day. . . ?"

CONFESSION TIME: In Mark 9:22-24, the father of a demon-possessed boy brought him to Jesus and said:

"Have mercy on us and do something if you can."

"If I can?" Jesus asked. *"Anything* is possible if you have faith."

The father instantly replied, "I *do* have faith; oh, help me to have *more!"*

Take a moment and confess to God any areas in your lives where you lack faith or wish you had more.

BIBLE TIME: "I prayed for faith, and thought that someday faith would come down and strike me like lightning. But faith did not seem to come. One day I read in the tenth chapter of Romans, 'Faith cometh by hearing, and hearing by the word of God.' I had closed my Bible, and prayed for faith. I now opened my Bible and began to study, and faith has been growing ever since." —Dwight L. Moody

We can never pray out of God's will when we pray God's Word. Read Mark 9:17-29 slowly a few times. Close your eyes and ask God to bring a main truth to the surface in each of your hearts. Then pray the Scripture back to God and allow Him to minister to your family. Your prayer might go something like this: "God, we know that a lot of our prayers address You the same way that the father in these verses did. We ask You to help—if You can. We ask You to work in our lives—if You can. Sometimes we don't even say if You can, but in our hearts, we think it. Please forgive us for that lack of faith. Please take what faith is in our hearts now, and strengthen it and multiply it. As the father said, 'I do have faith; help me to have more!' That's really our simple prayer today. Help us to exercise our faith as well, to use it so that we can see and hear more of You, for we know that is how our faith will grow stronger. By faith, we *know* You can and will work in our lives. In Jesus' name, Amen."

MEDITATION TIME: After praying the Scriptures, write down in a notebook any thoughts that God has impressed upon each of your minds. Perhaps think about this week's memory verse, and the words "confident assurance" and "certainty." How do these words describe faith?

INTERCESSION TIME—PRAYING FOR OTHERS: As you continue seeking answers for your faith, ask God to bring to your minds and hearts others around you who need to experience what faith is, or who need to see their faith grow. Don't forget other members of your family. Pray that they will honestly want to see their faith become stronger and more real every day.

PETITION TIME—PRAYING FOR YOURSELVES: Now, pray that God will reveal to each of you very specific crevasses in your hearts where your faith is weak. Ask Him to give you new experiences to strengthen your faith in those areas—even some tough experiences, if necessary. Thank Him for not giving you more than you can bear, only what He knows will increase your faith and trust in Him.

APPLICATION TIME: List in a notebook what steps your family can take in obedience to God this week to know and bolster your faith. Beside each step, note how obeying God in each circumstance can increase your faith in Him.

FAITH TIME: Faith is our positive response to what God has said. Spend a few moments praying through your eyes of faith. Tell God the positive things you see happening because of His goodness!

PRAISE AND THANKSGIVING TIME: Read 2 Thessalonians 1:11. Then praise God by recognizing who He is—a God who works in our lives. And thank God by recognizing what He has done—called us to be His children. God, like a good parent, rewards our obedience and faith in Him.

Family Time Throughout the Week

MONDAY—Do the Family Devotion Time. If you have time, get a start on the Family Worship section.

TUESDAY—Review the outline of faith from Hebrews 11 at the beginning of the Family Worship section. Do you see these characteristics of true faith in your own life? With your family at a mealtime or individually at bedtime, make a commitment to think of faith every time you turn on a light. Think of how much we take the power of electricity for granted. Each time you turn on a light, ask God to help you remember not to take your faith for granted. Ask Him to help you remember to use your faith, so that it will be strengthened and grow.

WEDNESDAY—As a family, talk about things that you are trying to accomplish which are impossible without God and faith. Is there anything God is calling you to do that your lack of faith is keeping you from trying?

THURSDAY—As a family, work together on the memory verse. Besides simply memorizing the words, take the verse apart phrase by phrase. Talk together about what different words mean. Help each family member grasp what this verse can really mean when we apply it to our lives.

FRIDAY—As a family, talk about what these words mean: "I believe in the sun, even when it does not shine; I believe in love, even when it is not shown; I believe in God, even when He does not speak." Talk about how we can live so that these words become real to each of us.

WEEK 13: FORGIVING MYSELF

Family Devotion Time

ACTIVITY: THE MEMORY GAME. Use a deck of playing cards or Uno® cards. Sort out about 20 pairs (40 cards). Make sure each card has at least one matching card; if you use regular playing cards, some cards may have more than one pair possibilities. Shuffle the cards and lay them out face down in a large rectangular shape (five rows of eight cards each works for 20 pairs).

> *When I **Forgive Myself**, I no longer feel bad about what I did wrong.*

Now play the memory game, taking turns turning over cards and trying to find pairs. If you find a pair, you keep those two cards. If you don't turn over a pair, you turn the cards back face down. The person to match the most pairs wins.

DISCUSSION: Depending on the size of your family and the amount of time to complete one game, you can play one or more games. After you've played for awhile, stop to discuss these questions. If your family likes the game, you can always play more after the prayer time.

• This game was called "The Memory Game." Do you think that you have a good memory or a bad memory?

• What's the very first thing you remember happening to you? How old were you?

• What's the strongest memory you have—it might be a very sad or extremely happy memory?

• Why do you think God gave us the part of our minds that helps us to remember things, even hard things like strong emotions and pain?

• Do you have memories you wish you could forget? Why?

Sometimes the person hardest to forgive is ourselves. And if we can't forgive ourselves, it's harder for God to use us. Not forgiving ourselves can make us bitter. We might even blame God or other people for the way we feel. The good thing is that God forgives us. That's the reason Jesus died on the cross for our sins—to make us right with God. And if God forgives us, can't we forgive ourselves? Think about what *this week's memory verse* says:

"He has removed our sins as far away from us as the east is from the west." —Psalm 103:12

FAMILY BIBLE TIME: Now read all of Psalm 103 aloud. Knowing how much God loves us and how He forgives us, how does it make you feel about God?

FAMILY PRAYER TIME: Encourage your family to pray simple sentence prayers as you raise these thoughts in their minds. If no one responds audibly, that's OK. They may be praying silently, and with this sensitive subject, that's fine. Once you've read through the list slowly, close in prayer.

"God, help us to think about our good memories . . ."

"God, help us to forget our bad memories . . ."

"God, as we think of areas where we just can't forgive ourselves for something we've done . . ."

". . . we ask You to help us remember Your grace and forgiveness . . ."

"We know that if we don't forgive ourselves, we're saying that Christ's work on the cross doesn't matter. We know better than that in our heads, help us to feel it in our hearts . . ."

Family Worship Time (optional)

Read this together with your family. But this week don't push anyone into a discussion he's not ready for yet. Be sensitive to the Holy Spirit's leading. Psalm 103 speaks eloquently and simply about God's forgiveness. But to apply the truth of this psalm's balm, we need to see ourselves through God's eyes. We may know the truth that God forgives us, but still we struggle with feelings of guilt and self-hatred. It's as if something is blocking what we know in our head—that God forgives us and we can therefore forgive ourselves—from what we feel in our heart. Here are some suggestions to move the truth of Psalm 103 from our heads to our hearts.

1. We need to adjust our view of God. He's not a taskmaster. He's tender with us and our feelings. He's not a legal accountant. He's lovingly devoted to us. He's not a performance-based God, keeping "score" on what we do. He's a loving-parent God, who finds pleasure and delight in watching us grow

We need to overcome any negative images we have of God stemming from our childhoods, church communities, and other authority figures. Then, we need to meditate on the truth of who God is from Scripture.

2. Find a safe, understanding, compassionate Christian who can be God's arms and legs and heart to you. Sometimes, receiving forgiveness from another person helps us to realize that God offers it as well, and that we can also forgive ourselves.

James 5:16 says, "Admit your faults to one another and pray for each other so that you may be healed." Confession is still a powerful way to make God's forgiveness tangible. If you feel frozen in your attempts to forgive yourself, consider telling your story to a mature, trusted Christian friend, pastor or counselor.

3. Be willing to change—to learn to live in freedom!

Emotionally, we may live so long under guilt and self-condemnation that the very idea of being free is threatening. We feel comfortable with what we know, and what we know is guilt. We adjust to our feelings of guilt and surrender the peace we could enjoy if we forgave ourselves. If we want to be released from guilt, we must change our thinking. We need a thorough cleansing of our thought processes. No more thinking, "I know what the Bible says about forgiveness, but. . . ." Every time we include a "but," we put one more bar in our prison of guilt. We need to get rid of the bars; we need to break out of the prison. We don't have to be there. But we have to want to get out.

If this describes what you're going through, what you're feeling, you might also meditate on John 8:32; Romans 8:1; Galatians 5:1; Hebrews 10:17, 18.

If you've had trouble forgiving yourself in the past, you may be emotionally spent right now thinking about the sin that you've found unforgivable. You may need a break to let God speak to you. Or you may sense that being able to forgive yourself is near, and you want to move on. At some point, spend some time going through these steps, either as as family or individually. They will help you gain a greater understanding of how and why you should offer yourself forgiveness.

PREPARATION TIME: Read Romans 8:1. Encourage each person to think about the areas or incidents from his past or present where he sometimes has feelings of guilt, shame or condemnation.

WAITING TIME: During your waiting time, let God love you, search you and show each of you exactly how you can have the strength to forgive yourself. Ask God to give you phrases that complete these sentence prayers:

"God, help me to feel Your love today, even sensing that You delight in me . . ."

"God, You have permission to reveal any hidden areas of hurt, unforgiveness or shame in my life . . ."

"God, is there anything that I need to know about forgiving myself as I enter this day. . . ?"

CONFESSION TIME: Read 1 John 1:9. Then individually confess your sin of unbelief of God's forgiveness for you: "Father, forgive me for holding myself in bondage, for keeping myself from You, and for limiting Your use of me."

Now read Hebrews 10:17-22. Picture each area where each of you needs to forgive yourself and leave it at the cross with Jesus. Picture Jesus taking the burden upon Himself and forgiving you. Receive His forgiveness, and turn and walk away in freedom.

BIBLE TIME: We can never pray out of God's will when we pray God's Word. Read Psalm 103:10-14 slowly a few times. Then close your eyes and allow a main truth to surface in your hearts. Pray the Scripture aloud and ask God to minister to each of you.

MEDITATION TIME: After praying the Scriptures, write down the thoughts that God has impressed upon your mind about His forgiveness and how it relates to forgiving ourselves.

INTERCESSION TIME—PRAYING FOR OTHERS: Pray for people that each of you knows who also have a difficult time forgiving themselves. If you've struggled in this area, you know how hard it can be sometimes to face even one more day with guilt. Pray that these people will sense and increase their understanding of God's forgiveness. Pray Hebrews 10:17-22 for each person by name.

PETITION TIME—PRAYING FOR YOURSELVES: If you've never really struggled with forgiving yourself, take time to thank God for that right now. Pray that He will keep you safe from the Enemy, that such a sin will not enter your life that you couldn't possibly forgive yourself for. Praise God for His gift of forgiveness.

APPLICATION TIME: List in a notebook what steps each of you can take toward obeying God even during times when you aren't sure you can forgive yourself. Note how being obedient is itself a step toward knowing your own forgiveness as well as God's.

FAITH TIME: Faith is our positive response to what God has said. Spend a few moments praying through your eyes of faith. Tell God the positive things you see happening because of His goodness!

PRAISE AND THANKSGIVING TIME: Read Hebrews 10:5-8 again. Now praise God by recognizing who He is—a willing sacrifice. And thank Him by recognizing what He has done—allowed us to forgive ourselves because He forgives us through the work of Christ on the cross.

Family Time Throughout the Week

MONDAY—Do the Family Devotion Time, and begin the Family Worship section.

TUESDAY—Work on memorizing Psalm 103:12. Make sure that you take some time to talk about what the verse means. Why do you think the psalmist used east and west to tell us how far sin is removed from us? Think of the sunrise and the sunset—they're not only on *opposite* sides of the horizon, they're separated by all of the daylight hours. How does this help our understanding of God's forgiveness?

WEDNESDAY—Read and meditate on Zephaniah 3:17, 18. How do you think God can feel this way about us? How can He find such delight—so much that He sings—in creatures who repeatedly fail Him? Does Christ have something to do with it?

THURSDAY—Read Romans 8:26-39. Then ask your family the questions in verses 31, 33, 34, 35, rephrasing them to aid understanding, if necessary. Then help your family seek the answers to the questions from the rest of the passage.

FRIDAY—Play the memory game again together as a family. As you play, talk through the discussion questions again. There may be members of your family who have gone through this week and have now realized that something is burning inside them that they need to forgive themselves for. Reopening the discussion may help them open up. If someone does begin to share areas where he cannot forgive himself, commit as a family to supporting and praying for this person, and to try to help him understand that God's forgiveness means he can forgive himself as well.

WEEK 14: FORGIVING OTHERS

Family Devotion Time

ACTIVITY: IT'S LONESOME OUT TONIGHT. Send everyone to his or her own room. Just have family members sit on their beds.

If you have children who share a room, encourage one of them to go into the bathroom or another room where no one else is right now. Each person, if possible, should be in a room by himself or herself.

> ***Forgiving Others*** *can make things right even when you've been hurt.*

Announce (loudly!) that you're going to spend your time together "apart" this week. Ask the first two discussion questions below as loudly as you can, and have family members shout back their answers. You might have to coax answers a little more than usual; no one will probably want to yell. If someone does answer, make sure everyone else can hear, or say, "Louder, please." And if you do have a lot of return shouters, be prepared for some strange looks from your neighbors the next day!

After you ask the first two questions, ask (loudly again!) for everyone to come to the room where you are, and you can complete your family time together there.

DISCUSSION:
• Why do you think it's important that we are able to have a good relationship with each other?
• Why would we want to do anything, like separate ourselves, to hurt our relationships with each other?
• Now that we're together, let's ask those two questions again. Why do we need good relationships? Why would we harm our relationships?
• What was wrong with trying to hold our time together

apart from each other?

• Besides trying to stay away from each other, can you think of any other ways we mess up our relationships?

• What about our attitudes and feelings toward each other. Can they affect our relationships?

• Do you think we have any right to hold grudges against other people when God offered us his forgiveness?

Even the "best" person in the world doesn't deserve God's forgiveness. Yet He offers it to everyone! Why, then, do we sometimes think it's OK for us not to forgive someone else? Only by further understanding God's forgiveness can we forgive others. That's why *this week's memory verse* encourages us:

"Be kind to each other, tenderhearted, forgiving one another, just as God has forgiven you. . . ." —Ephesians 4:32

FAMILY BIBLE TIME: Read Matthew 18:23-35. How is the king like God? How are we like the man who owed a lot of money?

FAMILY PRAYER TIME: Just as you did last week, encourage your family to pray simple sentence prayers as you raise these thoughts in their minds. If no one responds audibly, that's OK. They may be praying silently. Once you've read through the list slowly, close in prayer.

"God, right now we praise You for the good relationships we enjoy . . ."

"God, help us do our part to make any poor or weak relationships stronger . . ."

"God, forgiving others is such a big part of making relationships better. As we think of people who we just can't forgive for something they've done . . ."

" . . . we ask You to help us remember Your grace and forgiveness . . ."

"We know that if we cannot forgive others, we're saying that Christ's work on the cross doesn't matter. We know better than that in our heads, help us to feel it in our hearts . . ."

"Give us just one step we can take today to begin to forgive and put back together a bad or hurting relationship . . ."

Family Worship Time (optional)

This is a sensitive story that younger kids might not understand. If you are completing this section with kids younger than 12, you might want to move on to the paragraph following the next one.

There's a vast difference between forgiveness and trust. Forgiveness is given. Trust is earned. Betty has learned to apply this principle in her life. She became a Christian in her twenties, and God then began the process of revealing and healing in her life. As a child, Betty had been sexually molested by her father for several years. As soon as she was old enough, she left home and wanted nothing to do with her parents. In her growing relationship with Christ, she realized she needed to forgive her parents—her dad for molesting her, and her mom for denying it and not protecting her. However, Betty thought forgiving them would mean she would have to trust them and have a close relationship with them. Once she realized the difference between forgiveness and trust, she was willing for God to begin walking her through the healing process in order to forgive them.

Consider these biblical principles concerning forgiving others from the parable of the unmerciful servant in Matthew 18:21-35:

1. God offers unlimited forgiveness (verses 21-27).

2. God has given us mercy so we may extend it to others (verses 28-35).

3. God will turn us over to our own "prison" of bitterness if we are unwilling to forgive others (verses 34, 35).

4. God calls each of us to be responsible in every conflict to put things right by receiving or giving forgiveness (Matthew 5:23, 24).

Some of you may be sensing areas where you need to offer forgiveness to others. If so, spend some time going through the following steps so that God can prepare and teach you about how you can really forgive others who have hurt you.

PREPARATION TIME: Read Ephesians 4:30-32. Now silently think about the people who have hurt you or offended you. Try to remember the specific circumstances that led to the resentment or grudge you hold against them.

WAITING TIME: During your waiting time, let God love you, search you and show each of you how He wants you to forgive these people. Ask Him to provide appropriate answers to these simple statements:

Picture Jesus grieving with you, hurting with you when the offense happened. Picture Him taking the offense upon Himself and holding you in His arms as a parent would hold a hurt child.

Ask God to search your heart and reveal any sin that may be causing the grudge or wound to fester and keep from healing.

Ask God to show you His perspective of the other person and the entire situation.

CONFESSION TIME: Confess your sin of resentment, bitterness, self-pity, hatred, etc. Now, encourage each family member to spend some time alone to verbalize out loud to God His forgiveness of each person and what they did to Him. This sentence might help: "Because God forgives me, I forgive you, (person's name) for (what they did)"

BIBLE TIME: When we pray Scripture back to God we can be certain that we are praying in His will. Read Psalm 34:18-22 slowly a few times. Close your eyes and allow a main truth to surface in each of your hearts. Then pray the Scripture back to God and allow Him to minister to you. Your prayer might go something like this: "God, You know us so well. You know when we are hurting, when our hearts are breaking. Thank You for rescuing us when our sins get us down so far that we can't get up. We know that just because we know You doesn't mean we will escape from trouble. In fact, the Enemy will test us again and again. But You will give us the strength to withstand whatever trials come our way! Thank You for Your forgiveness. Help us to see that we are no better off than the wicked, though, if we don't also offer forgiveness. If we are truly serving You, we will forgive and offer pardon to those who wrong us, just as You have pardoned us. Help us to remember that and to offer it to others. In Jesus' name, Amen."

MEDITATION TIME: After praying the Scriptures, write down the thoughts that God has impressed upon your minds about offering forgiveness to others. Think especially about whether it matters if someone deserves your forgiveness or even asks for it. Did you deserve forgiveness from God? Didn't He offer it even before you asked?

INTERCESSION TIME—PRAYING FOR OTHERS: Pray for each person that you have forgiven today. Give everyone the option of praying silently. Pray that God will draw them to His love and truth, that they will see their need for Jesus' healing and forgiveness.

PETITION TIME—PRAYING FOR YOURSELF: Ask God to heal your hearts and to continue to wash away the wounds in His cleansing love and forgiveness. Ask Him to show each of you any other steps you need to take in this healing/forgiving process.

APPLICATION TIME: Some possible application steps:
• Share your hurts and pray with a trusted Christian friend.
• See a professional Christian counselor to work through any deeply wounded areas.
• Work through a Bible study course on forgiveness, either alone or with a family member or friend.

FAITH TIME: Faith is our positive response to what God has said. Spend a few moments praying through your eyes of faith. Picture yourself forgiven by God and free to love and forgive others. Express your gratitude to Him!

PRAISE AND THANKSGIVING TIME: Praise God by recognizing who He is—a merciful and faithful God. And thank Him by recognizing what He has done—allowed us to forgive others because He forgives us.

Family Time Throughout the Week

MONDAY—Do the Family Devotion Time. Work through the Family Worship section.

TUESDAY—Work together on your memory verse for this week. Make sure each person in the family understands what it means as well as memorizes it. If needed, take the verse apart phrase by phrase, and ask family members to define each word or phrase. Help younger children choose just a part of the verse to understand and commit to memory.

WEDNESDAY—Read Isaiah 53 after dinner with your family. Who is this passage about? How could anyone be treated so badly, yet make this kind of sacrifice—of His own life?

THURSDAY—Write down names of all the people you are not forgiving right now. Forgive each of them by working through the Preparation, Waiting and Confession Times in the Family Worship section above. At bedtime, ask family members individually if they are having these kinds of feelings of unforgiveness toward anyone. Help them to understand the need to forgive others, and to make the statement under Confession Time to you.

FRIDAY—Talk through the discussion questions at the beginning of this week again with your family. Are any of your answers different now that you've worked through this week's steps?

WEEK 15: GENTLENESS

Family Devotion Time

ACTIVITY: THE POWERFUL CLEANER. Before today's activity time as a family, fill a squirt bottle full of water. You might already have one around for plants or for ironing. When the family gathers, grab a roll of papers towels, the spray bottle of water, a bottle of window cleaner and then steer everyone toward a large

> ***Gentleness*** *means being strong enough to think of others before yourself.*

bathroom mirror. You may all feel a little silly standing together in front of the mirror, but this isn't necessarily a serious time. A few giggles are fine.

Have one member of the family spray half the mirror with plain water and another person spray half the mirror with the window cleaner. Pass out a couple of sheets of paper towels to each person, and wipe! Give everyone a chance to wipe the mirror on the side where there is plain water, and on the side where there is window cleaner.

DISCUSSION: Head back to the table, family room or living room, or wherever you typically have your discussions each week. Talk through the following questions:

• When you were cleaning the mirror, did you notice any difference in using just plain water and using the window cleaning liquid? Which was easier to use?

• Since the cleaner and water are both liquids, that doesn't explain why the cleaner seemed easier. So, talk about what might have made the cleaner work better.

• If you had to clean all the mirrors in your house once a week, would you rather use water or a glass cleaner?

• Now, what if you had to clean all the windows in a 50-story skyscraper? Would you rather use some kind of window cleaner or plain water?

• Why does having the right tool make things easier for us?

Having the right tools makes doing a job easier. It's easier to vacuum up crumbs up from a carpet than to sweep them up. A lot of people think that being gentle means that we have to be weak. But gentleness requires strength and power. In fact, those are the right tools for gentleness. We can be gentle when we're strong, when our power and strength are from God and controlled by God. Think of Christ and how gentle He was. Yet He was the strongest and most powerful man to ever walk the earth. He possesses the strength to carry every burden we could ever have. Read the words of *this week's memory verse:*

"Come to me and I will give you rest—all of you who work so hard . . . let me teach you; for I am gentle and humble. . . ."
—Matthew 11:28-30

FAMILY BIBLE TIME: Read Proverbs 15:4 from *The Living Bible.* Ask each family member to give examples of gentle words. How can they "cause life and health"?

FAMILY PRAYER TIME: Pray together as a family about being strong enough to be gentle. Ask God to help you see the difference between what the world sees as strength and God's view of strength. You can ask different family members to pray, or you can pray and others can join you silently.

Family Worship Time (optional)

Several years ago, Robert Ringer wrote a best-selling book called *Looking Out for #1.* Of course, most people probably could have written this book, and most really didn't need to read it! The same author wrote another book, *Winning Through Intimidation,* another title that hardly needed to be done, considering how many people already practice that philosophy.

From the titles, you can tell that both books had a similar message: To be powerful, you have to be tough. And to be tough, you've got to look out only for yourself.

That message is pretty different from "The meek and lowly are fortunate! for the whole wide world belongs to them" (Matthew 5:5), isn't it?

Well, here's a secret: Meekness is not weakness!

Dr. Martyn Lloyd Jones wrote, "The man who is meek is not even sensitive about himself. He is not always watching himself and his own interests. He is not always on the defensive . . . all that is gone. The man who is truly meek never pities himself, he is never sorry for himself. He never talks to himself and says, 'You are having a hard time, how unkind these people are not to understand you.' He never thinks, 'How wonderful I really am, if only other people gave me a chance.' Self-pity! What hours and years we waste in this! But the man who has become meek has finished with all that. To be meek, in other words, means that you have finished with yourself altogether, and you come to see you have no rights or desserts at all. . . . The man who is truly meek is the one who is amazed that God and man can think of him as well as they do and treat him as well as they do. That, it seems to me, is its essential quality."

Summed up another way, meekness—or gentleness—is power under God's control.

To grasp the idea that from being gentle comes true strength, spend some time going through these steps. As always, while it would be nice to go through all of the steps at one time, that doesn't happen in family life. Ask God to help you concentrate and learn even if you have to complete this in smaller chunks.

PREPARATION TIME: Reread the words of Jesus from this week's memory verse, and prepare yourselves to learn gentleness from Him.

WAITING TIME: During your waiting time, let God love you, search you and show each of you how you can be more gentle as you deal with people around you. Ask Him to give you phrases that complete these simple prayers:

"God, I feel Your love today, especially in the area of . . ."

"God, You have permission to reveal any areas in my life where I'm unwilling to be gentle . . ."

"God, is there anything I need to know about treating others with gentleness as I enter this day. . . ?"

CONFESSION TIME: Read Ephesians 4:2, 3. Then silently confess to God the times when you've not lived out these words, when instead you've been arrogant and brash, impatient and narrow-minded with those around you. Ask His forgiveness for the hurts you've cause others because you haven't been gentle.

BIBLE TIME: When we pray God's Word back to Him, we can be certain that we're praying for God's will. Read the verses above slowly a few times. Then close your eyes and ask God to bring a main truth to the surface in each of your hearts about gentleness. Now pray this Scripture and allow God to minister to you. Your prayer might go something like this: "God, make us humble, thinking of others before ourselves. Make us gentle, strong enough to think of others' needs before our own. Help us to be patient, secure enough that we hold our words and actions until we sense Your leading. Help us to bear with what we might consider 'faults' in other people's personalities. Most of all, we ask You, Holy Spirit, to reside in us and to lead us, especially when it comes to how we relate with people around us. Help them to see You and Your peace within us, not so they think we're great people, but so they will know more fully what it means to have You dwell within and work within. In Jesus' name, Amen."

MEDITATION TIME: After praying the Scriptures, write down in a notebook any thoughts that God has impressed upon your minds about gentleness. You may also want to read Philippians 2:4, 5; 2 Peter 1:7; James 3:16; and James 4:1, 2.

INTERCESSION TIME—PRAYING FOR OTHERS: Each of you should think about areas where you struggle with having a gentle approach. It's very likely that other people you know struggle in much the same way. Ask God to bring to your minds people who desire to have a gentle spirit. Pray that God will reveal to them exactly how they can exhibit gentleness.

PETITION TIME—PRAYING FOR YOURSELVES: Now make the same kinds of requests for yourself. If each of you sincerely desires to possess and display the gentleness of God, give God permission to work in your lives to change you into the caring and gentle people God desires.

APPLICATION TIME: Now list in a notebook what steps you think your family might take in order to have a spirit of gentleness. Beside each step, try to note how obedience to God can change each of you in the area of gentleness. Since obeying God is a positive action, try to write your steps in direct, active language. For example, if you've written down that one step is "carefully and patiently listening when someone else is talking," next to that write, "I will not cut people off before they finish what they're saying, and I will listen wholeheartedly, rather than listening halfway and formulating my next response while someone else is talking."

FAITH TIME: Faith is our positive response to what God has said. Spend a few moments praying through your eyes of faith. Tell God the positive things you see happening because of His goodness!

PRAISE AND THANKSGIVING TIME: Read James 3:17. Now praise God by recognizing who He is—a wise God who calls us to a life of wise and quiet gentleness. Also, thank God by recognizing what He has done—given us the strength and power to live quiet lives of gentleness.

Family Time Throughout the Week

MONDAY—Do the Family Devotion Time. Start on the Family Worship section.

TUESDAY—"Is my personality under God's control?" Talk together as a family about what gentleness doesn't look like (anger, jealousy, selfishness, and so on). Pray together, asking God to show each of you parts of your temperament that aren't under control.

WEDNESDAY—"Are my words under God's control?" Talk together as a family about language, and what kind of words you would expect to hear from a gentle person's mouth. Pray together, asking God to give you words that reflect a true gentle spirit that lies within each of you. Pray for that gentle spirit within to be genuine. Then, throughout the rest of the day and this week, carefully watch the things you say. Remember, each word is a gift.

THURSDAY—"Is my perspective under God's control?" Talk together as a family about the different ways we can see things—from a selfish perspective (how something affects *me*); from a selfless, yet imperfect perspective (how something affects others only); or from God's perspective (how something affects His kingdom and its work). What kind of perspective should we desire? How does our perspective change the way we look at ourselves and other people?

FRIDAY—"Are my responses under God's control?" Today, talk together about the different ways we can respond to circumstances in our lives. Do gentle people think about how they will react, or do they just blow up if something goes wrong? If we want to respond positively to any circumstances, how can we do that? Read Proverbs 16:32.

WEEK 16: GRACE

Family Devotion Time

ACTIVITY: A TWIST ON 20 QUESTIONS. Twenty questions is one of those games you can play just about anywhere, so this week's activity can take place wherever you like—at home, out for dinner, in the backyard. One family member thinks of a person, place or thing, and the rest of the family takes turns asking yes- or no-answered questions, trying to guess.

> **Grace** *means getting something you don't deserve.*

If this game doesn't seem appropriate for your family for some reason, you can also play a favorite board game or card game together. The game isn't as important as the final result.

When the family's game is over, declare the loser(s) to be the winner(s). If possible, even give the losers a prize or reward—like an extra dessert or the chance to pick a favorite meal to be made in the next week.

DISCUSSION: You might hear some grumbling from the winners. Good! That energy can help this week's discussion.

• This question is for the people who "won" the game, but didn't receive the reward: How did you feel when the loser(s) got the reward for losing the game?

• This question is for the losers, who turned out to be the real winners: How did you feel receiving the reward even though you had actually lost?

• What if other parts of life were like this game—it didn't matter how you performed and you still won a prize? How would you live differently?

• What about the way God relates to us? The Bible says, "The wages of [or punishment for] sin is death, but the free gift of God is eternal life through Jesus Christ our Lord" (Romans 6:23). Even though we're lost because of sin, and we really deserve to die, God gives us—free—eternal life through Christ. This is a definition of God's grace to us. Why does God offer us His grace?

• Since God had a plan so He could offer us His forgiveness and grace, why do you think it's so hard for us to offer other people around us our grace?

God's grace finds us just where we are in life, and that's where we are accepted. If anything was expected before we could receive grace, then it wouldn't be grace! So we don't have to try to be better before we are able to receive God's grace. Even more amazing, though, is that once we do accept God's grace, He gives us power to live beyond our own abilities. It's as though grace takes over and lets us do better. That's how we show grace to people around us—as we are able to do more than we thought we ever could. *This week's memory verse* says:

"God [gives] you everything you need and more, so that there will not only be enough for your own needs, but plenty left over to give joyfully to others." —2 Corinthians 9:8

FAMILY BIBLE TIME: To remind your family what God's grace cost Him, read Mark 15:25-40; 16:1-9.

FAMILY PRAYER TIME: Usually, it's pretty easy to accept a gift. But when the gift might change our lives and every way that we live, we might have to think about it a little longer. God offers His grace freely. But the results He leaves up to us. There are no strings attached to His grace that make us His puppets. Of course, He wants us to live differently so that others will see His grace. But He doesn't force us.

This week, pray together as a family that each one of you can know and experience God's grace. And pray that if you have accepted God's grace, that He will give you the desire to live for Him as well. Pray that each of you will allow God to work in your life in a life-changing way. Ask Him to use you so that others will also see His grace, and that they will want it as well.

Family Worship Time (optional)

Here are some truths about grace:
- God's grace is available because it is based upon Jesus' performance—not mine.
- God does not offer His grace to save me for what I can do for Him—He does it simply because He loves me.
- Part of receiving God's grace is dying to my "old husband" (the law). That means I stop relating to God based on my performance, and I start relating to Him based on grace.
- God's grace accepts me as I am, then enables me to live above my own ability.
- The ways I can serve God are actually greater under grace, because gratitude rather than guilt is the motivation.
- In order to receive and grow in grace, I need humility; I need to surrender myself to receive God's grace.

As you do each week, take some time to go through these steps, either on your own or with other members of the family. Do your best to work through these steps in the next few days.

PREPARATION TIME: Reread this week's memory verse. Think about the different areas of your lives—your personal life, family life, the relationships you have at church, work and/or school. Why is it so difficult for most of us to humbly share what we have with others when God provides it for free *and* He offers to meet every need and supply us with more than we need?

WAITING TIME: During your waiting time, let God love you, search you and show each of you His wonderful gift of grace. Ask Him to place in your hearts phrases that complete these simple prayers:

"God, I feel Your love today, especially in the area of . . ."

"God, in the area of living out Your grace, You have permission to reveal any wrong motive in my life . . ."

"God, as I go through this day and week, is there any area where I need to receive Your grace. . . ?"

CONFESSION TIME: "But he gives us more and more strength to stand against all such evil longings. As the Scripture says, "God gives strength to the humble, but sets himself against the proud and haughty." —James 4:6

Together, confess to God areas where you've been proud, boastful or arrogant, especially when it comes to your relationships with others.

Bible Time: We can never pray out of God's will when we pray God's Word. Read the verses above slowly several times, then close your eyes and allow a main truth to surface in each of your hearts.

Now pray the Scripture back to God and allow Him to minister to each of you. Your prayer might include these thoughts: "God, we're amazed to think of Your grace, and the strength and power you make available to us when we receive Your grace. You even give us power to stand up for good, to rid ourselves of evil things that might keep us separated from You. Help us to have the kind of faith it takes in Your grace and power to really cleanse us. Most of all, keep us humble, aware that this strength is from You and You alone, and that without it, we're right back where we started, with completely self-centered lives, full of empty boasting—and a lot of hot air. Again, please use Your grace within us to make us strong servants for only You. In Jesus' name, Amen."

MEDITATION TIME: After praying the Scriptures, write down in a notebook the thoughts that God is impressing upon your family's minds. Think about how grace, faith and strength (or power) are all related.

INTERCESSION TIME—PRAYING FOR OTHERS: Ask God to bring to your minds people who might need to know and experience His grace. Don't forget about the other members of your family. Pray that God will pour out a "greater grace" on those He brings to your minds.

PETITION TIME—PRAYING FOR YOURSELVES: Ask God to reveal areas of your lives where you are "performing" as if you've never received His grace. Then ask for His grace to change and empower each of you.

APPLICATION TIME: List in a notebook what steps your

family can take this week to live out God's grace in your lives. Beside each step, note how each area of your lives might look different as you live under God's grace, rather than your own performances.

FAITH TIME: Faith is our positive response to what God has said. Spend a few moments praying through your eyes of faith. Tell God the positive things you see happening in your family because of His goodness!

PRAISE AND THANKSGIVING TIME: "Now God says he will accept and acquit us—declare us 'not guilty'—if we trust Jesus Christ to take away our sins. And we all can be saved in this same way, by coming to Christ, no matter who we are or what we have been like." —Romans 3:22

Praise God by recognizing who He is—a God who loves us more than we can imagine! Thank God by recognizing what He has done—provided a way, through His grace, for us to have a restored relationship with Him.

Family Time Throughout the Week

MONDAY—Complete the Family Devotion Time. Also, get a start on the Family Worship section.

TUESDAY—Talk together as a family about how sufficient God's grace really is! It enables us to make it through tough times, and it empowers us to move forward in ministry and service. Now, think and talk about times when you've seen God's grace work in your own lives. How has God brought you through a difficult time? How has He given you strength to serve Him and minister to others?

WEDNESDAY—Reread James 4:6 under the Confession Time above. Some translations of the Bible call the "more and more strength" phrase "a greater grace." This means that the same grace that saved us is what will sufficiently enable us to face every other need in life! God wants to pour out doses of "greater grace" each day of our lives to give us His strength and power. But many of us struggle to receive anything beyond the grace that will save us. As a family, talk together about any areas of your lives where you need this "greater grace."

THURSDAY—As a family, take another look at this week's memory verse. Besides committing it to memory, take it apart and talk about what each phrase means. How can we really give up what we have and trust God to give us even more? What would doing that look like from day to day?

FRIDAY—If we want to live by grace and in God's grace, we really have to trust Him. Together with your family, think about these questions. Talk about them together. Do I consistently walk with a repentant heart, leaning on God? Do I really trust God and His unconditional grace for me? Pray together, asking God to help you trust Him and His grace to be more than sufficient for you every day.

Special note to parents: To know and experience God's grace, and many of the subjects discussed in this book, you and your children need to first experience the salvation that God offers through Jesus Christ. The Bible calls this being *born again.* Read John 3:1-21 to see Jesus' own explanation of what this means. Ask your kids if they know Jesus Christ as their Savior. Jesus will be our Savior—and give us eternal life—if we simply ask Him to be Lord of our lives. Above all, don't pressure your kids into doing anything they don't want to do. Pray for your kids, and be sensitive to God's leading. Ask God to prepare their hearts to talk about salvation, and He will.

WEEK 17: GRATITUDE

Family Devotion Time

ACTIVITY: TAKING INVENTORY. Provide a piece of paper and pen for everyone. You might also need to pair up an older child or parent with younger kids who can't write yet. The goal this week is to make a list of everything that you have and should be thankful for, yet maybe don't even think about.

> ***Gratitude** is being both thankful and grateful for what you have.*

Send family members to their rooms and instruct them to open their closet doors, dresser drawers and toy boxes. Mom and Dad might also take some time to go through other rooms of the house and open up closets, cabinets, and dressers. Now, sit down in the middle of the room and start listing things: clothes, shoes, bed, other furniture, toys, blankets and so on. Try to note especially the things that you use every day, yet you take for granted.

DISCUSSION: After all the members of your family have regathered, take some time to talk through these questions.

• Name some things on your list that you use every day.

• Is there anything on your list that was a gift from someone else in our family? What is it?

• Among the items that were gifts, is there anything for which you forgot to thank the person who gave it to you?

• Is there anything among the items on your list that you've never thanked God for providing?

• Why do you think that sometimes it's easier to give things to other people than to receive gifts?

• Do you think it can be hard to accept gifts from God? Why or why not?

God wants us to give with grateful hearts. He also wants us to receive gifts with gratitude—especially gifts that come from Him. He even wants our gratitude not only for what He does for us, but for who He is. That's why *this week's memory verse* says:

"Give thanks to him and bless his name. For the Lord is always good. He is always loving and kind. . . ." —Psalm 100:4, 5

FAMILY BIBLE TIME: Psalm 100 is filled with praise and thanksgiving for who God is and what He has done: "Shout with joy before the Lord, O earth! Obey him gladly; come before him, singing with joy. Try to realize what this means—the Lord is God! He made us—we are his people, the sheep of his pasture. Go through his open gates with great thanksgiving; enter his courts with praise. Give thanks to him and bless his name. For the Lord is always good. He is always loving and kind, and his faithfulness goes on and on to each succeeding generation."

From this passage, we can find seven biblical reasons for expressing our heartfelt gratitude to God:

1. God reveals Himself to us: "The Lord is God!"
2. God created us and is in control: "He made us."
3. We belong to Him: "We are his people."
4. God cares for us: "[We are] the sheep of his pasture."
5. God is good to us: "For the Lord is always good."
6. God's mercy never ends: "He is always loving and kind."
7. God is wonderfully faithful: "His faithfulness goes on and on to each succeeding generation."

FAMILY PRAYER TIME: As you look through each of your lists, encourage family members to pray simple prayers of gratitude to God for the things on their lists, especially the things they take for granted even though they use them every day. Remember, a bit of silent time during prayer time is OK; God listens to our thoughts as well as our audible words. Ask an older member of the family to close your prayer time, or do it yourself.

Family Worship Time (optional)

Anne Sullivan was born at Feeding Hills, Massachusetts. Born into a family afflicted with poverty, she was half blind. Then, at the Perkins Institute for the Blind, a brilliant operation restored Anne's sight. Thereafter she devoted herself to the care of the blind.

Meanwhile, down south a baby was born, a girl destined after early childhood never to see or speak or hear. This girl came under the care of Anne Sullivan, reluctantly at first. Yet with Anne's persistence, in two weeks, this girl had learned 30 words, spelling them by touching the hand of her teacher. As she grew and learned, this young woman grew to be known around the world—of course, we know her as Helen Keller. Teacher and pupil remained inseparable for 49 years.

Misfortune befell Anne Sullivan, who had become Mrs. Macy. What misfortune? She became blind. And now, the pupil taught the teacher how to overcome her lack of sight. She schooled her former teacher as devotedly as she had been schooled. Out of gratitude, Helen returned the grace to Anne.

Now spend some time going through the following steps. If you need a break or have interruptions, just commit to coming back and picking up where you stopped.

PREPARATION TIME: Think about this: The instant we are born, we already owe someone for nine months of room and board—and we never really pay that debt!

Are these sentences true in your life? "The more you have, the less grateful you are. Then, you begin to believe you deserve it; then you believe you need it; then you begin to demand it."

Think about your own attitudes of gratitude. Think about your personal lives, your family life, church life, and business or school life. In each of these areas, what are God's blessings for which each of you is grateful?

Also, think about some things that perhaps don't look like blessings. Are there areas where you acknowledge that God is in control and is teaching you something? Pray that what you learn causes you to grow.

In a notebook, list the blessings for which your family is grateful, and the areas that don't look like blessings. Beside the tough areas, leave room so that later you can record what you've learned.

WAITING TIME: During your waiting time, let God love you, search you and show each of you areas where He wants you to be grateful for what He's given you. Ask Him to bring into your minds phrases that complete the following simple prayers:

"God, I am particularly grateful for Your love because . . ."

"God, please show me anything I'm not grateful for but that You want me to be . . ."

"God, is there anything I need to know as I enter this day, an area You want me to no longer take for granted. . . ?"

CONFESSION TIME: The word "gratitude" comes from the same root word as "grace." Grace signifies the free and boundless mercy of God. Our word "thanksgiving" comes from the same root as "think." To *think* is to *thank.*

Take a few minutes together to think of areas, things or people you have taken for granted—or perhaps even felt that you deserved. Then ask God to replace your selfish thoughts with gratefulness.

BIBLE TIME: We can never pray out of God's will when we pray God's Word. Read Habakkuk 3:17, 18 several times. Then close your eyes and ask God to reveal a main truth to each of you. Now pray the Scripture back to God and allow Him to minister to you. After praying, your family might enjoy this modern-day version written by Dan Reiland:

Though the Christmas tree tilts, and traffic is insane,
The in-laws are here, and Lord, You know they're a pain.
Though my checkbook is empty, the car is on the blink,
My shopping's not done, Lord, I really need a drink.
Though Clinton is in office, and Carson has retired,
My boss is on the rampage and I may get fired.
Though the kids are screaming, and I'm in need of rest,
My waistline is growing, I'm just not at my best.
Though I've had the flu now for some 40 days,
And my doctor is sunning in Brazil until May.
And finally, though stressed far more than I please,
I promise to be grateful and down on my knees.

MEDITATION TIME: After praying the Scriptures, write down in a notebook the thoughts that God has impressed upon your minds about gratitude. Especially think about the many things we take for granted or even think that we deserve.

INTERCESSION TIME—PRAYING FOR OTHERS: During this step, ask God to bring to mind people in your lives who you take for granted. What are their needs? What doubts and worries do they have? Then pray these two things: First, that you will express to these people your appreciation for them and all the things they do for you; second, that they will find in their own hearts a gratefulness for all the things God provides for them and does for them.

PETITION TIME—PRAYING FOR YOURSELVES: Ask God to remind you of the times you've been ungrateful for all of His provision. Give Him permission to bring circumstances into your lives that may be unpleasant, but that will teach you and draw you closer to Him.

APPLICATION TIME: List in a notebook what steps your family can take this week to more adequately express your gratitude to God. Think again about everything you have—even pull out your lists from your family activity time—and commit to God that you will give thanks for something that you use each day.

FAITH TIME: Faith is our positive response to what God has said. Spend a few moments praying through your eyes of faith. Tell God the positive things you see happening because of His goodness!

PRAISE AND THANKSGIVING TIME: Reread this week's memory verse from Psalm 100. Then praise God by recognizing who He is—a God who is good, loving, kind and faithful. Also, thank God by recognizing what He has done—given us a desire and way to communicate our gratefulness for the blessings He provides in our lives.

Family Time Throughout the Week

MONDAY—Do the Family Devotion Time. If possible, get started on the Family Worship section.

TUESDAY—Work on finishing the Family Worship section. After a meal or with individual family members while getting ready for bedtime, talk about things we can be grateful to God for. Talk about God's provision of forgiveness and grace— salvation through Jesus Christ. Pray together, thanking God for this wonderful gift.

WEDNESDAY—Talk together as a family, at a mealtime or even during a snack time, about how hard it is to be grateful when things aren't going well. Why do you think God allows us to go through difficult times? What are some things we can learn from difficulty?

THURSDAY—Read the story of Helen Keller to your family (the first three paragraphs of the Family Worship Time section). Talk about how gratitude was shown by the people in this story.

FRIDAY—Review your memory verse. Do your best to take it apart phrase by phrase, asking what each phrase means and how it relates to gratitude. Use the outline of Psalm 100 under the Family Bible Time section of this week's study to help you understand the memory verse better as a family.

WEEK 18: THE HOLY SPIRIT

Family Devotion Time

ACTIVITY: THE AMAZING BUBBLE MAKER. This activity is kind of like a science experiment, but it's pretty simple. You need ¼ cup of water, ¼ cup of white vinegar, and ½ cup (divided into two equal portions) of baking soda.

First, have one of the kids pour the water into one of the portions of baking soda.

> **The Holy Spirit** is God—who lives right inside you and helps you.

Nothing, right? Encourage some stirring or shaking or whatever. The only real change is that you end up with baking soda paste. (You can save this for later and brush your teeth with it!)

Now have another child pour the white vinegar into one of the portions of baking soda. You won't have to do anything to get a reaction. It should bubble all over the place!

DISCUSSION: Now talk through these questions. As usual, the goal isn't to understand everything there is to know about the Holy Spirit—even theologians don't. But in a simple way, we can help our families understand how the Holy Spirit lives and works in our lives.

• Both of the liquids we used were clear, but which one made the baking soda bubble? Does anyone know why? (The baking soda is a base and the vinegar is an acid. In physical science, an acid will make a base react in some way.)

• Do we let things inside our lives that affect how we react?

• How do we react when our lives are filled with things that are not of God?

• How do you think our reactions change when the Holy Spirit lives inside us?

• What do you think those words mean—"the Holy Spirit lives inside us"?

The Holy Spirit is God, present on earth. He wants to live inside each of us. When the Holy Spirit lives in us, He affects everything about us. But He only acts within us when we invite Him to and give Him permission to. *This week's memory verse* says:

"Be filled instead with the Holy Spirit, and controlled by him." —Ephesians 5:18

FAMILY BIBLE TIME: Perhaps some younger family members aren't familiar with how God sent His Spirit to the early Church. Read Acts 2:1-21 aloud. Imagine what it must have been like that day in Jerusalem.

FAMILY PRAYER TIME: Ask your family to pray in short sentence prayers regarding the Holy Spirit, responding to each of these thoughts:

Pray that God will help you to realize that the Holy Spirit will have a positive influence in your life.

Ask Him to help you understand—or at least see—how the Holy Spirit works in your life.

Let God know that you want His Spirit in you and working through you.

Ask forgiveness for times when you've taken control back from the Spirit and given control to something else.

Family Worship Time (optional)

A. W. Tozer said, "Though every believer has the Holy Spirit, the Holy Spirit does not have every believer." If we've asked Christ to be our Savior, then He has given what He promised— the Holy Spirit right inside us. But we have to consciously relinquish control to the Holy Spirit. He doesn't force His way into the circumstances of our lives; we have to let Him into each circumstance.

In John 14:16-18 and 16:7-15, Jesus lists some very specific descriptions of the Person and ministry of the Holy Spirit. Christ reveals that the Holy Spirit's ministry will look very much like

His, except that the Spirit will indwell all believers at once. Also, if we let Him, the Holy Spirit will empower us to live and look like Jesus as well.

Probably the most unfortunate condition that exists in the church today is that many believers have reduced their lives and ministry to a safe, familiar routine—one that could be accomplished with simple human strength. If the Holy Spirit were suddenly removed from the earth, most of what we do would continue, unaffected by His absence.

A. W. Tozer writes: "The doctrine of the Spirit as it relates to the believer has, over the last half century, been shrouded in a mist such as lies upon a mountain in stormy weather. A world of confusion has surrounded this truth. This confusion has not come by accident. An enemy has done this. Satan knows that Spiritless evangelicalism is as deadly as modernism or heresy, and he has done everything in his power to prevent us from enjoying our true Christian heritage."

The Holy Spirit desires not only to indwell but to empower us; not simply to be in us, but to be on us, in power. He is a person, just like Jesus, who has a mind, will and emotions, and who wants to gift and enable every Christian for supernatural ministry.

Consider the following verses to understand the Holy Spirit's job description in your lives:

Helper (Comforter)—John 14:16
Guide (Counselor)—John 14:26
Foreteller (Revealer)—John 16:13
Empowerer (Power source)—Acts 1:8
Advocate (Lawyer)—Romans 8:26, 27
Enabler (Gift giver)—1 Corinthians 12:4-11

Now spend some time going through the following steps. Ask God to guide your time in study and communication with Him. Remember to listen for what God is saying and what He wants you to learn.

PREPARATION TIME: Read Zechariah 4:6. Then think about the areas of your lives where you haven't been experiencing the empowering of God's spirit, areas you've attempted to control and pull off in your strength. Specifically, think about how you've done this in your personal lives, your family life, your church or ministry life, and your school or professional life.

WAITING TIME: During your waiting time, let God love you, search you and show each of you areas where you're allowing the Spirit to work and areas where you're holding the Spirit back. Ask Him to bring to your minds phrases to help you complete the following simple prayers:

"God, today I know that I am walking in the power of the Spirit in these areas of my life . . ."

"God, You have permission to reveal any area in my life where I'm walking in the flesh . . ."

"Spirit, is there any new work that You need to do in me as I enter this day. . . ?"

CONFESSION TIME: According to Scripture, we can grieve, insult, resist and offend the Holy Spirit. One way we do this is by acting like Martha in Luke 10:38-42. Though she was attempting to serve Jesus, He wasn't impressed—because she was attempting to serve without first being served by Him. She was trying to do God's will, but her own way.

Confess together areas that you have initiated without the leading or power of God's Spirit.

BIBLE TIME: We can never pray out of God's will when we pray God's Word. Read Luke 24:49 slowly a couple of times. After reading, ask God to impress a main truth upon each of your hearts. Now pray this verse back to God. Your prayer might go something like this: "God, we thank You for Your promise of the Holy Spirit. We thank You for His work in our lives. We don't understand how He can be in us and in the person next to us and in believers all around the world. But by faith, we do accept that He is, because we know that He has worked in and through our lives. Unlike the disciples, we don't have to wait to tell others about how the Holy Spirit has filled us, because we can ask Him to fill us and control us every day. Thank You for His awesome power, power that even enables us to express our thanks to You now. In Jesus' name, Amen."

MEDITATION TIME: After praying the Scriptures, write down in a notebook any thoughts God has impressed upon each of your minds about the Holy Spirit. Especially think about how the Spirit is able to fill you and empower you. Think about what that means. Ponder how it works

INTERCESSION TIME—PRAYING FOR OTHERS: During this time think of two different kinds of people: First, those who know God and have the Holy Spirit in them but don't live like it. Second, those who don't know Christ personally and who need to invite the Holy Spirit into their lives. Pray that each person on these mental lists will take steps to allow the Holy Spirit to work in their lives.

PETITION TIME—PRAYING FOR YOURSELVES: Jesus promised that everyone who asked to "receive" or to be empowered by the Holy Spirit would be (Luke 11:13). But the issue we each must settle is: surrender. We don't move forward in control, but in submission; walking in the Spirit is more letting than trying. Pray that God would enable each of you to settle this issue in those areas you need to.

APPLICATION TIME: List in a notebook any steps you can take to "let" the Holy Spirit work in your lives. Think about and write down your daily routine—what areas do you tackle without even asking for God's help or blessing? Now beside those areas, list how you can let God's Spirit be in control.

FAITH TIME: Faith is our positive response to what God has said. Spend a few moments praying through your eyes of faith. Tell God the positive things your family sees happening because of His goodness!

PRAISE AND THANKSGIVING TIME: Reread this week's memory verse. Praise God by recognizing who He is—a God who is able to indwell each one of us. And thank God by recognizing what He has done—provided a personal, ministering part of Himself to work in our lives.

Family Time Throughout the Week

MONDAY—Do the Family Devotion Time. If possible, get started on the Family Worship section.

TUESDAY—With your family, read through the list that summarizes the Holy Spirit's job description in Christians' lives. Talk together about which of these areas you each experience most frequently. Why do you think you do? Which area do you not experience very often? Why not?

WEDNESDAY—Go back to the Preparation Time on the subject of the Holy Spirit. Ask family members who aren't completing the Family Worship section to think about the same questions in their own lives. Talk about why we may fail to experience the empowering of the Holy Spirit in certain areas of our lives.

THURSDAY—Talk about how day-to-day life would look different if all of us walked more consistently in the power of the Spirit. Spend time praying together again, asking the Spirit to work in you and through you. Pray for the other members of your family.

FRIDAY—Read Acts 1:8. This may be a familiar verse to some family members, but new to others. Talk about what each phrase means. How can each of you begin to live out the commission given in this verse?

WEEK 19: HUMILITY

Family Devotion Time

ACTIVITY: THE GREAT POPCORN SUCK-UP. For this week's activity, you need about a cup (or a handful) of popcorn, a brush or whisk broom and a dustpan, and a vacuum cleaner capable of handling popcorn.

Choose two family members to complete the activity, or take turns if you want everyone to have a chance.

> **Humility** *means thinking of others before yourself.*

Spread out the popcorn on the floor in two somewhat equal piles. Give one person the whisk broom and dustpan and the other person the vacuum cleaner. Now they will race to pick up the popcorn! Unless you have a professional janitor who is great at using a broom in your family, the person with the vacuum cleaner will most likely win.

DISCUSSION: Now comes the challenge for this week—relating power to humility. How can people who are humble possibly be powerful? Talk through these questions to get an idea of how humility and power are related:

• Which was easier: sucking up the popcorn with the vacuum cleaner or trying to sweep it up with a broom?

• If you could choose which "tool" to help you pick up the popcorn, which would you choose? Why?

• In your own life, in the usual day-to-day things you go through, which tool do you "feel" like you're using—the powerful vacuum cleaner or the slower broom and dustpan?

• Of course, it isn't quite so simple, but if you could choose tools to help you through day-to-day life, which one of these two would you pick?

Most of us go through the day trying to do a lot on our own. When we won't accept help, it's called pride. Pride is the opposite of humility. If we are too proud to ask for God's help, He can't help us. Then it's like using the broom and dustpan—we're just not powerful enough to do a very effective job of living each day. But if we set aside pride, and we're willing to be humble, God can work through us. That's like using the vacuum cleaner—a power source outside of us helps us do a much better job of making it through each day.

It's like *this week's memory verse* says:

"If you will humble yourselves under the mighty hand of God . . . he will lift you up." —1 Peter 5:6

FAMILY BIBLE TIME: The best example we have of humility is Jesus. He willingly left heaven and came to earth to die for us. Read Philippians 2:5-11. Notice that we are to have the same humble attitude that Jesus had.

FAMILY PRAYER TIME: During this prayer time together, emphasize the difference between our relatively puny power and God's amazing, awesome and unlimited power. Your family can silently or verbally repeat the phrases in this prayer as you read it aloud:

"God, help us to see how tiny and limited we are. Yet You care for us so much that You give us Your power. All You ask is that we set aside our own power and let You work through us. As 1 Peter 5:6 says, if we set aside our own desires, You can have Your way with us. Help us to realize what a good thing that is! Remind us of our pride and help us to give You control. Have Your way with us, God. In Jesus' name, Amen."

Family Worship Time (optional)

During the 1970s, Muhammad Ali reigned as the heavy-weight boxing champion for most of the decade. No one was more aware of his greatness than Ali himself. On countless occasions he would remind everyone of the phrase that almost became synonymous with him: "I am the greatest."

One day, however, after boarding an airplane, Ali met his

match. The flight attendant, walking the aisle to make sure that all the passengers had their seatbelts fastened, noticed that Ali had not fastened his. When she asked him to do so, he reportedly grunted: "Hmph! Superman doesn't need a seatbelt!" Unimpressed, the flight attendant just smiled and said, "Sir, Superman doesn't need an airplane." Quietly, Ali buckled his seatbelt.

This week's memory verse encourages us to humble ourselves so that God can work through us. But we miss God's counsel in the next verse about how we can humble ourselves: "Let him have all your worries and cares, for he is always thinking about you and watching everything that concerns you."

When we cast all of our cares on God, we are in absolute humility. We are trusting God to intervene, direct and empower all that we are concerned about.

Consider these contrasts between pride and humility:

• Pride demands equal rights. Humility sees life as a gift.

• Pride relies on personal effort. Humility relies on God's power.

• Pride is what religion is built from. Humility is required for Christians; God gets the glory.

• Pride focuses on measuring up. Humility focuses on undeserved mercy.

How do we enter into humility? First, we acknowledge our own weaknesses (2 Corinthians 12:9). Then we cast our cares on God (1 Peter 5:7).

Take some time going through these increasingly familiar steps, either alone or with another member of your family. Your goal is to exorcise pride and invite God to indwell you with His power.

PREPARATION TIME: Read Isaiah 57:15. In this verse, God says that He dwells in two places: the holy place and the lowly place.

Think about your personal lives, family life, church life, and your business or school life. Make mental lists, or write down areas where each of you struggles with human pride and self-centeredness in these areas of your lives.

WAITING TIME: During your waiting time, let God love you,

search you and show you His desires for your life in the area of humility. Ask Him to give you the right words to finish these simple sentence prayers:

"God, as I think about how humble I am or am not, I want to feel Your love and grace today, especially in the area of . . ."

"God, You have permission to reveal selfishness and arrogance in my life . . ."

"God, is there any 'care' that I need to cast on You as I enter this day. . . ?"

CONFESSION TIME: Paul Rader wrote, "Why does God want to humble a man or woman? Nobody can work for God until humility has taken hold of his life. Otherwise he magnifies himself out of all proportion to God."

John Ruskin wrote, "I believe that the first test of a truly great man is his humility. I do not mean by humility, doubt of his own power. But really great men have a curious feeling that the greatness is not in them, but through them. And they see something divine in every other man and are endlessly, foolishly, incredibly merciful."

Pray this simple prayer as your confession to God, either individually or together: "Lord, help me to be humble. Remind me to set aside my pride so that there's room for Your power in me! Work through me and be seen through me. Help me to extend every quality of Yours to those around me. In Jesus' name, Amen."

BIBLE TIME: We can never pray out of God's will when we pray God's Word. Read Psalm 51:16, 17 several times. Then close your eyes and allow a main truth to surface in each of your hearts. Now pray the Scripture back to God and allow Him to minister to your family. Your prayer might go something like this: "God, help us to sacrifice our pride to You. That's the only sacrifice You want from us, Lord. Thank You that we can approach You with broken hearts, ready for You to fill with Your own power. We're amazed again and again that You can work through us in such a way. In Jesus' name, Amen."

MEDITATION TIME: After praying the Scriptures, write down in a notebook any thoughts that God has impressed upon your minds about humility. Think again about how power and humility are related.

INTERCESSION TIME—PRAYING FOR OTHERS: Read Philippians 2:3. As God brings people to your minds, pray unselfishly for their success, for God's richest blessings to fall on them. Start now to set aside feelings any of you have of comparison and competition. Pray for God to finish His work in them, whatever that means in each individual's life.

PETITION TIME—PRAYING FOR YOURSELVES: During this time, talk to God about any obstacles in your lives that are preventing you from personal surrendering to Him. Be honest with God. Tell Him about your cares and acknowledge your need for Him in these areas. Most of all, ask God to work His will in and through each of your lives.

APPLICATION TIME: List in a notebook any steps your family can take toward obeying God in the area of humility. With each step, note how being obedient to God can help you all experience His power more fully every day.

FAITH TIME: Faith is our positive response to what God has said. Spend a few moments praying through your eyes of faith. Tell God the positive things you see happening because of His grace and power.

PRAISE AND THANKSGIVING TIME: Reread this week's memory verse. Now praise God by recognizing who He is— a mighty God who works in our lives. And thank God by recognizing what He has done—lifted you up and empowered you with *His* power.

Family Time Throughout the Week

MONDAY—Do the Family Devotion Time. Try to get started on the Family Worship Time.

TUESDAY—Read 1 Peter 5:6, 7. In these verses we are instructed to humble ourselves under God's mighty hand. Then we're told how to humble ourselves—by casting all of our cares on Him.

As a family, talk through and pray through the answers to these questions: In what areas of your life do you see yourself walking in humility? In what areas do you fail to walk in humility? Where do you try to control things rather than cast them on the Lord? What keeps you from handling the areas where you fail to be humble the way you handle areas where you walk in humility?

WEDNESDAY—Reread Isaiah 57:15. Note, once again, that God defines where He will dwell: the high and holy place, and the very lowly place. Two extremes, but two places that shed much light on God and our relationship to Him. Think through these questions together as a family: Why do you think God chooses to dwell among and give His grace to us when we are humble? How are "holy" place and the "lowly" place alike? Now, in your own words, pray that God will build you into a proper dwelling place for God; a place that is both holy and lowly.

THURSDAY—Reread Psalm 51:16, 17. Think about what kind of sacrifices we make so that we look good to others. Why do we confuse duties with the things God really wants us to wrestle with inside our hearts?

FRIDAY—Work on memorizing your memory verse together as a family. Also, take time to make sure everyone understands what the words mean. Take the verse apart phrase by phrase and talk about what each section means.

WEEK 20: IDENTITY IN CHRIST

Family Devotion Time

ACTIVITY: DOWN MEMORY LANE. For this week's activity, pull out all the old family photo albums. Just spend some time paging through the albums, looking at photos of extended family members and at photos of your immediate family in past years. It's especially fun to look at baby photos of your own family members.

> *Having an **Identity in Christ** means seeing yourself as better because Jesus lives inside.*

DISCUSSION: Talk about the following questions as you take a look at the past through photos:

• Of the other people in your family in these photos, who do you look the most like? What features are the most similar?

• Is there someone you know in your family who you act like? In what ways?

• What different things in our lives make us who we are?

• Are there any things that you see in yourself that you've gotten from another family member (the way you walk, the way you laugh, your eye or hair color, etc.) that you don't really like? Is there anything you can do about it?

• What do you think is your most Christlike feature or characteristic?

• Does having Christ live inside you make you a better or worse person? Why?

FAMILY BIBLE TIME: In 2 Corinthians 5:16-18, the apostle Paul says that if we have asked Jesus to be the Lord of our lives, we are given new lives. Read these verses in an easy-to-understand version. In a way, we become a new person who has never been seen before. The old bad things about us are gone. New good things take their place. For example, if we used to tell lies, we now have Jesus' power to tell the truth. Having Him inside us will remind us. Sadly, a lot of us keep living the old way. But we can apply the words of ***this week's memory verse*** and live based on what Jesus has done inside us:

"When someone becomes a Christian he becomes a brand new person inside. He is not the same any more. A new life has begun!" —2 Corinthians 5:17

FAMILY PRAYER TIME: Together as a family, ask God to help you remember your heritage. Also, ask God to help you realize that when you invite Him into your life, the past is erased in His eyes. Everything is forgiven and forgotten. God's forgiveness and this new life in Christ can free you to live with a new power to serve God. Does anyone want to ask God to live in their life? Now, thank God for your new identity and for the power and freedom that come with it.

Family Worship Time

When Victor Seribriakoff was 15, his teacher told him he would never finish school. Victor was told that he should drop out and learn a trade. He took the advice, and for the next 17 years he worked as an itinerant doing a variety of odd jobs.

Yet when Victor was 32 years old, an amazing transformation took place. A test revealed that he was a genius with an IQ of 161. Suddenly, he was no longer a dunce. He started acting like a genius. After that, he wrote several books, secured a number of patents and became a successful businessman. Perhaps the most significant event for the former dropout was his election as chairman of the International Mensa Society. The Mensa Society has only one membership qualification— a minimum IQ of 140.

What made the difference in Victor's life? What changed was the way he saw himself.

How many of us, as Christians, are like Victor? We live far beneath the privileges God has given us because we believe what the world says about us rather than what God says about who we are. Consider these truths about our identity in Christ, from 2 Corinthians 5:17, 18:

First, we have been given a new position—in Christ. This is mentioned more than 150 times in the New Testament. Second, we have new possessions—new spiritual resources inside. And finally, we have new potential—a ministry of reconciliation to the world.

As each of you ponders the identity you have in Christ, work through the following steps. As Christians, we sometimes think we don't deserve the privilege and promise that comes with knowing Christ. On our own, we don't. But after we invite Christ into our lives, God doesn't see us on our own anymore. He sees us as new too, because of what Christ did for us. As your family goes through these steps, keep in mind the goal of both seeing *and* accepting the promise of your identity in Christ.

PREPARATION TIME: Read Galatians 6:15. Now ask yourselves, "How have I allowed my identity as a 'new person' to affect my personal life, family life, church or ministry life, school or business life?" Ask God to increase the areas and time that each of you allow Him to live through you.

WAITING TIME: During your waiting time, let God love you, search you and show each of you where you can apply this week's lesson to your daily lives. Pray these simple prayers, asking God to provide the appropriate phrases to complete each sentence:

"God, today I affirm Your work in me as a new creature. I can see it especially in the area of . . ."

"God, You have permission to reveal any areas where I still live from my old identity . . ."

"God, is there any area of my self-image I need to focus on as I enter this day. . . ?"

CONFESSION TIME: "Since you became alive again, so to speak, when Christ arose from the dead, now set your sights on the rich treasures and joys of heaven where he sits beside God in the place of honor and power. Let heaven fill your thoughts; don't spend your time worrying about things down here. You should have as little desire for this world as a dead person does.

Your real life is in heaven with Christ and God." —Colossians 3:1-3

This passage calls you to three applications: to renew your perspective, to release your past, and to remember your purpose. Confess individually to God areas where you struggle to apply these verses in your own lives.

BIBLE TIME: We can never pray out of God's will when we pray God's Word. Read the above verses again slowly several times. Now pray the Scripture back to God and allow Him to minister to each of you. Your prayer might go something like this: "God, thank You for Your work on earth, and for Your resurrection. Because of it, we have entirely new lives. Help us to live like it! Help us to keep our focus on You and eternity. When the day-to-day things of our lives on earth get us down, help us to remember that our real lives are with You in heaven. And help us to live that truth out as we go through life day-to-day! In Jesus' name, Amen."

MEDITATION TIME: After praying the Scriptures, write down in a notebook the thoughts that God has impressed upon your minds. Especially focus on your identity. Think about what makes you who you are. How would each of you like to be different? Could fully accepting your identity in Christ make you more content with who you are?

INTERCESSION TIME—PRAYING FOR OTHERS: Read Ephesians 1:15-21. Ask God to bring to your minds others— including other family members—who need to understand the promises of this passage. Now, pray the verses back to God, inserting the names of those you're praying for.

PETITION TIME—PRAYING FOR YOURSELVES: Now pray the verses in Ephesians 1 for yourselves. Pray for wisdom and understanding so that you can accept these promises—and begin to live them because you believe they are true.

APPLICATION TIME: List in a notebook any steps your family can take toward obeying God in order to live as a people who have been given new identities.

FAITH TIME: Faith is our positive response to what God has said. Spend a few moments praying through your eyes of faith. Tell God the positive things you see happening because He has placed you in Christ and has changed your identity!

PRAISE AND THANKSGIVING TIME: Read 1 Corinthians 1:30. Then praise God by recognizing who He is—giver of life and salvation! And thank Him by recognizing what He has done—sacrificed Himself so that we can be made pure and holy in His sight.

Family Time Throughout the Week

MONDAY—Do the Family Devotion Time. Get started on Family Worship Time.

TUESDAY—It's amazing to think that more than 150 times in the New Testament, God refers to us in our new identity: *in Christ.* The words, "in Him," "with Him," or "in Christ" are everywhere in Paul's letters. With your family, look up the verses listed below and talk about what these different "in" phrases mean. If you use a study Bible, other verses will be cross-referenced. Notice that as Christians, in Christ we have wisdom, we are righteous, we have the same grace and power that Jesus experienced. The list goes on and on.

Romans 8:1, 2
Romans 12:3
1 Corinthians 1:30
2 Corinthians 5:21
Ephesians 1:19, 20
Ephesians 4:7

WEDNESDAY—Think and talk as a family about areas where it is sometimes difficult to accept our identity in Christ. Here are some areas to think about:

• What areas of your life do you struggle with healthy self-esteem?

• What other influences affect our ability to believe the promise of a new identity?

• Is there anything in your past (for example, a damaged

relationship or a work situation) that has made any area a struggle for you?

THURSDAY—After dinner, read Colossians 3:1-3 and the three applications listed above in the Confession Time to your family. Then discuss these questions:

• What are things that stop us from having a good self-image?

• What keeps us from letting go of our past?

• What are some ways we can serve God and have a ministry for Him?

FRIDAY—Like our salvation, our spiritual growth doesn't come by working for it, but by faith. Every step forward in God's Kingdom is a step of faith.

Experiencing our new identity in Christ requires us to simply accept God's promise by faith. Spend some time gathered together in silent prayer, asking God to help you accept these truths for your own life. Then, pray for other members of your family, that these truths are realized in their lives as well.

WEEK 21: INTEGRITY

Family Devotion Time

ACTIVITY: HIDE-AND-SEEK. For a designated block of time—
say 15 minutes or so—play hide-and-seek as a family. The
variation here is that one
family member, when he is
"it," gets to peek while the
others are hiding. Make sure
that this designated "peeker"
knows to peek discretely so he

> ***Integrity*** *means doing
> what is right even if no
> one sees you.*

isn't discovered. Remember, this is just a game. You're not
teaching that cheating is a good thing. The peeking is intended
to help your discussion time.

DISCUSSION: After the time is up, gather together as a family
and if it hasn't already been discovered, reveal the secret that
one person was peeking while the others were hiding. This
announcement should lead you easily into a discussion of these
questions:
- Was it fair for (name) to cheat?
- Even if we all didn't know (name) was cheating, was it OK?
- Do you think it's OK to cheat (or lie or do anything else
that we know is wrong) even if we're sure there's no way we'll
get caught? Why or why not?
- What about school or work—is it OK to do something
wrong because other people are doing it? Why or why not?
- How do you think we can stop ourselves from doing what
is wrong? How can we have integrity when other people around
us don't seem to have any?

Integrity means being honest, being fair, telling the truth. In
the Bible, it is called being righteous. As with many characteristics God wants us to have, integrity is both an action on our part

and a "letting" of God acting through us. ***This week's memory verse*** says we need to be honest, fair and tell the truth—have pure hearts—if we want to have a good relationship with God:

"Happy are those whose hearts are pure, for they shall see God." —Matthew 5:8

FAMILY BIBLE TIME: In 1 Kings 9:1-9, a conversation between Solomon and God reveals God's passion for integrity of heart, and how integrity translates into our lives. From this passage, we can reach four conclusions about integrity: First, God expects it from us. Second, integrity is a matter of the heart—we have to have integrity inside before we can show it outside. Third, God promises blessings for those who live lives of integrity. And finally, God also warns of consequences for those who live lives without integrity.

FAMILY PRAYER TIME: Pray together as a family about how you can be a family of integrity as well as individuals of integrity. Encourage family members to pray short sentence prayers, even prayers as simple as the definition for this week's topic. Remember that some silence during your prayer time is OK, even good. Allow individuals the time to think through what they want to say aloud. Also, remember that God knows our thoughts as well as hearing our words. Ask someone to close your prayer time, praying for each family member by name: "God, I pray that (name) will be someone who does what is right even if no one sees him/her."

Family Worship Time (optional)

Spend some additional time pondering the verses in 1 Kings 9, and meditating on the conclusions drawn from them. Then go through the following steps to gain a deeper understanding about integrity.

PREPARATION TIME: Read Psalm 15:1, 2. Now think about different areas of your lives, such as your relationships with friends, the way you handle your finances, your relationship with other members of your family, the way you do business or handle your professional or school life. Are there any issues that are keeping any of you from living a life of integrity?

WAITING TIME: During your waiting time, let God love you, search you and show each of you areas of strength and weakness when it comes to your personal integrity. Then pray these simple sentence prayers, asking God to place in each of your hearts the answers you need to give.

"God, I feel Your love today, especially in the area of . . ."

"God, I give You permission to reveal any area in my heart that does not have complete integrity . . ."

"God, is there anything I need to focus on in the various areas of integrity. . . ?"

CONFESSION TIME: Reread Matthew 5:8. Now, think about the areas of each of your lives that you need to confess to God concerning your personal integrity. Even consider writing these areas down in a notebook. These questions might help you think through your personal integrity:

• Do you always do what you say you'll do?
• Do you always tell the truth?
• Do you act the same when people are looking as when they're not looking?

You might even need to think in terms of percentages or ratios. One person's answer might be, "Nine times out of 10 I am the same person whether someone is watching me or not." If your answers are like this, confess the one time out of 10 that you fail.

BIBLE TIME: When we pray Scripture back to God, we can be certain we are asking for things within God's will. Read Matthew 5:8 again slowly a few times. Close your eyes and ponder what this verse is saying to each of you about integrity. Then pray the verse back to God and allow Him to minister to you.

MEDITATION TIME: After praying the Scriptures, write down in a notebook any thoughts God has impressed upon your family. The words are simple, but the meaning is deep. Allow God to communicate with your family through the words of the verse.

INTERCESSION TIME—PRAYING FOR OTHERS: Think about areas, even from those listed above, where any of you might have a difficult time in the area of integrity. It's very likely that those around you struggle in many of the same ways. Ask God to bring people to your mind, including members of your own family, who need God's guidance and strength and power to live lives of complete personal integrity.

PETITION TIME—PRAYING FOR YOURSELVES: Now ask God to help you in the same ways regarding your own personal integrity. Ask Him to give your family His guidance and strength and power to live lives that are marked by integrity.

APPLICATION TIME: Remember that integrity begins with honesty. List in a notebook any circumstances where any of you are not being honest with others, yourself or God. Then list what steps you might take to improve your track record, even if it means tough confrontations or eliminating circumstances from your lives that keep you from being people of integrity.

FAITH TIME: Faith is our positive response to what God has said. Spend a few moments praying through your eyes of faith. Tell God the positive things you see happening because of His goodness!

PRAISE AND THANKSGIVING TIME: Praise God by recognizing who He is—a God who unfailingly possesses the quality of integrity. And thank God by recognizing what He has done— given us a way to be pure in His eyes, and strength to be pure in the eyes of others.

Family Time Throughout the Week

MONDAY—Do the Family Devotion Time. If you have time, get started on the Family Worship section.

TUESDAY—Review Psalm 15:1, 2. Take the verses apart into shorter phrases, and as a family discuss what each part means. Try to understand the memory verse so that you each can apply it to your life. Don't allow it simply to be words you memorize.

WEDNESDAY—Meditate on Matthew 5:8. Talk as a family about what the simple words "those whose hearts are pure" mean.

THURSDAY—As a family, read Psalm 51:1-12. While David wrote this after committing a specific sin, it can be our prayer as well. Talk together about why God offers us His forgiveness and cleansing. How can that affect our integrity? Then, pray these verses back to God as your own prayer, perhaps with family members taking turns reading verse by verse.

FRIDAY—After a mealtime, talk with other members of your family about integrity and God's influence in our lives. How are these two ideas related? How can God's influence make us people of integrity?

WEEK 22: INTIMACY WITH GOD

Family Devotion Time

ACTIVITY: OBSTACLE COURSE. Set up your family room or living room so that it becomes an obstacle course. Move furniture and bring in other obstacles so that there is no direct route to you. The more complicated you can make it, the more fun the activity will be.

Now, have different members of your family start at the doorway or other designated starting point, and

> **Intimacy with God**
> *is gained by removing things in the way so God can be close to us.*

time how long it takes for each one to get to you. You can give each person two or three turns. If someone doesn't want to try, that person can be the official scorekeeper, recording each person's times.

DISCUSSION: After everyone has had a few turns, have them pull up a few of the obstacles around you for the discussion time. If this activity was a hit, you can play a few more times after the prayer time. But for now, encourage family discussion on these questions:

• Now that you've gone through the course a few times, are there any ways you found to improve your time?

• How would your time be different if we removed some of the things in the way?

• What happens when you have to go around so many things rather than walking directly to me?

• What if when you were at the starting point, there was a direct route to me? How would that affect your time and the time you aren't with me?

Why, no matter what we do sometimes, don't we feel any

closer to God? Could it be that we just do the same thing over and over? When we get stuck doing the same things day after day, we don't need to rely on God as much. We don't need God. So, we don't stay very close to Him. God makes Himself available to us. But we must take steps to be close to Him and to stay close to Him.

This week's memory verse says:

"When you draw close to God, God will draw close to you." —James 4:8

FAMILY BIBLE TIME: Read Ephesians 3:17-19 aloud, a phrase at a time. Encourage your family to restate each phrase to explain what it means to each of them.

FAMILY PRAYER TIME: Pray together as a family about drawing closer to God, about knowing Him better, about enjoying His presence in your life. Ask God to make His presence known to you at all times—even times when you don't expect it (or maybe even want it). You can ask other family members to pray, or you can pray and others can join you silently.

Family Worship Time (optional)

A few years ago, the *Boston Globe* interviewed Dennis Wise, an avid fan of Elvis Presley. His words of both passion and despair are striking:

"I loved Elvis. I followed him, his whole career. I have every album he has recorded, and seen every movie he's made. I once even bought some boots when I was in junior high school that looked just like his. The kids called them 'fruit boots.' But I didn't care—they looked like Elvis.

"Later, I even got a face lift, and a hair contour like his. I have won Elvis lookalike contests, and wanted him to notice, so I would storm the stage during and after concerts he would do. I don't think he ever saw me. I have ticket stubs from concerts, Elvis clippings from programs all over the world, and even some Elvis pillows from Japan.

"Yeah, Presley was, and is, my idol. My only regret was . . . that I never really saw him. I mean, really saw him. Sure, I went to concerts, but there was no contact. I once even climbed the walls around Graceland, the Presley mansion, to catch a glimpse of him. I think it might have been him that was walking through the house as I was looking through my binoculars. But I never really saw him. It's funny—all the effort I put into following him, yet I never could seem to get close."

So often, our efforts to get close to God sounds like Dennis Wise's efforts to get close to his idol. We want to experience intimacy with God, but if we are honest, we'd have to say: "It's funny, all the effort I put into following God, yet I can never seem to get close."

We can't just try to be like God. Our own efforts won't get us any closer. Instead, we need to build on these foundations:

• Intimacy with God is not automatic; rather it is the result of right choices.

• Intimacy with God begins with our own submission, humility and brokenness.

• It is our human nature to oppose God, so our efforts must be to move toward Him.

To help the concept of intimacy with God sink in a little more, work through the following, now familiar steps. Remember, ask God to help all of you concentrate and learn even if you can't go through all the steps in a single setting.

PREPARATION TIME: Read Exodus 33:11. Then reflect and respond to these questions: What things keep us from experiencing intimacy with God? What will it take for us to become more intimate with God? Have we bought into any "myths" about God that keep us distant? Are we really hungry for God, enough to act on what we need to do?

WAITING TIME: During your waiting time, let God love you, search you and show each of you how you can know more intimacy with Him. Ask Him to help each of you complete these simple sentence prayers:

"God, I feel Your love today, especially in the area of . . ."

"God, You have my permission to reveal any barriers in my life that keep me from closeness to You . . ."

"God, is there anything that I need to know that will enhance my intimacy with You. . . ?"

CONFESSION TIME: "I pray that Christ will be more and more at home in your hearts, living within you as you trust in him. May your roots go down deep into the soil of God's marvelous love; and may you be able to feel and understand, as all God's children should, how long, how wide, how deep, and how high his love really is; and to experience this love for yourselves, though it is so great that you will never see the end of it or fully understand it. And so at last you will be filled up with God himself." —Ephesians 3:17-19

After reading these verses again, confess areas in which each of you are alienated from the love of God. Confess areas in which each of you do not love God with all of your heart, soul, and mind. This may be done silently.

BIBLE TIME: Reread the verses from Ephesians slowly several times. Close your eyes and allow a main truth to surface in each of your hearts. Then pray the Scripture back to God and personalize it. Let each person do this. Your prayer might go something like this: "God, I want You to feel at home in my heart—not like a guest, but like someone who lives there. I pray that I can catch even a glimpse of what Your love is for me. I realize that until I am with You for eternity, I can never really know how far Your love for me extends. But help me catch just some of it. I want to know You. Fill me with Yourself and Your love, so that I can feel and enjoy Your presence. In Jesus' name, Amen."

MEDITATION TIME: After praying the Scriptures, write down in a notebook thoughts that God impresses upon your family about intimacy with Him. You might also meditate on Isaiah 43:1-4 and list what those verses reveal about intimacy.

INTERCESSION TIME—PRAYING FOR OTHERS: Pray for at least three people in your lives who you would like to see become intimate with God. Pray for revelation to come to them, and for them to experience what you've thought through today.

PETITION TIME—PRAYING FOR YOURSELVES: Pray for God to reveal Himself to each of you in fresh ways, and pray specifically for the barriers to be removed that stand between you and God.

APPLICATION TIME: In a notebook, list what steps you need to take in obedience to God, especially in areas that keep you from experiencing His intimacy. Leave room beside each step to list when that barrier is removed. Ask God to grant you His power to remove or destroy any barriers to intimacy with Him.

FAITH TIME: Faith is our positive response to what God has said. Spend a few moments praying through your eyes of faith. Tell God the positive things you see happening in your family because of His goodness!

PRAISE AND THANKSGIVING TIME: Reread Ephesians 3:17-19. From these verses, praise God by recognizing who He is—a God who loves us immeasurably and who lives inside us. Also, thank God by recognizing what He has done—He not only loves us, He gives us feelings so that we can experience His love and closeness.

Family Time Throughout the Week

MONDAY—Do the Family Devotion Time.

TUESDAY—Work on the Family Worship section. Together with your family, read Isaiah 55:6-9. How do you think we can make God's thoughts our thoughts, and His ways our ways? Talk about any roadblocks that can keep us away from God. What can be done about them? Are there steps you can take? Are there requests you can pray?

WEDNESDAY—Talk together as a family about the following statements. Do you think they're true? Why or why not? If they are not true, come up with statements together about intimacy with God that are true. Write them down in a notebook.

• Intimacy with God is just something you feel.

• If I know a lot of Scripture, then I am more intimate with God than someone who doesn't know it.

• If I feel close to God, then I must be really close to Him.

• If I'm a good person, I must be close to God.

• Intimacy with God is my possession as a Christian.

• If I am a deep and intense person or serve God with great fervor, then I must be close to Him.

Do any of these statements describe what you think intimacy with God is? Again, if these are not true statements, what statements would be true?

Pray together as a family and for each other that you would know true closeness to God.

THURSDAY—Together as a family, read Exodus 33:7-11. In this passage, Moses shows the price he paid to have an intimate friendship with God. Read the cost of intimacy with God, and discuss how you are doing at paying the price to be intimate:

1. You must be willing to get away from others sometimes to get close to God.

2. You must be willing to want to know God with all your heart.

3. You must be willing to let others watch you and know that you have a relationship with God.

4. You must be willing to learn to listen to what God says, and to obey Him.

FRIDAY—Reread this week's memory verse. After all that you've studied this week, these simple words might say all we need to know about intimacy with God. With your family, discuss what each phrase of this verse means. How can we make sure that "our hearts are filled with God alone"?

WEEK 23: JOY

Family Devotion Time

ACTIVITY: VOLCANO ERUPTION! Cover your table with newspaper to save time on clean up. Take some modeling dough and in a pie tin, form the dough into a mountain with a hole in the center to create a volcano. Fill the hole about half full with baking soda and pour in an equal amount of vinegar that is tinted with red food coloring. Watch the lava flow.

> **Joy** *is being glad when things are good—and when they're bad.*

You can repeat this activity several times so that different family members have a chance to make the volcano erupt.

DISCUSSION: Now spend a few minutes talking through the following questions about joy.

• Without looking it up in this book, what do you think joy means?

• What do you think happiness means?

• What is the difference between happiness and joy?

• Some people describe joy as "bubbling out." Can you ever think of a time when you were so glad that you couldn't keep it in? Tell us about it.

• Do you think joy is something we feel just when things are good? Why or why not? How can we feel any good feelings when life is going bad?

Joy is kind of weird, at least how we react to it is. God wants us to have it. It's right there for us to take. We want to have it. We like it when we feel joyful. Yet, sometimes we're afraid or shy about feeling it. Or maybe we are unable to obey God sometimes, and when we aren't obedient, the joy isn't there. Look at what **this week's memory verse** says:

"When you obey me you are living in my love . . . be filled with my joy. Yes, your cup of joy will overflow!" —John 15:10, 11

FAMILY BIBLE TIME: The true story is told of the translation of the New Testament from English into the Eskimo language. Problems arose for the translators when they encountered certain words in English for which there is no corresponding word in the Eskimo language. For example, there is a passage which tells us that the disciples are filled with joy on seeing Jesus. But since there is no word for "joy" in the Eskimo language, the translators had to find another way to express the meaning of the passage.

In their research, the translators discovered that one of the most joyful times for an Eskimo family is when the sled dogs are fed in the evening. The dogs come barking and yelping, running about and wagging their tails furiously. The children are squealing with delight, and the neighbors even become part of the happy commotion. It is altogether a "joyous" time.

The translators decided to use that daily event to help them convey the meaning of the biblical passage. As a result, when the passage is translated back into English, it reads: "When the disciples saw Jesus, they wagged their tails."

Why I can be joyful in spite of circumstances:
• Because God is with me—Isaiah 43:2.
• Because God has a plan for me—Psalm 50:15.
• Because God will help me—Psalm 43:5.

FAMILY PRAYER TIME: Part of experiencing joy is *rejoicing* in what God is doing in your life. That's why obedience is so important in knowing joy. If we're not living as God wants us to live, we have much less to rejoice about, and therefore less joy. Focus this week's prayer time on rejoicing. Before you pray, ask someone to list the many things you have to rejoice about. "Rejoice" means "give joy to." That's why we can rejoice together as we share the things in our lives that have brought about joy. As part of your rejoicing, be sure to thank God for His blessings, and His power and strength to help you live obediently.

Family Worship Time (optional)

Now spend some time going through these steps. Focus on knowing the joy of God, no matter how hard a time you seem to be going through.

PREPARATION TIME: Together, focus on the goodness of God. Think about the three reasons why each of you can be joyful in spite of your circumstances. Which one of the three fills you with the most joy? Which one do you tend to forget? Spend a few minutes and let God's joy flood your lives, regardless of your situation.

WAITING TIME: Read Zephaniah 3:17. Knowing that God takes great delight in you, allow Him to love you, search you and know each of you in an effort to grasp His joy. Ask Him to give you answers to these simple sentence prayers:
"God, I feel Your love today, especially in the area of . . ."
"God You have permission to reveal any wrong motive in my life that might steal away my joy . . ."
"God, You know what potential difficulties I will face today. Prepare my heart for them and give me joy regardless of my situation . . ."

CONFESSION TIME: Every relationship needs joy, not happiness. Think about these contrasts: Happiness is external; joy is internal. Happiness is based on chance; joy is based on choice. Happiness is based on circumstance; joy is based on Christ.
As you ponder these contrasts, confess to God areas in which any of you seem to lack joy.

BIBLE TIME: We can never pray out of God's will when we pray God's Word. Read Romans 5:1-11 slowly a couple of times. Then close your eyes and allow a main truth to surface in each of your hearts. Pray the Scripture back to God and allow Him to minister to you.

MEDITATION TIME: After praying the Scriptures, meditate on these thoughts together:

1. Joy comes from understanding truth—verse 2.
2. Joy comes from having a hope in the future—verse 2.
3. Joy comes from seeing the big picture—verses 3-5.
4. Joy comes from being accepted—verse 9.
5. Joy comes from having peace with God—verse 11.

INTERCESSION TIME—PRAYING FOR OTHERS: Think of people who seem to lack joy in their lives. Ask God to give them joy in spite of the circumstances they may be facing. Remember, "The joy of the Lord is our strength."

PETITION TIME—PRAYING FOR YOURSELVES: Think about the areas where any of you lack joy. Now ask God to give you joy in spite of the circumstances you are facing.

APPLICATION TIME: List in a notebook the steps your family can take to feel more joy this week. Read through the "Joy comes from . . ." list under the Meditation Time above. Look at the verbs (understanding, having, seeing, being). Are you able to claim those actions in your own life? Ask God to help you live them out.

FAITH TIME: Faith is our positive response to what God has said. Spend a few moments praying through your eyes of faith. Tell God the positive things you see happening because of His goodness!

PRAISE AND THANKSGIVING TIME: Read John 15:11. Now praise God by recognizing who He is—a joy-giving God. And thank God by recognizing what He has done—put His joy in us, in spite of whatever we're going through.

Family Time Throughout the Week

MONDAY—Do the Family Devotion Time together as a family. Work on the Family Worship section.

TUESDAY—Read John 15:1-11. Talk as a family about the things Jesus mentions in these verses that will give us joy. Read the story at the beginning of the Family Bible Time section to your family. Now ask the same questions you asked during the discussion time yesterday. Does this story help everyone understand joy a little better?

WEDNESDAY—Read 2 Peter 1:7. Talk together as a family about ways you can focus on giving rather than receiving. How can this bring you joy? How can joy come from giving something away?

THURSDAY—Read Colossians 3:13 and Romans 5:3, 4. Today, talk together about ways that you can focus on healing rather than hurting. How can this bring you joy? How can joy come out of painful situations?

FRIDAY—Read Psalm 62:8 and Philippians 4:4. Today, talk about ways that you can all focus on God's power rather than your problems. How can this bring you joy? How can joy come out of problems?

WEEK 24: KINDNESS

Family Devotion Time

ACTIVITY: THE GREAT GIVEAWAY. Instruct the members of your family to head to their rooms. Everyone should bring back to the family time together two or three things that they no longer need or use.

When everyone is back together, put all the items in a box. Sometime this week, go together as a family to a

> **Kindness** *is more than a feeling—it's showing others how much you love them.*

Goodwill or Salvation Army or another donation center and give your items away. Even better, you could pick items that a family in your church needs, or items you think several families might need. You could then go as a family to deliver these items personally, or donate them to the families anonymously through your church.

DISCUSSION: As you load your items into boxes, talk through these questions as a family.

• How does it make us feel when we are able to be kind, for example, such as when we give something away?

• Have you ever been on the receiving end of someone else's act of kindness? How did that make you feel?

• Why do you think we need to do more than just think about being kind—why do we need to act out our kindness?

• Why do you think it's important for Christians to show acts of kindness?

• What is the greatest act of love and kindness ever?

God wants us to become more like Christ every day. One way we can be like Christ is to show kindness to others. Jesus was kind even to those who were not kind to Him. Even when

He lost patience with both His friends and His enemies, He treated them with respect and kindness. God has demonstrated His love and kindness to us through Christ. How should we respond? *This week's memory verse* tells us:

"In response to all he has done for us, let us outdo each other in being helpful and kind to each other and in doing good." —Hebrews 10:24

FAMILY BIBLE TIME: One day a man came to Jesus and asked Him what the most important verse was in the Bible. Listen to what He said (read Matthew 22:34-40). Jesus said, "Love God and love your neighbor as yourself." That's the whole essence of Christianity. What was Jesus saying? He was saying that nothing matters more than relationships. *Nothing.* Your relationship to God and to other people.

Jesus also said that what distinguishes a Christian is love. Others will know that you are His disciples simply by how you show your love. The word for love in action is "kindness." Kindness is simply love in action. It is not a feeling. It is something you do.

FAMILY PRAYER TIME: Pray together in short, simple sentence prayers for opportunities to demonstrate your kindness individually and as a family. Pray for God to reveal to you those who most need your acts of kindness. Close your prayer time, asking God to give your hearts the right attitude when it comes to giving of yourself, that no one will give reluctantly or because they expect a pat on the back or a reward.

Family Worship Time (optional)

Stephen Grellet—the name may not sound familiar. Grellet was born in France. He was a Quaker, and he died in New Jersey in 1855. That's about all we know about him, except for a few lines he penned that have made him immortal: "I shall pass through this world but once. Any good I can do, or any kindness that I can show any human being, let me do it now and not defer it. For I shall not pass this way again." Consider these four ways that Jesus demonstrates His kindness to us:

1. He understands my weakness—Hebrews 4:15, 16.
2. He tells me the truth—John 8:32.
3. He forgives my sin—Romans 3:23, 24.
4. He affirms my worth—Psalm 139:16, 17.

The following steps will help the idea of kindness sink in more clearly. Spend some time completing these with other members of your family. Remember to let God speak to you through each step.

PREPARATION TIME: "Be kind to each other, tenderhearted, forgiving one another, just as God has forgiven you because you belong to Christ." —Ephesians 4:32

Ponder this thought: Wouldn't it be wonderful if Christians were known by their kind spirit instead of their judgmental spirit?

WAITING TIME: During your waiting time, let God love you, search you and show each of you how He wants you to demonstrate kindness. Ask Him to help each of you complete these sentence prayers with phrases appropriate to your own lives:

"God, I feel Your love today, especially in the area of . . ."

"God, You have permission to reveal any wrong motive in my life . . ."

"God, as I enter this day, who do You want me to show kindness to. . . ?"

CONFESSION TIME: Think about these questions:

"Am I kind to others when I see their weakness?

"Do I tell the truth in love?"

"Do I affirm the worth of those around me?"

As a family, spend a few moments confessing to God those areas where each of you fails. Remember, be honest. God already knows your hearts. He just wants to make sure *you* know them.

BIBLE TIME: Read the story of the good Samaritan in Luke 10:29-35. Ask yourselves, "Would I react like the priest, the Levite, or the Samaritan?"

Now pray the Scripture back to God and allow Him to minister to each of you. Your prayer might go something like this: "God, help us to be good neighbors. Help us to know that anyone who needs an act of kindness is our neighbor. Open our eyes so that we see the needs of those around us, even those people who are not easy to love. Of course, help us to be safe, but don't let that concern stop us from responding when Your Holy Spirit is telling us to help someone. Help us to have attitudes of kindness so that when someone has needs, we can put Your love into action and show kindness. In Jesus' name, Amen."

MEDITATION TIME: After praying the Scriptures, write down in a notebook the thoughts that God has impressed upon your mind. Especially focus on the action part of kindness. Remember that kindness is more than a feeling, it is an act.

INTERCESSION TIME—PRAYING FOR OTHERS: Ask God to bring to your minds people who need an act of kindness this week. Think of someone who is going through a time of grief, of financial difficulty, of struggle at work, of tough times in a relationship. Pray for that person, and that God will help you demonstrate kindness to that person this week.

PETITION TIME—PRAYING FOR YOURSELF: Pray back to God the sentences listed under the Confession Time. Ask Him to make you into people who are kind to others when you see their weaknesses, people who are willing to tell the truth with a loving attitude, and people who affirm the worth of other people around you.

APPLICATION TIME: In a notebook, list some steps your family can take to obey God in the area of kindness. Think of the people you prayed for during the intercession time. List exactly what you will do to demonstrate kindness to them. Leave room to make notes of how your obedience in this area will draw your family closer to God and make you more prepared to show kindness in the future.

FAITH TIME: Faith is our positive response to what God has said. Spend a few moments praying through your eyes of faith. Tell God the positive things you see happening because of His goodness!

PRAISE AND THANKSGIVING TIME: Read Romans 3:23, 24. Now praise God by recognizing who He is—a kind and forgiving judge. And thank God by recognizing what He has done—providing a way, through faith in Jesus Christ, that we can be declared "not guilty" of our sins.

Family Time Throughout the Week

MONDAY—Do the Family Devotion Time. If possible, get started on the Family Worship section.

TUESDAY—God's Word teaches that success in life, plus failure in relationships, still equals overall failure. As a family, talk about your relationships—with each other and with people outside your family. Are there any places where you are failing? Talk about how acts of kindness can help your relationships be more successful.

WEDNESDAY—As a family, work on memorizing your memory verse. Talk about each of the phrases. What does it mean to "outdo each other"? Read a few verses before the memory verse, Hebrews 10:18-23. Now ponder together as a family, what does the phrase, "in response to all he has done for us" mean?

THURSDAY/FRIDAY—In Matthew 25:35, 36, Jesus says that on the Judgment Day, the one thing you'll be judged for is how you treated other people. This is the heart of what it means to be a Christian—love in action. Talk about a family that your family might minister to. Raise the question on Thursday at dinnertime, and encourage your family to think of other families who might need acts of kindness. On Friday at dinner, decide on a family, and talk about what your family can do to meet their needs.

WEEK 25: LIFE PURPOSE

Family Devotion Time

ACTIVITY: THE BIG BUILDUP. Use a Nerf ball or another soft ball that can be thrown in the house. Or use a bean bag or even a clean pair of socks rolled into a ball.

Sit in a circle and toss the ball to someone across the circle. The person the ball is tossed to must then say something good about the person who tossed the ball. It can be something simple, such as "Joey is good at building with Legos®," or "Ashley likes to make people laugh," or "Jessica is good at keeping her room clean."

> **Life Purpose:** *trying to be everything that God wants you to be.*

DISCUSSION: Talk through these questions. What God wants us to be may not be the same as our jobs or what we like to do. But it helps to look at the things that make us who we are to figure out what God might want us to do with our lives:

• What was your favorite thing someone else said about you?

• Of all the things that someone else said about you, which do you think is something that God has given you?

• Is there anything someone said that might be what you want to do someday? For example, if someone told you that you are good at baseball, do you think you might like to play for a Major League team someday? If someone said that you are good at making sick people feel better, do you think you might want to become a doctor or a nurse?

• Do you think there's a difference between the things you like to do, and what God wants you to do?

The Bible gives us a lot of insight into what God wants us to do with our lives. Here are three things to think about concerning your life purpose:

1. Your purpose is designed by God, to glorify God.

2. Your purpose will fit with the gifts God gives you.

3. Your purpose will happen because of God's power, not your own.

These truths line up nicely with *this week's memory verse:*

"God . . . will keep right on helping you grow . . . until his task within you is finally finished. . . ." —Philippians 1:6

FAMILY BIBLE TIME: Psalm 139:1-6 reminds us of how important we are to God. We need to remember this as we think about what He wants us to do with our lives.

FAMILY PRAYER TIME: Pray together for the lives represented in your family. Ask each person to pray for the person on his left. Each of you can thank God for who that person is and for the good things about him. Pray that he will learn exactly what God wants him to do with his life.

Family Worship Time (optional)

The great composer Peter Illich Tchaikovsky put a sign on the gate to his home: Visiting hours Monday and Tuesday between 3 and 5 p.m. Other times please do not ring.

In effect, Tchaikovsky was saying, "I'm a composer. This is how I'm going to bless the world—not by idle conversation." He knew his purpose and lived his life to the fullest according to his purpose.

The life each of you has been given is a gift from God. You are a steward of every minute contained in that gift.

Read Ephesians 3:1-8. Here you'll see that Paul clearly knows his purpose and the power behind it. Of course, his ultimate purpose is to know, love and obey God—the same ultimate purpose we all share. But his specific purpose is to preach the Gospel.

Spend some time going through the following questions. The discovery of your life purpose is more than a one-time process. But by investing a little bit of time now, you can be well on your way to one of the most important discoveries you will ever make.

PREPARATION TIME: Encourage each family member doing the Worship Time to think through the following questions to begin to "frame up" his life purpose:
• What are your spiritual gifts? (Scan through Romans 12-14 for descriptions of spiritual gifts.)
• What is your passion?
• What are you good at?
• What ministries has God used you in?
• If you could do one thing with your life, where you had a guarantee that you wouldn't fail, and money didn't matter, what would it be?

WAITING TIME: With this topic, your real waiting time could be weeks or months to fully know God's mind and heart on your purpose in life, but start here!
During your waiting time, let God love you, search you and show each of you His desires for your lives. Ask Him to help each of you formulate answers to these simple sentence prayers:
"God, how can I know more fully that You created me on purpose, with a purpose . . ."
"God, I give You permission to reveal anything that I may be doing or not doing that might block Your purpose for me . . ."
"God, show me Your plan for my life . . ."

CONFESSION TIME: Individually pray this simple prayer: "God, I confess that I have wasted my time and talent in the following ways . . ."

BIBLE TIME: We can never pray out of God's will when we pray God's Word. Read Psalm 139:1-6 slowly a couple of times. Now, close your eyes and ask God to bring a main truth to your heart. Then pray the verses back to God and allow Him to minister to each of you, specifically asking God—who knows you better than you know yourselves—to reveal His purpose for your life to you.

MEDITATION TIME: After praying the Scriptures, write down

in a notebook any thoughts that God has impressed upon your minds. Especially concentrate on how awesome it is that God knows each one of us in such detail and in such a personal way. Thank Him for this amazing attribute of His.

INTERCESSION TIME—PRAYING FOR OTHERS: Think about the family activity you did at the beginning of this section. As you think about the good things that your family said about each other, pray that even those statements will help each person in your family to become all that God wants him to be. Pray that God will reveal His purpose for each one's life, and that each family member will be willing to take appropriate risks in order to live out His purpose.

PETITION TIME—PRAYING FOR YOURSELVES: Individually think about what your family members said about you during the activity time. Was anything said that surprised you? Sometimes, God's purpose for our life is different than anything we've ever thought of. Ask God to help you be open to His leading and to clearly show you what He wants you to do for Him and what He wants you to be.

APPLICATION TIME: List in a notebook any steps each of you might be able to take to live out your life purpose. Again, remember that purpose and career aren't necessarily the same. Your job could be a garbage collector, but your purpose could be completely different. Perhaps your purpose is to serve others with your gift of hospitality, something you cannot easily carry out in your job. If anyone is struggling with what his life purpose is, commit to concentrating on the questions in the Preparation Time every day for the next few weeks. Write down your answers and pray over them daily. Specifically ask God to reveal His purpose for your life *and* how you are to live out that purpose.

FAITH TIME: Faith is our positive response to what God has said. Spend a few moments praying through your eyes of faith. Tell God the positive things you see happening in your family because of His goodness!

PRAISE AND THANKSGIVING TIME: Reread this week's memory verse, and praise God by recognizing who He is—a God who works directly in your life. Also, thank God by recognizing what He has done—carefully and strategically planned your purpose in life.

Family Time Throughout the Week

MONDAY—Do the Family Devotion Time.

TUESDAY—Rcad Psalm 139:1-6 again, after a mealtime or with individual members of your family at bedtime. Now pray these words for members of your family who aren't doing the Family Worship section in their presence. Let them know that you believe these words, and that God really can be trusted with their future.

WEDNESDAY—Read John 17:1-4 together after a mealtime. Talk together about what Jesus' life purpose was and is. How did Jesus know this so clearly? How do you think we can know our purpose in life more clearly?

THURSDAY—Read Acts 20:18-24 together after a mealtime. Talk together about what the apostle Paul's life purpose was. How could Paul know his purpose so clearly? How does this help us discover our own purpose in life?

FRIDAY—Review your memory verse. Talk together as a family about what this verse means. Memorize the words, and also take the verse apart and have the goal of understanding the verse. Pray together that God will help you apply the verse to your lives as well.

WEEK 26: LORDSHIP

Family Worship Time

ACTIVITY: A FEW OF MY FAVORITE THINGS. Just a couple of weeks ago, your family members went to their rooms to pick a few things they didn't need or want anymore, and your family gave those items away as an act of kindness.

> **Lordship:** *Putting God before yourself, even letting Him "own" you.*

This week, send the members of your family to their rooms and ask them to pick out two or three of their favorite things and then come back to wherever you're having your family devotional time. Assure them before they go that they get to keep these items!

Do a bit of "show and tell" once everyone has re-gathered. Have each person show his favorite things and tell why it is such a cherished possession. If it is something that has a use, have the owner demonstrate it.

DISCUSSION: When you're finished with your "show and tell" time, talk through the following questions together as a family. These simple questions are meant to help you gain just a little better understanding of what Lordship means:

- What makes your most favorite item your most favorite?
- I promised that we wouldn't have to give away our favorite possessions, but think for a minute. What if I now said we each were going to give away our most favorite thing—how would you feel about that?
- How do you treat your most cherished item—do you toss it around carelessly, or do you make sure it is safe and secure?
- What would you be willing to give up—other things you have, brothers or sisters!—in order to keep your favorite thing?

Lordship is simple. It could also be called ownership. Because of the price that Christ paid on the cross, God owns us. We are His. But God is the kind of owner who doesn't want us unless we want Him to have us. So Lordship can be hard to put into practice. But we're promised, as in *this week's memory verse,* that if we allow God to be in control, He will treat us as a cherished child, providing exactly what we need:

"Don't worry at all about having enough. . . . Your heavenly Father already knows perfectly well that you need them, and he will give them to you if you give him first place in your life and live as he wants you to." —Matthew 6:31-33

FAMILY BIBLE TIME: Read Matthew 8:1-3. What did the leper say to Jesus? How does this show he knew Jesus was in control? What did Jesus do?

FAMILY PRAYER TIME: Pray together as a family that you would have the attitude of Mother Theresa, that well-known servant of people: "You will never know that Jesus is all you need until Jesus is all you've got."

Ask God to help you remember that each of you belongs to Him. Thank Him for all He provides. Ask Him to help you not just make Him a priority in your life, but to make Him *the* priority in your life. Pray for Him to show you clearly how He wants you to live. Be prepared for the answer—how He wants you to live is written clearly all over Scripture and demonstrated daily in the lives of many committed Christians around you. Thank Him for these direct answers to your prayer.

Family Worship Time (optional)

What is Lordship? Consider what these verses say, discussing them as a family or with your spouse.

1. Submission to God's will—Matthew 8:2.
2. Placing God first in your life—Matthew 22:36-40.
3. Accepting responsibility and accountability—Matthew 25:14-30.
4. Doing God's will—Matthew 7:21-27.
5. Personal obedience regardless of the cost—John 21:15-23.

In a little church in Eastern Europe before the downfall of communism, about a hundred people had gathered to worship God on a beautiful Sunday morning. They had just finished a prayer, when suddenly, with a loud bang, communist soldiers burst through the front door, submachine guns in hand. They made their way to the front of the church, calling the people gathered there "the filth of the earth" and "parasites ruining the glorious revolution," Then the soldiers shouted that the time had come to rid the nation of them.

Acknowledging that there might be some who did not really believe all this religious nonsense, the soldiers gave the people 60 seconds to leave the room. There was silence. Then, suddenly, about half of the congregation rushed to the doors, some even through the windows, to get out in time. The minute was over, and deeper silence fell upon the remaining half of the congregation as they stared down the muzzles of the submachine guns.

Unexpectedly, the men dropped their guns and said, "Brethren, we have come to worship with you! But first, we had to get rid of the hypocrites!"

One word separated the people who stayed from those who left: Lordship!

Author S.M. Lockridge identifies three classes of people:

1. Those who neither call God Lord nor do the things He says.

2. Those who call him Lord but do not do the things He says.

3. Those who call him Lord and do the things He says.

Then he notes: "Christ's Lordship is based on His ownership.

God didn't have to put His signature on the corner of a sunrise;

Nobody else is going to cause the sun to rise . . . He's the owner.

God didn't have to put a laundry mark on the lapel of a meadow . . . He's the owner.

God didn't have to carve His initials on the side of the mountain . . . He's the owner.

God didn't have to put a brand on the cattle of a thousand hills . . . He's the owner.

God didn't even have to take out a copyright on the songs that the birds sing . . . He's the owner!"

Spend time as a family communicating with God through these steps. Try to grasp more thoroughly what Lordship means.

PREPARATION TIME: Commit yourselves to the Owner right now. Hannah Whitehall Smith said, "It is generally much less difficult for us to commit the keeping of our future to the Lord than it is to commit our present. We know we are helpless as regards the future, but we feel as if the present was in our own hands, and must be carried on our own shoulders; and most of us have an unconfessed idea that it is a great deal to ask the Lord to carry ourselves, and that we cannot think of asking Him to carry our burdens too."

WAITING TIME: During your waiting time, let God love you, search you and show each of you His desires in the area of Lordship. Ask Him to help you complete these simple sentence prayers:

"God, I feel Your love today, especially in the area of . . ."

"God, You have permission to reveal any uncommitted area in my life . . ."

"God, is there anything that I need to know about my willingness to serve You as I enter this day. . . ?"

CONFESSION TIME: Lordship in your life means that your words and your walk are the same. If any of the following thoughts speak to your hearts and show inconsistencies in your lives, spend time confessing these areas to God. Read them aloud, allowing time for silent prayer after each one.

- You call Me Master, and obey Me not.
- You call Me Light, and see Me not.
- You call Me Way, and follow Me not.
- You call Me Life, and desire Me not.
- You call Me wise, and acknowledge Me not.
- You call Me fair, and love Me not.
- You call Me rich, and ask Me not.
- You call Me eternal, and seek Me not.
- You call Me gracious, and trust Me not.
- You call Me noble, and serve Me not.
- You call Me mighty, and honor Me not.
- You call Me just, and fear Me not.
- If I condemn you, blame Me not.

BIBLE TIME: When we pray God's Word to Him, we can know that we are praying in His will. Read Luke 6:46-49 slowly several times. Close your eyes and allow a main truth to surface in each of your hearts. Then pray the Scripture and allow God to minister to you.

MEDITATION TIME: After praying the Scriptures, write down in a notebook any thoughts that God has impressed upon your minds about Lordship. Think more about ownership. Think of all the things you own—what if they could choose not to let you own them at certain times? What if you owned something but a friend always borrowed it and kept it most of the time? Can you really say you are the owner?

INTERCESSION TIME—PRAYING FOR OTHERS: Reread the list under the Confession Time above. Can you think of anyone one of you knows—even a member of your immediate family—who seems to be struggling in any of these areas? Is there someone who makes one of the claims yet doesn't display what should be the resulting qualities in his life? Ask God to show that person how he can make his words and his walk the same.

PETITION TIME—PRAYING FOR YOURSELVES: Now do the same thing for yourselves. Under the Confession Time, you confessed inconsistencies in your life. Now ask God to remove them. Ask Him to help mold you into a person who He owns, who claims the characteristics and demonstrates the behavior, who talks the talk and walks the walk when it comes to Lordship in your life. Again, allow time for family members to pray silently.

APPLICATION TIME: In a notebook, list any steps your family needs to take in obedience to God this week. Are there any other areas where you've not invited God to take control in your life? Or can you be instrumental in helping someone understand that God won't make us into His puppets, but He does want us to willingly submit to His Lordship?

FAITH TIME: Faith is our positive response to what God has said. Spend a few moments praying through your eyes of faith.

Tell God the positive things you see happening because of His goodness!

PRAISE AND THANKSGIVING TIME: Reread this week's memory verse. Praise God by recognizing who He is—a God who know us and our needs. And thank Him by recognizing what He has done—met our needs when we submit to His Lordship.

Family Time Throughout the Week

MONDAY—Do the Family Devotion Time together. Get started on the Family Worship section.

TUESDAY TO FRIDAY—Lordship is a hard issue to put into practice in your life, in part, because you first have to determine what parts of your life you are withholding from God. Spend this week settling the "Who's number one issue." Study the Lordship Ladder, read one or two of the Scriptures each day and discuss them with your family. Have the goal of climbing up this ladder toward knowing God's peace.

The Lordship Ladder

Peace	Romans 8:1
Total Surrender	Romans 12:1, 2
Hunger for Righteousness	Matthew 5:6
Partial Surrender	Luke 9:57-62
Wrestling	Romans 7
Seeking	Matthew 6:33
Unstableness	James 1:8

WEEK 27: LOVE

Family Devotion Time

ACTIVITY: VALENTINE'S DAY ANY DAY. Come to your family's time together prepared with scissors, glue, markers, magazines that can be cut apart, construction paper (red and white are favorites). Yes, you're all going to make Valentines, just like you did when you were a kid! It doesn't matter what time of year it is now; the idea is to express your love to another member of your family.

> ***Love*** *means choosing to show others how much you care for them.*

Put the names of your family into a hat, and have each person draw out a name. That is the one he/she will construct a Valentine for. Fold the construction paper into a greeting-card shape, and make your own card. You can use photos of families from magazines, write out a favorite Bible verse or saying, or draw your own pictures. You might need to help younger members of the family, but let them keep the identity of their secret Valentine to themselves.

When everyone is finished, exchange your cards. Take a few minutes to read the cards, and to thank the other person for making it and for their expression of love.

DISCUSSION: After you've had a chance to read the card from your secret Valentine, talk through these questions as a family:

- How does it feel to have someone show his love to you?
- How do you think it would feel if no one loved us?
- Do you think love is just a feeling? If it's more than a feeling, what is it?
- If you want someone to love you, do you have to do

anything? Don't you at least have to accept another's love?

• If you want to express your love to someone else, does that person have to do anything? How would you feel if he rejected your love?

Love is more than a feeling. We also show it. It's even a command from God. While we might say we love someone, even more important is how we show our love in our actions. Love is showing someone that we really care for him. Of all the qualities we can show as Christians, love is most important. In its purest form, love is a reflection of God through us to others. That's why **this week's memory verse** says:

". . . Let us stop just *saying* we love people; let us *really* love them, and *show it* by our *actions.*" —1 John 3:18

FAMILY BIBLE TIME: Read John 21:15-17. If anyone knows the story of Peter denying Jesus, have him explain how it fits in with this story. What did Jesus want Peter to do to show his love for Jesus?

FAMILY PRAYER TIME: During your prayer time together, take turns praying in simple sentences. Perhaps other family members can pray after you say each of the following phrases: "Offer God thanks for the other members of your family who love you." "Thank God for friends who unselfishly show their love to you." "Pray for one person to whom you need to demonstrate God's love." "Ask God to give you the exact actions so that this person can see your love and the love of God through you."

Now close your family time with thanksgiving and praise for God, who is the perfect Giver of love.

Family Worship Time (optional)

C. S. Lewis wrote that to love at all is to be vulnerable. Love anything and your heart will certainly be wrung and possibly broken. If you want to be sure of keeping it intact, you must give your heart to no one. Lock it up safe in the casket or coffin of your selfishness. But in that casket—safe, dark, motionless, airless—it will change. It will not be broken, but it will become unbreakable, impenetrable, irredeemable.

Scripture is full of verses about love—about God's love for us and about how we are to love others. Here are two important thoughts when it comes to our love:

1. Love is a matter of choice—Colossians 3:14.

Again, if love were just a feeling or an accident, then God couldn't command it. He wouldn't command us to do something that was just a feeling. But He can command an action in our lives.

2. So, love is also a matter of conduct—1 John 3:18.

We are to demonstrate our love, not just claim that we love others.

The following steps will help you understand love—the biblical idea of love—more clearly. Of course, the world has its own erroneous definitions of love. But we want to strive to display the kind of love defined in Scripture.

PREPARATION TIME: Read 1 Corinthians 13:13. Keeping in mind that love is a matter of choice and of conduct, take a few moments to discuss these two questions:
- In what areas do I find it easy to love?
- In what areas do I find it difficult to love?

WAITING TIME: Jesus didn't just say, "Love one another." He said, "Love one another as I have loved you."

The best example that helps us understand God's love is the cross of Christ. On the cross, Jesus defined *agape* love. Did He die a shameful and humiliating death for a humanity that loved Him? No, for a world that hated Him. The Roman soldiers couldn't wait to confiscate His clothes. The Jewish religious leaders were so envious of His presence and character that they had wanted to kill Him for a long time. Pilate just wanted to wash his hands of the whole affair. And the crowd ranted and raved for Him to be crucified. And you and I would have been in there somewhere.

Still, Christ gave His life out of the purest unconditional love right at His darkest moment of human hatred. This was not and is not human love. It is the love of God, in Christ, who quietly died in love in the face of screams of hate, and who loves us to the end in spite of that hate.

During your waiting time, let God love you, search you and

show each of you His love. Ask Him to give you the right words to finish these simple prayers:

"God, I feel Your love today, especially in the area of . . ."

"God, because of Your unconditional love to me, You have permission to reveal any wrong motive in my life . . ."

"God, is there anything about receiving or giving love that I need to know as I enter into this day. . . ?"

CONFESSION TIME: Read John 21:15-17 again and have each person put in his own name wherever Simon Peter's name is. Do this several times, concentrating on areas where your love falls short in relationship to God. Now individually confess these areas to God.

BIBLE TIME: Read 1 Corinthians 13:1-8 slowly a few times. Close your eyes and allow a main truth to surface in each of your hearts. Then pray the Scripture back to God and allow Him to minister to you. Ask God to supply your family with the kind of love described in these verses.

MEDITATION TIME: After praying the Scriptures, write down in a notebook any thoughts God has impressed upon your mind. Which words describe your feelings and acts of love? Positive words like patient, kind, true, loyal? Or negative words like jealous, envious, boastful, proud, haughty, selfish, rude. Which words describe the kinds of actions each of you would like to receive? Which describe the actions you'd like to give?

INTERCESSION TIME—PRAYING FOR OTHERS: Ask God to bring to mind people you find hard to love. Ask God to give each of you new feelings for them. Ask Him to help you think of ways that you can actively express your love to them.

PETITION TIME—PRAYING FOR YOURSELVES: Pray that God's *agape* love—the work of Christ on the cross—will be seen in and through your lives. Ask God to help each of you love others so much that they will want to know why you are able to have that much love.

APPLICATION TIME: In a notebook, list what steps your

family can take this week to obey God's command to love others. How can you demonstrate your love for another person? Is there someone in your immediate family who especially needs to feel and know your love this week? Write down actions your family might take so that others see your love.

FAITH TIME: Faith is our positive response to what God has said. Spend a few moments praying through your eyes of faith. Tell God the positive things you see happening in your family because of His goodness!

PRAISE AND THANKSGIVING TIME: Read Ephesians 4:2, 3. Praise God by recognizing who He is—our leader and example of love. Also, thank God by recognizing what He has done— provided a way for us to know His love, and for us to express love to others around us.

Family Time Throughout the Week

MONDAY—Do the Family Devotion Time. Also, work on the Family Worship section.

TUESDAY—Read these paragraphs to your family after a mealtime:

Have you figured out that your actions make your feelings? By the way you act, you can change the way you feel. People have said: "I don't love him/her anymore," or "I don't love my parents/kids anymore. What's wrong with me?"

The answer is, "Begin to act like you love them."

Their response might be, "Act like I love them? How can I act like I love them when I don't *feel* like I love them?"

This is one of those things we've got all wrong. The way we act can change the way we feel about other people. When we begin to act in kindness toward others—showing compassion, tenderheartedness, forgiveness—it can change the way we feel about them.

Now, talk together about ways we can act toward others that will show them our love. What are some simple actions we can take, even if we don't *feel* like loving someone else?

WEDNESDAY—Read the paragraphs under Waiting Time,

and talk about God's ultimate example of love—Christ's work on the cross. Then take some time after a mealtime or at bedtime to thank God again for His love.

THURSDAY—Reread 1 Corinthians 13:1-8. Talk about the words used here to describe love. Ask family members to help define the words, perhaps by talking about what actions could be described by each word. For example, "Love is patient."—Being patient means I'm willing to wait my turn for the bathroom. Then pray that God will help you to live out these actions to show your love to other members of your family.

FRIDAY—Henry Drummond wrote, "You will find as you look back upon your life that the moments when you really lived are the moments when you have done things in the spirit of love." Commit to each other that you will all really live this weekend, because you'll make every effort to do things in a spirit of love.

WEEK 28: MARRIAGE

Family Devotion Time

ACTIVITY: MOM-AND-DAD COUPONS. This activity has a benefit, but just for the parents present! Have everyone make a coupon for mom and dad.

Mom and dad should make coupons for each other—G-rated ones, please!

> ***Marriage*** *is a wedded, committed relationship between a man and a woman in love.*

The coupons can be for services or chores or gifts. Some suggestions:

Garbage-person coupon: This certificate entitles one month of garbage collection and dumping duties from Sarah.

Room Cleaner: This coupon means the bearers (Mom and Dad) will not have to ask me to clean my room for three months.

Childcare (From a teen with younger siblings): This certificate entitles holders to one night of free babysitting while they go out on a date.

Pooper-scooper: I promise to clean out the cat's litter box (ugh!) for the next three weeks.

Dad to Mom—Kitchen helper: This certificate entitles my wife to the next four Monday evenings out with friends, because even the best of marriages need time apart, too.

DISCUSSION: Take a few minutes to discuss these questions with your family:

• Why do you think God made marriage?

• Do you think it's important for people to stay married their whole lives? Why?

• What do you think is the most important part of being

married? What are some things about marriage that aren't important?

• Do you plan to get married someday? What kind of person would you like to marry?

God created marriage—right at the beginning of everything. And the Bible doesn't give us any reason to think He has changed His mind about marriage. If a man and a woman have the kind of marriage God talks about in the Bible, they have become a team. They might disagree on things, but they act like one person. As *this week's memory verse* says:

"A man leaves his father and mother and is joined to his wife in such a way that the two become one person." —Genesis 2:24

FAMILY BIBLE TIME: Here's some advice God gives to us as parents. Listen to it and think about how important marrying the right person is. (Read Ephesians 5:21-33 aloud. Answer any questions your children might raise about this passage.)

FAMILY PRAYER TIME: For this prayer time, do something a bit different. Pray for your spouse, thanking God for him or her. Then take turns praying for each of your children by name. Pray that God will lead each one to the person He wants them to marry. Pray for those people, whoever they are, that God will work in their lives and draw them closer to Him. Thank God that He created marriage, and that He knows the future. Ask Him to guide and direct each of your lives so that you will always walk with Him, including your marriage and family life—even if that's many years away for your kids.

Family Worship Time (optional)

Older kids who usually complete this section each week can take this week off. But it would be great if you would pray each day for your parents' marriage.

In Ephesians 5:21-33, the apostle Paul gives us clear guidelines for Christian marriages. And though these guidelines can be humanly challenging, they are fully achievable with the power of the Holy Spirit.

From this passage, we can agree on these three biblical truths about Christian marriages:

1. Husbands and wives are first subject to the Lordship of Jesus Christ, and then mutually subject to one another.

2. The husband is the spiritual leader of the home in the same way that Christ is the leader of the church. Therefore, he must bring these qualities to his role in the marriage—he must be: loving, sacrificial, caring, responsible, committed and consistent.

3. It is the desire of God's heart to do whatever it takes to keep the marriage together, and for couples to experience His love through their spouses.

To gain a deeper understanding of what it means to maintain and commit to a biblically based marriage, work through the following steps. This week, if you are married, you may decide you want to work through these steps with your spouse.

PREPARATION TIME: Read Ephesians 4:26-31. Now look through the list below and check to see if there are areas where you are struggling within your marriage.

- Unresolved conflict
- Children
- Finances
- In-laws
- Kindness/respect
- Communication
- Not in love
- Spouse is not a Christian
- Spiritual growth
- Previous marriage problems
- Other

What are the top two or three areas where you are struggling? Confess these areas to God, and, if appropriate, to your spouse as well.

WAITING TIME: During your waiting time, let God love you, search you and show you and your spouse fresh perspectives regarding your marriage. Then ask Him to help you complete these simple sentence prayers:

"God, I feel Your love today, especially through my spouse, because . . ."

"God, You have permission to reveal any issue that I have not forgiven or that needs to be forgiven in my marriage relationship . . ."

"God, is there anything that I need to know about my relationship with my spouse as I enter this day. . . ?"

CONFESSION TIME: Read Colossians 3:12-14. Now confess to God—together or alone—any areas that are hurting, or at least not helping your marriage.

BIBLE TIME: We can never pray out of God's will when we pray God's Word. Read Philippians 2:1-5 slowly a few times. Now, close your eyes and allow a main truth to surface in your hearts. Then pray the Scripture back to God and allow Him to minister to you.

MEDITATION TIME: After praying the Scriptures, write down any new thoughts that God has impressed upon your minds about marriage. Think too about the example He provides with Christ as the bridegroom and the church as the bride (Revelation 21:2,9).

INTERCESSION TIME—PRAYING FOR OTHERS: Together, ask God to bring to mind married couples you know who are struggling with their marriages. The idea here isn't to judge or gossip, but to really pray that healing and strengthening will take place where it needs to. Ask God to help the husband and wife renew their commitment to each other. If these couples have children, pray for them, too. Ask God to bring healing to them, as well as understanding of what their parents are going through. Most of all, ask God to draw these families closer to Him, to strengthen them, to heal their relationships.

PETITION TIME—PRAYING FOR YOURSELVES: Pray for your own marriage. Reread the biblical truths about marriage under the first part of the Family Worship section. Do these statements describe your marriage? Are you fulfilling your role as God intended? Pray for any areas where you are failing, and ask God to bring you success as you lean on Him. Praise Him for areas where you are doing well, and ask Him to protect and strengthen you there.

APPLICATION TIME: In a notebook, list some steps you each can take this week to obey God in the area of strengthening your marriage. Note how your obedience in this area will draw you closer to God and to your spouse.

FAITH TIME: Faith is our positive response to what God has said. Spend a few moments praying through your eyes of faith. Tell God the positive things you see happening because of His goodness!

PRAISE AND THANKSGIVING TIME: Read Colossians 3:18-21. Praise God for who He is—the Creator of marriage and family. And thank Him for what He has done—let us in on His plans for how our family relationships can and will work if we follow His plans.

Family Time Throughout the Week

MONDAY—Do the Family Devotion Time together. Work on the Family Worship section as you have time.

TUESDAY—Finish up the Family Worship section. As a family, after dinner, pray together for the marriages within your family: your own, grandparents, aunts and uncles, extended family and so on. If marriages are hurting or have broken up, pray for God's healing, forgiveness and grace. If your marriage is hurting or in trouble, reassure your children that you want God's will for your whole family.

WEDNESDAY—Evaluate yourself compared to the characteristics and qualities in Colossians 3:12-14. Which one will you work on today? These qualities aren't just limited to marriage, so everyone in the family can do this.

THURSDAY—Write a letter to your spouse describing your commitment (see Matthew 19:5, 6). Children can write a letter to their parents describing what they most appreciate about watching their parents' marriage relationship. Younger children may want to draw their home, and especially how they feel about their mom and dad.

FRIDAY—Work together on your memory verse for the week. As you sometimes do, break the verse down into phrases and discuss their meanings. Help your family both to memorize and understand the words of the verse.

WEEK 29: PAIN

Family Devotion Time

ACTIVITY: PUTTING A BITE ON IT. Your kids might know how to do this already. After everyone has gathered together, issue these instructions. Put the tips of your little fingers between your upper and lower teeth, just to each side of your front teeth. Now, apply just a little bit of pressure. Don't bite. You shouldn't actually feel any pain, just pressure. Do this for about 20 seconds.

> ***Pain** is the hurt we might feel on the outside—or in our hearts.*

Now take your fingers out of your mouth, and immediately press the fingertips together, pressing with pretty good pressure. Oddly, this will most likely hurt more than when you had your fingers in your mouth.

DISCUSSION: Take a few minutes and talk through these questions together:

• Why do you think we have pain in our lives?

• Do you think life would be better for us if we didn't have pain?

• Would we be able to feel good if we never experienced pain? If you weren't ever sick, would you know how good it feels to get better? If no one ever hurt your feelings, would you really know how good it feels to have people not say bad things to you?

• In your life, what's the most painful thing you ever went through? What were the most painful feelings you ever had?

• Do you think that you learned anything from this time of hurt? What was it?

Pain is weird. It can build up for a long time without

hurting. It's like the activity with our little fingers. The fingers didn't hurt at first, and they didn't hurt when we put them between our teeth. But they hurt when we added the pressure of putting them together. Pain and hurt—especially the hurts we feel inside—can build up. Sometimes we feel them when we aren't ready for them. But this kind of hurt can be OK. God can teach us something when we feel hurt. But we have to be open to His teaching. *This week's memory verse* tells what we can learn through our pain and hurt:

"This short time of distress will result in God's richest blessing upon us forever and ever!" —2 Corinthians 4:17

FAMILY BIBLE TIME: In Psalm 119:65-72, the psalmist zeroes in on the healing process of God's Word when we face pain, hurt and sorrow. Pain is seldom our welcomed friend, but it seems to come calling upon every single one of us at some point in our lives. So the issue is not whether or not we can avoid it. We can't. The issue is: how will we respond to it when it arrives in our lives. In Psalm 119, we are given a "perspective on pain" in our lives:

• God always deals with us rightly and fairly (verse 65).

• Meditating on God's Word will bring us the discernment we need (verse 66).

• Pain and hurt are markers in our life that indicate how intimate we are with God (verse 67).

• God's nature is only good, and all that He does is good (verse 68).

• We must ignore lies about ourselves and recognize the truth (verses 69, 70).

• Pain and hurt, though never fun, are to motivate us to find truth (verse 71).

• God's Word is to be treasured as central in the healing process (verse 72).

FAMILY PRAYER TIME: Pray for the other members of your family right now, even asking if you can take turns praying around your family circle. Is someone in your family going through pain or hurt right now—maybe a friend has moved away or someone has died? Pray that each of you will understand what God is trying to teach you. Also, thank God for the times when you aren't hurting inside. Close your prayer time by asking God to help you understand more and more throughout this week why we have to learn to live with pain.

Family Worship Time (optional)

As your family thinks about why we go through pain and suffering in our lives, take some time to go through the following steps. Ask God to teach you through this process.

PREPARATION TIME: Read Psalm 119:67. Think together about your personal lives, your family life, your church or ministry life, and your business or school life. Can you think of any principle or truth God has taught any of you through pain in each of these areas?

WAITING TIME: During your waiting time, let God love you, search you and show each of you what He wants you to learn about the hurts we experience. Ask Him to provide simple, heartfelt answers to these statements:
"God, I need to feel Your love today, especially in the area of . . ."
"God, You have my permission to reveal any bitter attitude or wrong motive in my life . . ."
"God, is there anything that I need to know as I enter this day. . . ?"

CONFESSION TIME: Read Psalm 22. Have you ever felt like the writer of this psalm? Individually, confess to God areas where you've felt hurt or pain or sorrow, and you were unwilling to trust Him to teach you and deliver you from your hurt.

BIBLE TIME: We can never pray out of God's will when we pray God's Word. Reread Psalm 119:65-72 several times. Close your eyes and ask God to point out a main truth to each of you from these verses. Then pray the Scripture back to God and allow Him to minister to your family.

MEDITATION TIME: After praying the Scriptures, write down

in a notebook any thoughts that God has impressed upon your minds. Spend a few moments meditating on these truths. Throughout the week, come back to this step to reflect and meditate on these thoughts concerning pain and how you deal with it.

INTERCESSION TIME—PRAYING FOR OTHERS: Read James 5:16. Now ask God to bring to your minds anyone—including members of your family—who needs healing for pain they are experiencing right now. Ask God to help them understand how He wants to use this experience of pain or sorrow to teach them.

PETITION TIME—PRAYING FOR YOURSELVES: If any of you are facing pain and hurt right now, especially in a relationship, thinking through these statements might help you understand what God is trying to teach you:

1. Start by facing the facts. (What's happened? Don't rationalize.)

2. Forgive as much as can be forgiven. (Hurt is legitimate, but ask for and expect release.)

3. Seek the healing of memories. (God doesn't intend you to carry hurt.)

4. Find a caring community (an accountability group or support group).

5. Believe that God isn't bound by the limits and failings of our human relationships. Instead, He is generous, forgiving, trustworthy and truthful.

Pray that God will enable each of you to learn from your experiences, and will help you be forgiving of those who hurt you.

APPLICATION TIME: In a notebook, list any steps your family needs to take in obedience to God this week. Is there someone who is hurting who you need to reach out to and surround with your love? Can you be instrumental in helping someone understand that though God doesn't cause our pain, He does allow it so that we can be drawn closer to Him? How can you demonstrate or explain this principle in a loving, patient, understanding way?

FAITH TIME: Faith is our positive response to what God has said. Spend a few moments praying through your eyes of faith. Tell God the positive things you see happening because of His goodness!

PRAISE AND THANKSGIVING TIME: Reread this week's memory verse. Praise God by recognizing who He is—a God who can heal our hurts. And thank Him by recognizing what He has done—provided blessings we can know for all eternity.

Family Time Throughout the Week

MONDAY—Do the Family Devotion Time, and get started on the Family Worship section.

TUESDAY—Reread Psalm 119:65-72, and the statements about this passage in the Family Bible Time. Talk together as a family about which statement you have experienced most in your personal life. Then discuss which statement you've struggled with the most. Pray together as a family, expressing to God the pain you've felt in your lives, how you've responded to your hurts, and how the pain and what you've learned from it has changed you.

WEDNESDAY—Review your memory verse together as a family. Check how everyone is doing on memorizing it, and help younger members of the family. Also, talk through what the verse means, if necessary, taking it apart phrase by phrase and defining what different sections mean.

THURSDAY—As a family, talk through this statement: If you are facing pain and hurt right now, God desires to heal you. How do you think we can accept this truth and live by it?

FRIDAY—Reread James 5:16. Within your family, are there any faults or sins that you need to confess to each other and to God? Have a quiet time together after dinner. Declare that tonight is a "safe" night. Allow people to share their shortcomings openly and without judgment—either tonight or after tonight. Ask for forgiveness if you've hurt another family member. Pray together as a family for healing.

WEEK 30: PARENTING

Family Devotion Time

ACTIVITY: HUNT AND CLIP. Give each person a pair of scissors and a stack of magazines. This week, the activity is to look for photos from either advertisements or articles which show parents and children together.

> **Parenting** *is loving kids enough to teach them to do right.*

Encourage everyone to look specifically for photos that show families having a good time together, that somehow portray families interacting and showing their love for one another.

Have a short "show and tell" time, where each person holds up the photo(s) he has cut out, and describes what he thinks the family is doing.

DISCUSSION: Now, as a family, talk through these questions together:

• How are the parents in your photos showing their love for their kids?

• How are the kids showing love back to their parents?

• If you had to draw or describe a picture of what love between parents and children looks like, what would you draw? What situation would be pictured?

• Why do you think some parents seem not to love their kids?

• If you had to draw a picture of a home where this love seemed to be missing, what would it look like? What would the parents and the children be doing (or not doing)?

Christian parents are called to a very special mission. They are given the responsibility to raise their children into responsible adults. They are also commanded by God to raise their children into adults who will follow God. As *this week's memory verse* says:

"Teach a child to choose the right path, and when he is older he will remain upon it." —Proverbs 22:6

FAMILY BIBLE TIME: Parenting is at the same time the most challenging and rewarding journey moms and dads ever embark on. The apostle Paul shares a few simple truths in Ephesians 6 to help guide us on our journey.

"Children, obey your parents; this is the right thing to do because God has placed them in authority over you. Honor your father and mother. . . . If you honor your father and mother, yours will be a long life, full of blessing. And now a word to you parents. Don't keep on scolding and nagging your children, making them angry and resentful. Rather, bring them up with the loving discipline the Lord himself approves, with suggestions and godly advice." —Ephesians 6:1-6

This passage gives us three biblical guidelines for Christian parenting:

1. Children are to honor and obey their parents.

2. Parents are not to treat their children harshly. They are to freely give them generous amounts of unconditional love.

3. Parents are to seek God's will and wisdom in raising their children. We are to teach them to obey God, and to love Him and serve Him.

FAMILY PRAYER TIME: With your kids, pray that they will understand that the obedience you demand from them, and the discipline you deliver, are meant to help them grow up to love, serve and obey God.

Family Worship Time (optional)

(Children who usually complete this section each week can take this week off. But it would be great if you would pray each day for your parents.)

Charles Francis Adams, a 19th Century political figure and diplomat, kept a diary. One day he entered: "Went fishing with my son today—a day wasted." His son, Brook Adams, also kept a diary. On the day his father took him fishing, Brook Adams made this entry: "Went fishing with my father—the most wonderful day of my life!"

Parents just never know what a few moments spent with their children mean.

The following steps will help you identify areas where you're doing well as a parent, and areas where you can use some improvement.

PREPARATION TIME: Read this week's memory verse again. Read through the following list and think about any issues you are wrestling with in raising your children. Why?
Discipline
Self-control (yours)
Spiritual growth
Peer relationships
Self-esteem

WAITING TIME: During your waiting time, let God love you, search you and show you areas of your life where your parenting skills need to change. Ask Him to help you complete these simple prayers:

"God, I feel Your love today, especially in the gift You have given me of my children . . ."

"God, You have permission to reveal any area in which I need to improve as a parent . . ."

"God, grant me wisdom to know how to train my children according to Your will. . . ?"

CONFESSION TIME: Read Psalm 103:13 and Proverbs 31:10, 28. Confess the areas of your life as a parent (a role model) that would not be pleasing to God.

BIBLE TIME: We can never pray out of God's will when we pray God's Word. Read Deuteronomy 6:1-7 to yourself a couple of times. Close your eyes and allow a main truth to surface in your heart. Then pray the Scripture back to God and allow Him to minister to you. Your prayer might go something like this: "God, help me to know exactly what to teach my children. There are so many things going on in the world today, and so many influences in kids' lives. But You remain unchanged. Help me to teach them to love You. Help me to model my love for You. Help me to model Your love for me and for them. I do love You with all my heart, soul and might. I want my kids to know that fervent love for You as well. Help me to speak well of You always, so that they know of my love and honor and respect for who You are and all You have done for me and my family. In Jesus' name, Amen."

MEDITATION TIME: After praying the Scriptures, write down in a notebook whatever thoughts God has impressed upon your mind about parenting. Perhaps focus on the example and model we provide for our children.

INTERCESSION TIME—PRAYING FOR OTHERS: This week, praying for others may be easy or it may be difficult. It depends on how well you know your kids. Pray a prayer of thanksgiving and blessing for your children, and pray specifically for their needs.

PETITION TIME—PRAYING FOR YOURSELVES: Ask God to help you know your kids better, so that you can bring their needs directly before Him. Also, pray for your skills as parents. Pray that you will model appropriate attitudes and behaviors for your kids. If you are part of a two-parent family, thank God for your spouse who shares parenting duties and joys with you. If you are a single parent, thank God for the joys you know as well. Also, pray for additional strength as you face some parenting struggles alone.

APPLICATION TIME: In a notebook, list any steps you need to take this week to improve your parenting skills. List any behaviors you need to change so that you become more like the parent described in Ephesians 6.

FAITH TIME: Faith is our positive response to what God has said. Spend a few moments praying through your eyes of faith. Tell God the positive things you see happening because of His goodness!

PRAISE AND THANKSGIVING TIME: Reread Psalm 103:13. Praise God by recognizing who He is—a God of compassion. Also, thank God by recognizing what He has done—provided the example of a perfect parent.

Family Time Throughout the Week

MONDAY—Do the Family Devotion Time. Get going on the Family Worship section.

TUESDAY—Write down the top five most important values you want to teach your children (such as honesty, positive attitude, kindness). Talk together as a family about how you're doing as a parent. It can be tough to listen to your children give you a "performance review." But it can also be very enlightening!

WEDNESDAY—Spend extra time today praying with your children. A general time guideline: for each year of age, spend one minute praying praying with your child.

THURSDAY—Read Philippians 2:3. Talk together as a family about what this verse means for both parents and children.

FRIDAY—Review your memory verse. As you've done other weeks, make sure that everyone in the family works to understand the verse as well as to memorize it. Ask family members to provide simple definitions for each phrase of the verse.

WEEK 31: PASSION

Family Devotion Time

ACTIVITY: HANDS OFF! This week's activity might not be so fun for your family, simply because they have to wait. It's not an exercise in patience—in fact, that will come next week.

Start a few minutes before your family's gathering time by making a batch of popcorn. You know how popcorn is— the delicious odor wafts

> ***Passion*** *is wanting something so much you think of it more than anything.*

through the house, making your family look like a bunch of cartoon characters carried along in mid-air on the fragrance to the place where you gather!

But here's the catch. This bowl of popcorn just sits in the middle of the table until after the discussion and prayer time are over. No one touches or sneaks a bite! You don't have to be cruel; let them know that everyone can eat it after prayer time. But not until then!

DISCUSSION: While everyone's mouth waters and they just seem to stare at the popcorn, try to talk through these questions.

• What are you thinking about right now?

• Why is it so hard to think of anything else but eating that popcorn?

• Can you think of any other time when you could only think about one thing? Was there ever a time that you wanted something so badly that it completely filled your brain?

• Do you think that this kind of desire can ever be a good thing?

• Can you think of something good you might want so much that it seems to push everything else out your mind?

Passion can be a good thing. If we want what God wants for us, that's great. Sometimes the Bible uses the word *zeal* for passion. Zeal is a desire to please God, to do what He wants us to do, especially when we help other people. God wants us to have this kind of passion! As **this week's memory verse** says:

"[Jesus] died . . . [to] make us his very own people, with cleansed hearts and real enthusiasm for doing kind things for others." —Titus 2:14

FAMILY BIBLE TIME: Read Philippians 3:13, 14. Talk about how passionate athletes are in trying to win a game. As Christians, we should be that passionate about serving Jesus.

FAMILY PRAYER TIME: Pray together as a family, encouraging other family members to say short sentence prayers after you say these phrases: Thank God for sending Jesus to die for our sins. Ask God to protect us and keep us from sinning. Ask God to make us His, to use us. Thank Him for a cleansed heart and the privilege of serving Him. Pray that He will give us enthusiasm, passion, zeal as we serve Him by helping others.

Family Worship Time (optional)

The starting point of all achievement is desire. Weak desires bring weak results, just as a small amount of fire makes a small amount of heat. If you find yourself lacking in persistence, your weakness might be fixed by building a stronger fire under your desires.

Among the great number of books authored by C. S. Lewis is the highly provocative *The Screwtape Letters*. In this book, Screwtape briefs his nephew Wormwood on the subtleties and techniques of tempting people. The goal, he counsels, is not wickedness but indifference. Screwtape cautions his nephew to keep the prospect, the patient, comfortable at all costs. If he becomes concerned about anything of importance, Wormwood is to get him to think about his lunch plans; not to worry, it could induce indigestion.

And then Screwtape describes his own job in these definitive terms: "I, the devil, will always see to it that there are bad people. Your job, my dear Wormwood, is to provide me with the people who do not care."

It might seem that Wormwood and his peers are succeeding! As Tony Campolo writes: "We are caught up at a particular stage in our national ethos in which we're not only materialistic, but worse than that—we're becoming emotionally dead as a people. We don't sing, we don't dance, we don't even commit sin with much enthusiasm. Kierkegaard once said this age will die, not from sin, but from a lack of passion. There is a deadness everywhere. High schools are apathetic. Colleges are apathetic. I mean, everybody's gone to sleep." (*Publisher's Weekly,* Sept. 6, 1991)

Jesus had a warning along that line for the church at Ephesus. While acknowledging their accomplishments, hard work and doctrinal purity, He looked them right in the eyes and said, in effect, "You're doing all this stuff in my name, but I don't think you even love Me anymore" (see Revelation 2:1-6).

The remedy? How can you regain passion and zeal? Stop dead in your tracks. Set aside your preoccupations. Turn around. Remember your first commitment to your Lord. Do the things you used to do in that first flush of wholehearted surrender and joy. And watch yourself!

If any of you misses the passion you used to have—or if you never had it—work through the following steps. Ask God to use these now familiar steps to light a new fire within each of you.

PREPARATION TIME: Read Philippians 3:7-16. Now reread verses 13, 14. As you begin going through these steps this week, ask God to help keep each of you focused on the future, on "the end of the race" and "the prize."

WAITING TIME: During your waiting time, let God love you, search you and show each of you His desires in the area of your passion. Ask Him to reveal to you phrases that complete these simple prayers:

"God, I feel Your love today, especially in the area of . . ."

"God, You have permission to reveal any apathetic spirit in my life . . ."

"God, is there anything that I need to 'feel about zeal' as I enter this day. . . ?"

CONFESSION TIME: There's an old story about the man who tried to save Sodom from destruction. The city's inhabitants ignored him, and a friend asked mockingly, "Why bother everyone? You can't change them."

"Maybe I can't change them," the man replied, "but if I shout and scream, it may prevent them from changing me!"

Let each person answer these questions for himself:

• Has your love grown cold for God?

• Do you carry a burden for people who don't know Christ as Savior?

• Do you find joy in serving God?

Confess silently to God areas where each of you find yourselves silent, no longer screaming and shouting; the fire is missing. Remember, be honest with God. He already knows your hearts.

BIBLE TIME: When we pray God's Word back to Him, we can be certain that we're praying for God's will. Reread Philippians 3:7-16 slowly a few times. Then close your eyes and allow God to bring a main truth to the surface of each of your hearts regarding passion. Now pray this Scripture back to God, personalizing it. Allow God to minister to each of you through this prayer.

MEDITATION TIME: After praying the Scriptures, write down in a notebook any thoughts that God has impressed upon your minds about passion. Reread Philippians 3:10. How does the apostle Paul say he has experienced power and freedom?

INTERCESSION TIME—PRAYING FOR OTHERS: Can you think of people your family knows who are passionate about their faith in God? Ask God to bring situations into their lives so that their "fire" doesn't die down or go out. What about Christians who seem to lack even a spark of enthusiasm about their faith? Pray that God will bring circumstances into their lives that will renew their zeal and stoke their fires.

PETITION TIME—PRAYING FOR YOURSELVES: Which of the phrases above describes each of you? Are you a Christian with a burning passion, or one who lacks even a spark? Pray the same things for yourselves, that God will give you circumstances to keep your fires burning for Him or to light that first flicker.

APPLICATION TIME: List in a notebook what steps your family can take toward obeying God in the area of passion and enthusiasm. Remember, like so many qualities of our lives as Christians, passion is shown by your action. For example, it will be shown by a great desire for personal holiness. It will reflect the attitude of Matthew 5:29, 30. Read this verse and ask God to help each of you become obedient in your zeal for Him.

FAITH TIME: Faith is our positive response to what God has said. Spend a few moments praying through your eyes of faith. Tell God the positive things you see happening in your family because of His goodness!

PRAISE AND THANKSGIVING TIME: Read Philippians 4:12. Praise God by recognizing who He is—Provider of our Savior. Thank God by recognizing what He has done—worked inside each of us to make us what He wants us to be.

Family Time Throughout the Week

MONDAY—Do the Family Devotion Time, and begin the Family Worship section.

TUESDAY TO FRIDAY—Below are some great verses on passion. They each tell of a work that God puts within us to make us different. Each day this week, read these verses to your family, perhaps after dinnertime. Talk about how all of us, not just adults, can have a passion to serve others and serve God. Together, ask God to do a work within you that you cannot do for yourselves. Pray for each other as well.

- Job 38:36
- Psalm 4:7
- Isaiah 42:1
- Isaiah 63:11
- Jeremiah 31:33
- Jeremiah 32:40
- Ezekiel 11:19
- Ezekiel 36:26, 27

Remember, God works from the inside out, not the outside in. He does a work in our hearts. He changes our thoughts and attitudes, which changes our choices, which changes our actions, which changes our very lives.

God never asks you to do a work outwardly unless He has first done a work inwardly. But it is our responsibility to respond. When God has worked in our lives, then we are to adjust our lives to His agenda, not ours.

WEEK 32: PATIENCE

Family Devotion Time

ACTIVITY: THE INCREDIBLE FACE OFF. This week, no props or preparation needed! No food involved!

Remember the game you played when you were a kid, where you just sat nose-to-nose with someone, staring directly in his eyes, and the first one who laughed was the loser? That's the activity for the week.

> ***Patience* means waiting for others without getting mad at them.**

Just pair off family members. For 10 or 15 minutes, play this game. Usually, the time that two people can look at each other without laughing gets shorter and shorter, and typically ends with both people laughing. That's OK. Wow, family devotions where laughter is OK, even welcome!

DISCUSSION: After you're all tired of looking each other in the face, talk through these questions as a family:

• Did you notice that the longer we tried to look at each other without laughing, the harder it got and the shorter the time was?

• Why is it that sometimes the harder we try at something, the harder it becomes?

• Do you think that you're a patient person? Why or why not?

• Do you think God wants us to be patient? Why is that such an important thing?

• What are some ways we can be more patient? Can you tell me what it looks like to be patient?

It's wise to be patient and foolish to be quick-tempered. You can't talk about patience without talking about anger. Patience means "slow to get angry." As *this week's memory verse says:*

"A [patient] man controls his temper. He knows that anger causes mistakes." —Proverbs 14:29

FAMILY BIBLE TIME: Job gives us the greatest lesson in patience in the Bible. If you have a children's story Bible, read a condensed version or the summary of Job's story. Remind your children of the circumstances: Though Job is wise, rich and good, terrible things happen to him. Yet throughout his suffering, he never quits believing that God cares for him. Read Job's response to his friends in Job 19:25-27.

FAMILY PRAYER TIME: Encourage your family to pray in short sentence prayers about patience:

Pray that God will put into each of you a desire to be patient.

Ask Him to show you how impatience and anger are not part of someone who knows and loves Him.

Tell Him about times when you've lost your patience and become angry at others—someone in your family, at school or work, at church.

Pray that He will help you control your temper and anger.

Family Worship Time (optional)

Franz Joseph Haydn wrote a musical piece that requires the flute player to sit quietly for 74 measures and then come in exactly on the upbeat of the 75th. Gerald Johnson, historian and writer, who plays the flute in the Baltimore Symphony, says that a composer who expects a man to wait that patiently and perform that precisely is looking for a rare individual.

Patience means "long wrath—slow anger." Really. Half the Greek word for patience is "anger," and the other half is "long" or "slow." Patience means to handle your anger slowly.

Wouldn't it be great if we lived in a perfect world? Unfortunately, we don't, so we have to deal with one of the secrets of healthy relationships—patience. We all need patience in an imperfect world.

God is calling each of us to be patient, in fact, to be "a rare individual."

Now spend some time together completing these increasingly-familiar steps. Don't let their familiarity allow you to skip or skim. Take the time to really work and study and contemplate each step and the progression of steps. You can apply your patience here too!

PREPARATION TIME: Anger is one letter from danger. When you lose your temper, you lose.

The Bible is very specific about the damage that uncontrolled anger does. Read these verses from Proverbs: 11:29; 14:17; 14:29; 15:18. Then talk about the areas in your lives where you most quickly display anger. Where are you most patient?

WAITING TIME: Eugene Peterson, in his book, *A Long Obedience in the Same Direction,* wrote: "One aspect of this world that I have been able to identify as harmful to Christians is the assumption that anything worthwhile can be acquired at once. We assume that if anything can be done at all, it can be done quickly and efficiently. Our attention spans have been conditioned by 30-second commercials and 30-second abridgments."

How impatient have we become? Contrast the above thought with the words of Exodus 34:6: "I am Jehovah, the merciful and gracious God . . . slow to anger and rich in steadfast love and truth."

During your waiting time, let God love you, search you and show each of you His desires in the area of patience. Ask Him to reveal to you phrases that complete these simple prayers:

"God, I feel Your love and presence today, especially in the area of . . ."

"God, You have permission to reveal any wrong motive in my life, any area where I am quick to anger . . ."

"God, is there anything that I need to know as I enter this day? Prepare me for trials that will require patience . . ."

CONFESSION TIME: Read Ephesians 4:26, 27. Individually confess any anger you might be holding in your life right now. Again, remember, God already knows your heart. But confession is healthy and a first step in healing what you're feeling.

BIBLE TIME: When we pray God's Word back to Him, we can

be certain that we're praying for God's will. Read Ephesians 4:26, 27 again slowly a few times. Then close your eyes and ask God to bring a main truth to the surface in each of your hearts about how patience and anger are related. Now pray this Scripture and allow God to minister to you. Your prayer might go something like this: "God, help us today. We know there are times when we're angry, and we know that You want us to be patient instead. Our anger even becomes sin when we hold grudges, so help us to release to You the times when we become angry. Help us not to hold our anger within, suppressing it and letting it fester and grow. Most of all, we pray that Satan will not get even a foothold in our lives because of our temper. We invite You to be in control of our lives, including those areas where we are quick-tempered. In Jesus' name, Amen."

MEDITATION TIME: After praying the Scriptures, write down in a notebook any thoughts that God has impressed upon your minds about patience. Focus on how anger is the opposite of patience. And if we are angry we are not supposed to deny it or suppress it. The quickest way to rid ourselves of anger is to confess it to God!

INTERCESSION TIME—PRAYING FOR OTHERS: Ask God to bring to your minds people who need to learn to be patient. Don't use this as a time to judge them, but as a time to pray for them. Pray that they will see their need to be "slow to anger." Ask God to place circumstances in their lives that teach them patience.

PETITION TIME—PRAYING FOR YOURSELVES: Read James 5:7-12. Do any of you see any qualities in this passage that characterize your attitudes? Are you patient? Courageous? Or do you grumble and criticize? Ask God to replace undesirable qualities with desirable ones in your lives.

APPLICATION TIME: List in a notebook what steps your family can take toward obeying God in the area of patience. Note how being obedient is itself a step to help you be patient.

FAITH TIME: Faith is our positive response to what God has said. Spend a few moments praying through your eyes of faith. Tell God the positive things you see happening because of His goodness!

PRAISE AND THANKSGIVING TIME: Reread the simple words of Exodus 34:6. Then praise God by recognizing who He is—a merciful and gracious God. And thank Him by recognizing what He has done—provided us with patience through His great and unfailing love for us.

Family Time Throughout the Week

MONDAY—Do the Family Devotion Time. Get started on the Family Worship section, and work to finish it in the next couple of days.

TUESDAY—Read Isaiah 40:28-31. Talk together as a family about what these verses mean. What does it mean "to wait upon the Lord"? How can our waiting allow God to give us strength?

WEDNESDAY—Talk together about the "50/20 principle." When a situation comes that is just not fair, read Genesis 50:20. How can having this attitude—that God can make good out of a bad situation—make a difference in our lives?

THURSDAY—Read Romans 15:5. Talk together about any areas of your lives where it is hard to be patient. Commit together that you will each rely on God's help to be patient.

FRIDAY—Read and meditate on the following:

We are in such a hurry that many of us cannot imagine our lives without Federal Express, when it absolutely, positively, has to be there overnight. What would we do without Federal Express?

What would we FedEx addicts have done a hundred years ago? Back then they didn't have Federal Express, they had Pony Express. I can see the commercials now: "Pony Express—when it absolutely, positively has to be there in three months." Can you imagine waiting three months for a package? We have trouble waiting three days.

The bad news is this: God rarely uses Federal Express to build character. He doesn't overnight or fax character to us. It takes time to build character. Lots of time. That's why He is taking so much time in your life. God isn't in a hurry.

Can you believe God took 40 years to build character into Moses? Most of us want character in 40 minutes, and even then we're impatient. Maybe God's motto is, "When it absolutely, positively has to be there in 40 years." Moses was in a hurry to free the children of Israel. He was sure God had placed him in his unique position so that he could have an unusual ministry. And he was right—but he was off on the timing.

God is not in a hurry when it comes to our lives. He will take all the time necessary to do a deep and lasting work in our lives. Because we're in a hurry, that seems hard on us. Like Moses, we may even be in a hurry to do a good thing. But God is not in a hurry.

Listen to this word of encouragement: You are right on schedule. Maybe not on your schedule, but on God's schedule. He knows precisely what He is doing. Every trial has a beginning, a middle, and an end. You cannot determine where you are in your trial, but God knows exactly where you are. He is moving you along at just the right pace. Someone once said that everything is in walking distance, if you have enough time.

As far as God is concerned, we've got the time. Take it.

WEEK 33: PEACE

Family Devotion Time

ACTIVITY: REMOTE POSSIBILITIES. This activity requires a television set with a remote control. If you don't have one, don't go buy one! You'll just have to talk through the activity instead of doing it. Or you can talk through what would happen if you did the same thing to the telephone.

> ***Peace** is not worrying because you know God is in control.*

Go to the room where your TV set is. Take the remote control and randomly punch in two numbers. Did you get a station that your TV even receives? Let other family members have a turn punching in numbers randomly. Now, take out your program listing. Look at the day and time it is right now, and choose a program that's on. Punch in the numbers of that channel.

Voila! The program you were looking for. Good reception. Exactly what you were hoping to find.

DISCUSSION: These questions and the Family Worship Time are to help you and your family connect the concepts of peace and God being in control.

• What happened when we just punched in any numbers on the remote?

• How was it different when we punched in the numbers of a channel we had looked up?

• What would happen if you picked up the phone, closed your eyes, and just punched any numbers?

• Why do you think it's important that we be in control?

• What would happen if there weren't laws, say for speeding, and people could drive unsafely and out of control?

• How would the world be different—for example, the relationships between countries—if we didn't have laws?

If we are out of control, we will never know peace. But even if we *are* in control, we may not know peace. We need to put God in control. Peace is from the Hebrew word, *shalom,* which means a sense of order and well-being, a feeling of wholeness. Peace happens when we obey God and are sure that He is in control. The promise of God's peace is contained in **this week's memory verse:**

"He will keep in perfect peace all those who trust in him." —Isaiah 26:3

FAMILY BIBLE TIME: Have you ever heard the expression, "get your goat?" It comes from the horse-racing industry of past years. Horse owners would often stable a goat with their racehorse because the presence of the goat seemed to keep the horse calm. But if someone got the goat before the race, the horse owners believed their horse would lose its poise and blow the race.

When you allow someone who annoys you to shake you out of control, you let them "get your goat."

God's promise in Isaiah 26:3, this week's memory verse, is that if we allow ourselves to be under the control of God's peace, we can keep our goat!

Read Isaiah 48:17, 18. If we want to know "peace like a flowing river," we must gladly submit, with a willing spirit, to God's teaching, directing and commanding. The Prophet Isaiah immediately goes on to state that there is "no peace . . . for the wicked" (48:22). Those who reject what is best, and disregard God's ways, will know nothing of the sense of well-being they would have known if they had lived their lives in obedience.

FAMILY PRAYER TIME: Pray together as a family that you will discover this week how to let God be in control of your lives, so that you can know His perfect peace. Ask Him to remind you, to give you nudges each day, that turn your thoughts to Him. Thank Him for allowing us to know peace in a world that is full of turmoil and pain.

Family Worship Time (optional)

The following steps will help your family more completely understand God's peace, and help you begin to see how you can experience it in your own lives:

PREPARATION TIME: Think about your own lives for a minute. How much peace do you experience? In your personal lives, family life, church or ministry life, business or school life, do you have difficulty experiencing peace? Why?

WAITING TIME: During your waiting time, let God love you, search you and show each of you His desires in the area of knowing His peace. Ask Him to reveal to you phrases that complete these simple prayers:

"God, I feel Your love today, especially in the area of . . ."

"God, You have permission to reveal any wrong motive in my life, especially anything that is keeping me from knowing Your peace . . ."

"God, is there anything that I need to know as I enter this day, any situation I may encounter where letting You remain in control will be difficult. . . ?"

CONFESSION TIME: Read Philippians 4:6, 7. This passage calls for us to pray about everything, especially our worries. Together confess to God any worries that you are keeping control of, not surrendering to Him. Ask for His help.

BIBLE TIME: When we pray God's Word back to Him, we can be certain that we're praying for God's will. Reread the familiar verses from Philippians 4 again slowly a few times. Then close your eyes and ask God to bring a main truth to the surface in each of your hearts about peace. Now pray this Scripture and allow God to minister to each of you. Your prayer might go something like this: "God, we do give You our worries. We give everything to You. We realize that it's wrong to claim to be Yours, but then to hold on to pieces of our lives, even our worries. Thank You for wanting to know our needs, and thank You for every answer to prayer You give—even those that we're not expecting! Please help us to know and experience Your wonderful peace. We may not understand it, but we can certainly enjoy it and rejoice in it! Thank You for the quiet and rest and peace You provide to those who trust in You. In Jesus' name, Amen."

MEDITATION TIME: After praying the Scriptures, write down in notebook any thoughts that God has impressed upon your mind about His peace. Also, read Matthew 6:25-34, and focus on the five steps to inner peace revealed in these verses:

1. Relax yourself (verse 25).
2. Value yourself (verses 26, 28-30).
3. Accept yourself (verse 27).
4. Focus yourself (verses 31, 32, 34).
5. Consecrate yourself (verse 33).

INTERCESSION TIME—PRAYING FOR OTHERS: Together think about people you know, including members of your own family, who seem to be going through difficult times, even a time of torment or turmoil. Pray for them, asking God to place in them a sense of peace. Pray that these people will be broken in such a way that they will gladly give control back to God, surrendering their worries and troubles to Him. Pray that even in this time of strife, they will be able to rejoice and praise God for His gift of peace.

PETITION TIME—PRAYING FOR YOURSELVES: Ask the same questions of yourselves. Is there an area where any of you seem unwilling to give God complete control? Do your lives feel like the remote control when you punched in random numbers, with no sense of order or well-being? Ask God to break your spirits, so that you are willing to give Him complete control. Thank Him for the anticipated experience of knowing His perfect peace.

APPLICATION TIME: List in a notebook what steps your family can take toward obeying God in the areas of control and peace. Acknowledge that obedience to God is the first step to knowing His peace. Work this week and in following weeks to allow God to be in control of every area of your lives—even the smallest, day-to-day areas.

FAITH TIME: Faith is our positive response to what God has said. Spend a few moments praying through your eyes of faith. Tell God the positive things you see happening because of His goodness!

PRAISE AND THANKSGIVING TIME: Reread Isaiah 48:17, 18. From these verses, praise God by recognizing who He is—a God who knows what's best. Thank Him by recognizing what He has done—given us peace and righteousness when we follow His commands.

Family Time Throughout the Week

MONDAY—Do the Family Devotion Time and begin the Family Worship section.

TUESDAY—Discuss this thought with your family: There are three types of people: Those who bring nothing to God in prayer; those who bring some things to God in prayer; and those who bring everything to God in prayer.

Which type are you?

WEDNESDAY—Reexamine your memory verse for this week. Talk through it as a family as well as memorizing it. Pray together again that God will help you make the words of this verse a reality in your life.

THURSDAY—Talk together as a family about any situations within your home that are stressful. Perhaps even make a list. It can be as simple as four or five people sharing one bathroom every morning, or as complicated as siblings or a parent and a child not being able to get along. Pray that God will bring His peace over your home. If you are trying to retain control, pray that God will give you the strength to turn the situation entirely over to Him.

FRIDAY—Pick up the discussion you began yesterday. What actions can you and other members of the family take to resolve the situation? Is anyone unconvinced that God's peace can prevail? Review some of the Scripture verses in this lesson that promise God's perfect peace. Talk about how you can practically apply these to your situation—remember that the Bible isn't outdated, and its advice applies to you, today!

WEEK 34: PROBLEMS

Family Devotion Time

ACTIVITY: THE QUESTION GAME. This week, the activity is pretty much just a discussion, so the line between it and the discussion time will seem pretty blurry. So, let's combine them.

DISCUSSION:
- What would you do if someone broke your favorite toy? Your bike? Your Walkman®?

> ***Problems*** *are questions about my life I can't figure out the answers to.*

- How would you feel if someone hit you for no apparent reason?
- What would you do if someone kept picking on you at school, or kept putting you down at work?
- How would you feel if you wanted something really bad, but your parents/spouse/God said, "No, you'll have to wait for it"?
- What do you think your biggest problem is? Does one of these questions describe it? Or do you have bigger problems?

Problems happen. We might as well admit it. Sometimes we have problems that are pretty easy to live with. Other times, we might make more out of problems than we need to. Think about the questions we just talked about. These problems might make us feel bad, even put us through a bit of a trying time. But maybe they're not all that serious. What about more serious problems, ones that have the potential to change our lives or even threaten us? What if someone close to us is very sick or dies? What if we hurt so bad inside that we aren't sure we can tell anyone else about it?

Scripture promises that even these problems have their bright side—reward from God. As **this week's memory verse** says:

"Happy is the man who doesn't give in and do wrong when he is tempted, for afterwards he will get as his reward the crown of life that God has promised those who love him." —James 1:12

FAMILY BIBLE TIME: As a family, read James 1:2-14 together. This passage sums up our problems in two simple sentences:

Problems are inevitable. But, problems have a purpose.

Talk together about any problems someone in the family might be facing. Try to figure out why God is allowing these problems to occur right now.

FAMILY PRAYER TIME: Pray together as a family about the problems you are facing—whether big or small. Pray that God will help you sort out the answers to the minor problems, and will give you perseverance until the major ones end. Thank Him for His promise of a reward when you stick through a challenging situation.

Family Worship Time (optional)

Did you ever hear about the man who, before he could get out of his house and head for work, had four long-distance calls? Everyone seemed to have a problem. And everybody wanted him to get on a plane that day to help out. He finally told his wife to forget about his breakfast. He rushed out of the house as fast as he could. But when he stepped into the garage he discovered his car wouldn't start. So he called a taxi.

While he was waiting for the taxi, he got another call—this time from Chicago—about another problem. Finally, the taxi came and he rushed out, piled his gear into the backseat and yelled, "All right, let's get going."

"Where do you want me to take you?" the taxi driver asked.

"I don't care where we go," the man shouted. "I've got problems everywhere."

A group of psychiatrists met together in Buffalo to define life. After a week of discussion, here's the definition they came up with: "Life is stress and you'd better like it."

Scott Peck said, "This is a great truth, one of the greatest truths. It is a great truth because once we truly see this truth, we transcend it. Once we truly know that life is difficult—once we truly understand and accept it—then life is no longer difficult. Because once it has been accepted, the fact that life is difficult no longer matters. Most do not fully see this truth that life is difficult. Instead they moan more or less incessantly, noisily or subtly, about the enormity of their problems, as if life were generally easy, as if life *should* be easy."

Discuss each of these questions briefly: Do you find life easy or difficult? What about the problems you face? Do you find it easy to surrender them to the Lord, or do you like to hold on to them like a ratty old security blanket? Spend some time going through the steps below, to help you identify your problems, and to understand how you can surrender them and even benefit from them.

PREPARATION TIME: List the problems each of you wrestle with in your personal lives, family life, church or ministry life, business or school life.

WAITING TIME: During your waiting time, let God love you, search you and show each of you His desires when it comes to the problems you face. Ask Him to reveal to you phrases that complete these simple prayers:

"God, I feel Your love today, especially in the area of . . ."

"God, You have permission to reveal any issue in my life that may be a cause to my problems . . ."

"God, is there anything that I need to know as I enter this day, any problems I may face that You can prepare me for now. . . ?"

CONFESSION TIME: Read James 1:2-12. Privately confess to God problems that have caused each of your spirits to sag and kept you from a letting Him build strong Christian character within you.

BIBLE TIME: We can know that we're praying for God's will when we pray His Word back to Him. Reread James 1:2-4 slowly a few times. Then close your eyes and ask God to bring a main truth to the surface in each of your hearts about the problems you face. Now pray this Scripture back to God and allow Him to minister to each of you. Your prayer might go something like this: "Dear God, even when life is relatively good, it seems bad. Sometimes we look at our checkbook or schoolwork or business, and we see all kinds of difficulties and problems. Why do we have to face them? Well, from now on, we resolve to be happy to face them—well, OK, maybe not happy, but we will rejoice in spite of needing to face them. For when times are hard and troubles are mounting, You work in us. You grow in us. Qualities that are good, like patience, increase within us. So, let it grow. Allow us to face any problems that draw us closer to You, for You will build our character, making us strong, full, complete, and ready for anything! In Jesus' name, Amen!"

MEDITATION TIME: After praying the Scriptures, write down in a notebook any thoughts that God has impressed upon your mind about problems. Do you think it matters if the problems we face are big ones or little ones? Or can God use any situation to help us grow closer to Him?

INTERCESSION TIME—PRAYING FOR OTHERS: Who do you know, even among your family, who is facing problems today? Together ask God to provide His peace for that person. Pray that the truths you are learning will somehow be revealed to this person. Pray that the problems will draw him closer to God, rather than push him away. Pray for his attitude, that he will recognize the character that is being developed inside him.

PETITION TIME—PRAYING FOR YOURSELVES: What about each of you? What troubles are you up against? Surrender your problems to God, and anticipate what He wants to teach you through this difficult time. That's what you can rejoice about.

APPLICATION TIME: List in a notebook what steps your family can take toward obeying God in the area of problems. If any of you have a habit of not letting go of your problems, write down how you can surrender every one to God. Make this commitment: "When I have a problem, I don't own it. It's God's." God gives us sound minds—but He will teach us as He guides us through resolving things we face.

FAITH TIME: Deep in our hearts we agree with Lucy in the "Peanuts" comic strip when she says, "I don't want ups and downs. I want ups and ups and ups!"

Faith is our positive response—one of those "ups and ups"—to what God has said. Spend a few moments praying through your eyes of faith. Tell God the positive things you see happening in your family because of His goodness!

PRAISE AND THANKSGIVING TIME: Read Hebrews 12:10-13 Praise God by recognizing who He is—a loving, properly disciplining Father. Thank God by recognizing what He is doing—building character, His own, into our lives.

Family Time Throughout the Week:

MONDAY—Do the Family Devotion Time. Also, get started on the Family Worship section.

TUESDAY—James 1:2 states that we are to cultivate an attitude of joy regarding problems. Talk as a family about how we can have joy in the midst of our problems.

WEDNESDAY—Memorize this quote by Nena O'Neill: "Out of every crisis comes the chance to be reborn." As Christians, what do you think these words mean?

THURSDAY—Talk together again about the problems you discussed under the Family Bible Time. After a few days, do you have any new insights about why God is allowing these problems in your life?

FRIDAY—Learn this formula together. You might even take time to let each member of the family write it on an index card. A good spot to keep it is in your personal Bible.

Problems are . . .

P redictors
R eminders
O pportunities
B lessings
L essons
E verywhere
M essages
S olvable

WEEK 35: PURE IN HEART

Family Devotion Time

ACTIVITY: SOAP AND PEPPER. Take a small bowl of water and sprinkle pepper on the water surface. You can use quite a bit of pepper, and this will still work.

Now take just a single drop of dish soap and put it on the end of your finger or on another family member's finger. Now put just the tip of the finger into the pepper-filled water. "Cool!" is the likely reaction from your family when the pepper quickly moves to the sides of the bowl, leaving the middle of the water clear.

> **Pure in Heart:**
> *Being so clean on the inside that it shows on the outside*

DISCUSSION: Now, spend a few minutes talking through these questions together:

• If you had to make a comparison of the water and pepper to sin in our lives, what would each ingredient represent?

• What would the soap represent? Isn't it neat that Jesus doesn't just move our sins aside—He cleanses them and washes them completely out of our lives?

• Why do you think God needs to be able to see our hearts as clean and pure?

• What happens to us when our hearts are not clean?

• Is there is anything we can do, any sin we can have in our hearts, that God wouldn't be able to make it pure? Why?

In the Bible, *heart* is often used to refer to our spiritual lives. As sinners, our hearts are unclean. If we ask God to cleanse our hearts, through the blood of Jesus Christ, God then sees us as pure and holy. Our sins are gone. We are forgiven. *This week's memory verse* tells what happens:

"Don't keep looking at my sins, erase them from your sight. Create in me a new, clean heart, O God, filled with clean thoughts and right desires." —Psalm 51:9, 10

FAMILY BIBLE TIME: Psalm 51 is David's prayer for forgiveness. Read verses 1-10 and talk together about how God will forgive us no matter how "bad" our sin might be. (If it seems appropriate, briefly outline David's sin with Bathsheba and his murder of her husband in 2 Samuel 11.)

FAMILY PRAYER TIME: If we don't know Jesus Christ as our Savior, our hearts cannot be made clean. Only because of Christ's work on the cross can we be pure in God's sight. That can only happen if we accept this wonderful gift from God. This week, pray together that every member of your family will understand what this means, and that anyone who has not asked Jesus to save them from their sins will do so this week. Ask the Holy Spirit to work in the lives of those who don't know Christ, to soften this heart to receive Christ. For those who know Christ, pray that their commitment to God will be renewed, that they'll remember Christ's sacrifice on the cross to save them from sin. Praise God for this marvelous plan that He put in place so that we can know and love Him.

Family Worship Time (optional)

Max Lucado writes:

I can still remember the first time I saw one. I had gone to work with my dad—a big thrill for a ten-year-old whose father worked in the oil fields. I sat in the cab of the pickup as tall as I could, stretching to see the endless West Texas plain. The countryside was flat and predictable, boasting nothing taller than pumpjacks and windmills. Maybe that is why the thing seemed so colossal. It stood out on the horizon like a science-fiction city.

"What's that?"

"It's a refinery," Dad answered.

A jungle of pipes and tanks and tubes and generators—heaters, pumps, pipes, filters, valves, hoses, conduits, switches, circuits. It looked like a giant Tinker-Toy set. The function of that maze of machinery is defined by its name: It refines. Gasoline, oil, chemicals—the refinery takes whatever comes in and purifies it so that it's ready to go out. The refinery does for petroleum and other products what your "heart" should do for you. It takes out the bad and utilizes the good.

Read Matthew 5:8 and Matthew 15:18, 19. Now consider together these three biblical truths from these verses:

1. Jesus' listeners knew that the heart represented the person each of us has inside. In Jesus' day—and today as well—the heart was thought of as the seat of the character.

2. Our prayer should be like David's—"Create in me a new, clean heart."

3. The order is clear—First, purify the heart. Then you will see God. We usually reverse the order. We try to change the inside by altering the outside.

How can we change from the inside out? Work through the following steps to discover how our hearts can be made pure.

PREPARATION TIME: Jesus gave us the plan for changing our hearts in the Beatitudes. Read the following together:

1. Admit our poverty, our need of Him—Matthew 5:3.

2. Admit our sorrow, grieve our sin—Matthew 5:4.

3. Admit our desire to be changed by Him, to be used by Him—Matthew 5:5.

4. Admit our hunger to be filled with His heart —Matthew 5:6.

WAITING TIME: During your waiting time, let God love you, search you and show each of you His desires when it comes to purifying your lives. Ask Him to reveal to you phrases that complete these simple prayers:

"God, I feel Your love today, especially in the area of . . ."

"God, search my heart and see if there be any hurtful or harmful way in me . . ."

"God, is there anything I need to know about the condition of my heart as I enter into this day. . . ?"

CONFESSION TIME: Read Luke 6:45. Reflect on what has come out of your mouths. Confess any areas of your hearts these words might be revealing.

BIBLE TIME: When we pray God's Word back to Him, we can be certain that we're praying for God's will. Read James 3:13-18 slowly a few times. Then close your eyes and ask God to bring a main truth to the surface in each of your hearts. Now pray this Scripture back to God and allow Him to minister to each of you.

MEDITATION TIME: After praying the Scriptures, write down in a notebook any thoughts that God has impressed upon your minds about being pure in heart.

INTERCESSION TIME—PRAYING FOR OTHERS: Ask God to bring to your minds the names of people who are struggling either with accepting the truth that only Christ can really heal their hearts, or people who have accepted this truth, but don't seem to be applying it in their lives. Ask God to work in the hearts of both kinds of people. Pray for them by name, asking God to reveal Himself to each one so that they can accept His gift that will result in the purifying of their hearts, or if they've already done so, that they can live so that others see on the outside what has taken place on the inside.

PETITION TIME—PRAYING FOR YOURSELVES: Encourage each family member to spend some time alone today, considering these questions: Where do you stand with God? Do you feel that your heart is pure? Why or why not? Remember, God knows you better than you know yourself. He knows how to meet your needs before you even know you have a need. Ask God to work in your life right now to reveal Himself to you too. Pray that He would also help you live so that others—on the outside—will see the changes that have taken place on the inside.

APPLICATION TIME: List in a notebook what steps your family can take toward obeying God in the area of keeping your hearts pure. Read Psalm 51:12, 13. How do you think God can make us willing to obey Him? Do you really have that desire?

FAITH TIME: Faith is our positive response to what God has said. Spend a few moments praying through your eyes of faith.

Tell God the positive things you see happening in your family because of His goodness!

PRAISE AND THANKSGIVING TIME: Praise God by recognizing who He is—our God of salvation! And thank God by recognizing what He has done—when we ask, He has worked in each of us to make us pure and holy in His sight!

Family Time Throughout the Week

MONDAY—Do the Family Devotion Time. Work on the Family Worship section.

TUESDAY—Work together on your memory verse. Make sure everyone in the family understands what the words mean as well as working on committing it to memory. Remember that it's OK to simplify or shorten the verse for younger children.

WEDNESDAY—Read the Beatitudes in Matthew 5:1-12 to your family. Someone has called these the "Be Attitudes." How can the attitudes we have affect who we are and how we act? Talk through how being humble, being in mourning, and being meek can be good qualities or attitudes to have. Pray together that God will give each of you this kind of heart.

THURSDAY—If possible, talk through the plan of salvation. Again, if someone doesn't know Christ as his Savior, he can't experience having his heart made pure. This might be a good day to talk with members of your family individually, perhaps at each one's bedtime. Ask if each person knows that Jesus lives in his heart. Ask how he knows. If you feel satisfied with the answer, have a prayer time emphasizing what Christ has done for each of you. If you're not satisfied with someone's answer, talk through how he can accept Jesus Christ, and pray together if he desires to accept Christ.

FRIDAY—Repeat the family activity. Talk together as a family to see if anyone has any questions about how God works in our hearts to cleanse and purify us.

WEEK 36: SELF-CONTROL

Family Devotion Time

ACTIVITY: PUPPET SHOW! This week, make finger puppets. Plan to feel a little silly, but your younger kids especially will love this activity.

Draw faces on everyone's forefingers with washable markers. Family members can choose to draw whatever expression they want to on

> **Self-Control** means taking responsibility for what you think and do.

their finger-faces. If they're having a sad day, they might choose to draw a sad face. Or they might want to draw a happy face if they would really rather be happy.

Make sure everyone participates in this activity, or they can't participate in the discussion time either. That's right! You're going to do the discussion time with finger puppets! As the "leader," you will ask the discussion questions using your "puppet," and family members will respond with their "puppets." Prayer time can be done without fingers if you like (though God might enjoy that show too!).

DISCUSSION: Talk through these questions together to help your family understand what self-control is:

• Just like we're able to wiggle our fingers to make our finger puppets work, do you think we're able to control what we do?

• Do you think we are also able to control what we think about?

• Are there some things—either that we do or that we think—that we are not able to control? Examples? Why?

• Do you think we can *learn* to control some of the things we can't?

• Would it be good to work on those things? For example, if

you get mad really easy, would it be good to learn how not to get angry so easily? Why?

Self-control is another weird thing Christians can have happen to them. While all of us have some things in us that we can learn to control, there are some parts of our lives that are just outside of our power and ability to control. Yet God provides His help, through the Holy Spirit. As **this week's memory verse** says, self-control comes from being under the Holy Spirit's control:

"When the Holy Spirit controls our lives he will produce this kind of fruit in us: love, joy, peace, patience, kindness, goodness, faithfulness, gentleness and self-control. . . ."
—Galatians 5:22, 23

FAMILY BIBLE TIME: Proverbs 25:28 says, "A man without self-control is as defenseless as a city with broken-down walls." What does this mean?

Anything uncontrolled can harm your relationships:
• Uncontrolled anger—Proverbs 29:11
• Uncontrolled spending—Proverbs 21:20
• Uncontrolled ambition—Proverbs 23:4

FAMILY PRAYER TIME: As a family, talk together about the things that happen every day that seem out of anyone's control. For example, do you seem to get angry a lot? Are there times when you're not polite to other family members? Do you some-times have trouble holding on to money or material possessions?

Pray together for these problems, that each of you would surrender yourself to the Holy Spirit's control, and as a result, discover more self-control in your lives. If you have uncontrolled anger, pray that the Spirit would help you slow and control it. If you are sometimes rude or offensive, pray that God through the Holy Spirit would help you be more polite and kind. If you are struggling with out-of-control spending, pray that God would help you learn how to be in control of your finances. Thank God for this supernatural power that He provides through His Holy Spirit working right inside each of us.

Family Worship Time (optional)

The word for self-control comes from a Greek root word meaning "to grip" or "take hold of." This word describes people who are willing to get a grip on their lives and take control of areas that will bring them success or failure.

When areas of our lives spiral out of control, we are like the man in this short poem, titled "Your Competitor":

"An enemy I had, whose face I stoutly strove to know,
For hard he dogged my steps unseen, wherever I did go.
My plans he balked, my aims he foiled,
He blocked my onward way.
When for some lofty goal I toiled, he grimly said to me, Nay.
One night I seized him and held him fast, from him the veil
  did draw,
I looked upon his face at last and lo . . . myself I saw."

Why is self-control important? Because it can harm ourselves and our relationships. And we can't just wait for "someday" to come along when we'll practice self-control. As H. P. Liddon writes: "What we do upon some great occasion will probably depend on what we already are; and what we are will be the result of previous years of self-discipline."

Work through the following steps together to gain a better understanding of how we Christians can practice self-control as Scripture describes it.

PREPARATION TIME: Abraham Lincoln said, "I will get ready and then perhaps my chance will come." Too often our disciplines have not been developed and an opportunity is missed.

Begin spending this time with God by thinking through areas in each of your lives that are not developed.

WAITING TIME: During your waiting time, let God love you, search you and show each of you His desires for you in the area of self-control. Pray these simple prayers back to God, completing each sentence as He leads you:

"God, I feel Your love today, especially in the area of . . ."

"God, You have permission to reveal any undisciplined area in my life . . ."

"God, is there anything that I need to know about self-discipline as I enter this day. . . ?"

CONFESSION TIME: Right now determine to take responsibility for the undisciplined areas of your lives. Begin to confess to God those areas where each of you lacks self-control. Also, confess areas where you need to surrender to the Holy Spirit's control, areas you just can't handle on your own. Ponder this too, in preparation for the next step: Are there areas you control wrongly? Are there areas where you practice self-discipline, but that would benefit from being under the Spirit's control?

BIBLE TIME: We can know that we are praying for God's will when we pray His Word back to Him. Read Galatians 5:19-26 slowly a few times. Then close your eyes and ask God to bring a main truth to the surface in each of your hearts about self-control. Now pray this Scripture back to God and allow Him to minister to you. Your prayer might go something like this: "God, we pray for all the times when we should surrender ourselves to You. When we think of the potential within us if we don't surrender: potential for impure thoughts, for lust rather than love, to worship things and beings over You, hatred, fighting, jealousy, anger, selfishness, complaining, criticizing, withdrawing just to those who listen to us—and even worse things! Help us to surrender control of our lives to the Holy Spirit, and we pray that He will produce the kind of fruit within us that can be used by You. Help us to follow the Holy Spirit's leading in every part of our lives. In Jesus' name, Amen."

MEDITATION TIME: After praying the Scriptures, write down in a notebook any thoughts that God has impressed upon your mind about self-control. Read this poem, and discuss this: Does self-control mean focusing on only ourselves? Is it selfish?

I would be true, for there are those who trust me;
I would be true, for there are those who care;
I would be strong, for there are those who suffer;
I would be brave, for there is much to dare.
I would be friend of all—the foe, the friendless;
I would be giving, and forget the gifts;
I would be humble, for I know my weakness;

I would look up, and laugh, and love, and lift.

INTERCESSION TIME—PRAYING FOR OTHERS: Can you think of someone one of you knows who seems to have it all together: someone who is organized, happy most of the time, pretty confident and so on? Now, try to think if this person is selfish or giving to others. If he seems selfish or self-centered, pray that God would help him see that no matter how much he's in control of himself, he won't really have control until he surrenders to the Holy Spirit. Again, this concept really takes God's Spirit to help us understand it—how can we give up ourselves so that we can be in control; how do we surrender freedom so that we can truly be free? But pray for the Spirit to put this understanding in this person's heart. On the other hand, if this person seems selfless and gives freely to others, yet seems in control of things, it's a good sign that he is living under the Spirit's control already. Pray that this person will be strengthened, and that he will always keep on surrendering his life to the Spirit's control, and that the "fruits" that result will be used for the glory of God alone.

PETITION TIME—PRAYING FOR YOURSELVES: Encourage each person to do some self-examination. Think about yourself. Do you match either of the descriptions of others in the above step? If so, pray the same ways for yourself. If not—if you feel that you don't have much control in your own life—take time now to surrender to the Holy Spirit's power. Pray that God will bring the fruit of the Spirit (Galatians 5:22, 23) to bear in your life, too.

APPLICATION TIME: List in a notebook what steps your family can take toward obeying God in the area of self-control. Think about how being obedient is itself a step toward self-control.

FAITH TIME: Faith is our positive response to what God has said. Spend a few moments praying through your eyes of faith. Tell God the positive things you see happening in your family because of His goodness!

PRAISE AND THANKSGIVING TIME: Reread Galatians 5:25. Now, praise God by recognizing who He is—a living and indwelling God. And thank Him by recognizing what He has done—provided His power to lead in every part of our lives.

Family Time Throughout the Week

MONDAY—Complete the Family Devotion Time. Get to work on the Family Worship section.

TUESDAY TO FRIDAY—The great theologian John Wesley developed these "Four Questions" for weekly class meetings. For the next four days, encourage your family to respond to them. You can rephrase them into your own words, but these can be a tool for any accountability group any of you might meet with. And in this setting, your family is an accountability group—one designed by God!

1. What known sins have you committed since we last met? If there are such, what shall we do about it?

2. What temptations have you faced?

3. How were you delivered from these temptations?

4. What have you thought, said or done, of which you are uncertain whether it was sin or not?

Another tool you can use to spark discussion and hold each other accountable is this self-discipline strategy:

• List your three weakest areas.
• Which one hurts you the most?
• Work on that area daily.
• Have someone hold you accountable.
• Chart your progress.

Again, if you're willing to be vulnerable and open with each other, your family is the best accountability group you can find.

WEEK 37: SERVANTHOOD

Family Devotion Time

ACTIVITY: THE RESTAURANT GAME. This week, the activity involves role-playing. Younger kids especially like to do this; older ones might need some coaxing.

Role-play the different people in a restaurant. Assign family members to be customers, waiters, cooks and so on. More than one person can be customers, and you can

> ***Servanthood*** *is seeing and taking care of what others need.*

take turns acting out the different roles.

If your family has flown a few times, you can also role-play an airplane flight. Some family members are passengers and others are the crew of flight attendants and pilot, copilot and navigator.

With either game, the purpose is to take care of the customers' needs. The people playing the waiters or the flight attendants should make an effort to try to anticipate what the customers are going to need even before they ask for something.

DISCUSSION: We don't have a lot of models of servanthood left in our society. Serving others seems to have been replaced by watching out for ourselves. However, good waiters and flight attendants are two exceptions. Discuss these questions about your activity and what it means to be a servant.

• Which do you think is easier, taking care of our own needs, or taking care of what other people need?

• Why do you think we should care about the needs of other people? Think especially about why we should care about people we don't even know.

• What are some ways we can serve people, besides waiting

on them like a waiter or flight attendant does?

• What are some ways we can make sure we know about what other people need? How can we build relationships with others so they are comfortable telling us what they need?

When we serve others, we are also serving God. We need to ask God to help us see what other people need. And when we do help others, we shouldn't brag about it. If we are really servants, God will receive the glory. As this week's memory verse says:

"Work hard and cheerfully at all you do, just as though you were working for the Lord. . . ." —Colossians 3:23

FAMILY BIBLE TIME: Read John 13:1-17. Explain that in Bible times, when people came to visit, a servant usually washed their dirty feet. What do you think Jesus was trying to teach His disciples by washing their feet?

FAMILY PRAYER TIME: As a family, pray together for ways that you can serve each other within your family, and for ways that you can serve people outside of your family. In simple sentence prayers, ask God to guide you to recognize the needs of each other. Pray that those whom you serve will be blessed by your work. Pray that your own work will be blessed because it is God's work. And finally, pray that God will receive the glory from the ways you serve Him through others.

Family Worship Time (optional)

Reread John 13:1-17. This passage describes how Jesus was able to serve others—even teach them through His service—near the end of His earthly life and ministry.

After you read this passage, together look for the verses here that illustrate these biblical principles of servanthood:

1. Security in God is the basis for servanthood.
2. We love people when we serve them.
3. We lead by serving and serve by leading.

Now, take some time to go through these steps so that you will be more open to God's leading regarding your service. Keep in mind these three principles as you work through the steps.

PREPARATION TIME: Read Luke 17:7-10. Now think about the familiar areas of your lives that are often a part of this time: your personal lives, family life, church life, and business or school life. In each of these areas, who are the people God is calling you to serve?

WAITING TIME: During your waiting time, let God love you, search you and show each of you His desires in the area of servanthood. Ask Him to give you appropriate, personal answers for each of these simple prayers:

"God, I feel Your love today, especially in the area of . . ."

"God, are there any areas or people I am serving with the wrong motive. . . ?" (For example, we may have the wrong motive if we are offended by no gratitude or acknowledgment.)

"God, is there anything I need to know as we enter into this day, any one or any way You want me to be prepared to serve. . . ?"

CONFESSION TIME: Read Colossians 3:23, 24. Together or individually confess to God any areas where you are not serving wholeheartedly as though you were directly doing your work and service for Him.

BIBLE TIME: We can know we are praying for God's will when we pray His Word back to Him. Read Mark 10:43-45 slowly a few times. Then close your eyes and ask God to bring a main truth to the surface in your hearts about being a servant. Now pray this Scripture back to God and allow Him to minister to each of you. Your prayer might go something like this: "God, we want to be great in Your eyes. Thank You for this amazing truth in Your Word, that if we want to be great, we have to be servants. We must even be like slaves. Help us to be like Christ, to think of our lives not as something for others to serve, but as something that is here to serve others. Show us exactly where and when and how to serve others best. Again, may You receive the glory. In Jesus' name, Amen."

MEDITATION TIME: After praying the Scriptures, write down in a notebook any thoughts that God has impressed upon your minds about servanthood.

INTERCESSION TIME—PRAYING FOR OTHERS: Can any member of your family think of someone you know who is "too big for his britches"? In other words, who has made himself self-important? Does this person seem to think that others are below him, there only to serve him? If you've had bad feelings for this person, ask God to forgive you for those. Now, pray that God would place within this person a change of heart, a desire to serve rather than be served. A desire to be "great" in the eyes of God. Pray for your own attitude as well. Pray that you can serve this person with good and godly motives so that he can see how biblical servanthood works.

PETITION TIME—PRAYING FOR YOURSELVES: Do you find yourselves unwilling to serve? What is it that keeps us from wanting to serve others—perhaps a fear of hurt or ridicule? Ask God to help each of you overcome any fears you might have about serving other people. Ask Him to remind you of the blessings that will be yours for your service. Pray for specific people to come to your mind whom God wants you to serve.

APPLICATION TIME: List in a notebook what steps your family can take toward obeying God in the area of servanthood. Remember the biblical principles from John 13:1-17.

FAITH TIME: Faith is our positive response to what God has said. Spend a few moments praying through your eyes of faith. Tell God the positive things you see happening because of His goodness!

PRAISE AND THANKSGIVING TIME: Reread Mark 10:45. Praise God by recognizing who He is—the Servant-Messiah. And thank Him by recognizing what He has done—gave His life so that we might have life.

Family Time Throughout the Week

MONDAY—Do the Family Devotion Time. Get started on the Family Worship Time.

TUESDAY—Work together on memorizing Colossians 3:23.

Remember to make sure that everyone in the family understands what this verse means. Talk about practical ways you can make the words come alive in your life, rather than just letting them be words you've memorized.

WEDNESDAY—Talk together as a family about a family who needs you to serve them. You might even think of a creative, unexpected way to serve them—washing their car, taking them meals, doing their yardwork, painting their house. Then set up a time in the next two weeks to go do your service together as a family.

THURSDAY—Read 1 Peter 5. Talk about what qualities of leadership are mentioned here. How are the qualities of a leader and a servant the same? How are they different? Do leaders make good servants? Do servants make good leaders?

FRIDAY—Go out to eat if you can, if not tonight, sometime this weekend. Watch the waiter who serves you. How does he do at seeing your needs before you even know you have them—does he fill your water glass, bring extra napkins, check back on you—before you ask him to? After your meal, let him know how much you appreciated his service. You might even let him know that your family is studying servanthood, and thank him for his example.

WEEK 38: SHARING YOUR FAITH

Family Devotion Time

ACTIVITY: A SPECIAL LETTER. Supply the whole family with writing paper and pens. If you have younger children, you might ask if they want drawing paper and crayons or markers.

Now, each person should think of someone he loves who he thinks doesn't know about God, especially about how Jesus is able to save us from our sins if we invite Him

> ***Sharing Your Faith*** *means believing in God so much that you have to tell your friends about Him.*

into our lives. Then write a letter to that person, telling him how great God's love is.

You don't need to know a lot of Bible verses or even know step by step what someone must do to accept Christ as Savior. Instead, just tell or draw what Jesus means to you. Tell how He works in your life. Tell about His love for you.

If the person receiving the letter cares about you, he will be happy to read of your relationship with God. And who knows, he might just want the same kind of relationship too.

DISCUSSION:

• Why do you think it's important to tell other people about Christ?

• Is telling others (or writing to them) the only way people can see what Christ means to us?

• Have you ever heard of the word *witness?* What do you think it means?

• Here's a deep one: Why do you think God wants us to tell others about Christ and let them see His work in us? God is all-powerful, so why didn't He think of a better way for people to learn about Christ?

Sharing our faith means being witnesses of our faith. In court, witnesses tell exactly what they've seen. As Christians, we are witnesses by telling others exactly what we've seen God do in our lives. Sometimes, we are so excited and enthusiastic about God's work within us that we can't contain it; before we even tell others about it, they see it. God wants us to be His witnesses, to testify about what He's done for us, as it says in *this week's memory verse:*

"When the Holy Spirit has come upon you, you will receive power to testify about me with great effect. . . ." —Acts 1:8

FAMILY BIBLE TIME: Read together Acts 8:26-40. Discuss how each of you can be more like Philip this week.

FAMILY PRAYER TIME: During this time of prayer, remember to pray for the letters you wrote during the activity time. Pray that the heart of the receiver will be prepared ahead of time to listen to the message of the letters. Ask God to fill in the blanks so that the receiver has understanding of the message.

Also, pray for other opportunities for sharing your faith. Pray for people in your family, for friends, for classmates, for neighbors who may need to see Christ's love demonstrated through an individual or your whole family. Ask God to make you strong witnesses for Him, filled with the power and sensitivity that the Holy Spirit gives.

Family Worship Time (optional)

The story is told of an apprentice demon, soon to be sent to earth on his first mission, who is preparing for a last-minute strategy session with his master.

The young demon is a fast learner. He has realized that the unbelieving world is already in his master's power and that it would be a poor use of his time and resources to focus his schemes on the lost. Rather, his strategy is to focus on neutralizing the Christians in their evangelistic work.

"They could do the most harm," he reasons, "so I must keep

them from the destructive work, modeled so well by Paul 2,000 years ago, of 'opening the eyes of the unbelieving that they might turn to God from Satan'" (Acts 26:18). He shudders at the thought of Paul's success.

The demon then shares his strategy with his master. "I'll try to convince Christians that there is no such thing as sin," he says. "Then they will stop sharing the Good News. The answer will soon become irrelevant if I eliminate the question."

"This is only a part of my plan," says Satan, "but it cannot be the focus, for most of our enemies realize the reality of sin. Even those in our power sometimes, in rare moments of clear thinking, realize sin's destructiveness. You'll confuse some of the enemy, but not all of them on this."

"Well then, I'll convince the church that there is no hell, that even if there is sin, there are no eternal consequences."

"Good thinking," replies Satan. "You will confuse some with this, but still, the prospect of judgment is so ingrained in men, even those in our power, that this will not neutralize the enemy. Most will see through the deception."

The young demon thinks for a moment, and then a look of triumph floods his face. "I've got it! I'll convince them that there is no hurry. They can have their doctrines of sin, heaven and hell. I'll just help them rationalize away their lack of conviction on these matters by whispering in their ears, 'There is no hurry; don't inconvenience yourself. Save it for later.' They are all so prone to be concerned with their own cares and problems anyway, that they will buy right into it."

"You have done well," says Satan. "You will see great success in neutralizing the enemy with this strategy." (C. S. Lewis)

Acts 1:8 gives us God's command and perspective on sharing our faith:

1. We are all commanded to be His witnesses.

2. Witnessing is an indication that the Holy Spirit is in control of our lives.

3. Witnessing begins in our local area, and then reaches beyond.

Spend some time going through these steps together in order to make the sharing of your faith completely in line with God's plan for how the world discovers Him.

PREPARATION TIME: Read 1 Peter 3:15. Now think about who the people are in each of the following areas of your lives that God might be calling you to be ready to share your faith with? Think of people in your personal lives, your family, your church life, people at your business or school.

WAITING TIME: During your waiting time, let God love you, search you and show each of you His desires in the area of sharing your faith. Then ask Him to help you complete these simple sentence prayers:

"God, I feel Your love today, especially in the area of . . ."

"God, search me and show me where I've lost my sense of urgency and heart for the lost . . ."

"God, is there anything I need to know about sharing my faith—perhaps someone You want me to witness to—as I enter this day. . . ?"

CONFESSION TIME: Read 2 Corinthians 5:18. Do you think it's a privilege for you to share your faith? Do you have God's heart and passion for the lost? Confess to Him how you really feel. Are you apathetic? Are you afraid? Ask Him to help each of you overcome the obstacles in your life.

BIBLE TIME: We can know that we are praying for God's will when we pray His Word back to Him. Read Romans 1:16, 17 slowly a few times. Then close your eyes and ask God to bring a main truth to the surface in each of your hearts about sharing what you believe with others. Now pray this Scripture back to God and allow Him to minister to you. Your prayer might go something like this: "God, when we think that someone cared enough for us—and for You—to share the Gospel with us, we are really humbled. We're not ashamed of the Gospel, but for some reason, we sense a lot of other roadblocks in our lives that keep us from sharing our faith. We ask You today to remove those roadblocks, prepare our hearts to share the Good News of the Gospel, and then help us simply to let others know that faith in You can save them, give them eternal life, allow them to spend eternity with You in heaven. Thank You for this amazing gift! In Jesus' name, Amen."

MEDITATION TIME: After praying the Scriptures, write down in a notebook any thoughts that God has impressed upon your minds about sharing your faith. Rather than feeling "guilted" into sharing your faith, think of all the love—God's and someone else's—that brought you to Christ. How can you not do the same for others who you love?

INTERCESSION TIME—PRAYING FOR OTHERS: Together list non-Christians and intercede on their behalf. Look up 2 Corinthians 4:3, 4 and pray it for the people you think of. Pray that whatever is hindering them from seeing their need for Christ would be removed.

PETITION TIME—PRAYING FOR YOURSELF: During this time, think of the circumstances of when you accepted Christ. Think back through the way God prepared your heart and through the chain of events that took place leading up to that moment. Thank God for the way He works.

APPLICATION TIME: List in a notebook what steps your family can take toward obeying God in the area of sharing your faith. Reread Acts 1:8. Though this verse isn't written as a command, it is. It's almost just a simple expectation that God has of us. Again, if we have the power of the Holy Spirit, how can we *not* tell others about it and let them see it in our lives?

FAITH TIME: Faith is our positive response to what God has said. Spend a few moments praying through your eyes of faith. Tell God the positive things you see happening in your family because of His goodness!

PRAISE AND THANKSGIVING TIME: Read 2 Corinthians 5:18 again. Now praise God by recognizing who He is—giver of life through the Savior. And thank Him by recognizing what He has done—given us the privilege of being a part of His plan for others to know Him.

Family Time Throughout the Week

MONDAY—Do the Family Devotion Time. Get started on the Family Worship section.

TUESDAY—Memorize Acts 1:8. With other family members, get out a map of the Holy Land during New Testament times. Find the places mentioned in the verse. Notice how the geographic names form ever-widening circles out from Jerusalem. Now get out a map of your city or state. Can you substitute appropriate names into Acts 1:8 to personalize it for your family? List your neighborhood, your city, your state, your country—and to the ends of the earth.

WEDNESDAY—Read aloud the story, under the Family Worship Time, about the devil's assistant's plan for stopping the spread of the Gospel. Discuss which obstacles some of you may have let land in your way. Ask if any of you have the idea that you'll always have later to tell others about Christ. Discuss some things that might happen to prevent you from being able to share your faith later. How can you regain a sense of urgency to share your faith now?

THURSDAY—Mail the letters and drawings you created during the family activity time. As you send them off, pray again for the people who will receive your letters. Let God know that you are open to sharing more with them if that is part of God's plan.

FRIDAY—Review your memory verse. As always, make sure that everyone understands the meaning of the verse, in addition to memorizing it.

WEEK 39:
THE SOVEREIGNTY OF GOD

Family Devotion Time

ACTIVITY: THE PRAYER BANK. Start a prayer bowl or a prayer box. This will help you all see how God answers prayer.

If you want to use a prayer box, let the younger members of your family decorate it. Place a supply of index cards or scrap paper near the box. Start by spending some time now thinking of prayer requests.

> **The Sovereignty of God:** *believing that God rules your life— and the world.*

They should be personal, related to your family. Write down the requests on the cards, and agree as a family that you will all pray for the requests. Decide on a certain number each day—one or two or whatever. When someone has prayed for the request on the card, place the card in a pile next to the bowl or box. When all the cards have been prayed through, place them back in the box. Family members can add requests for as long as you decide to keep the box or bowl going. Also, you can leave space on the cards to write down the answers, or use the backs of the cards.

DISCUSSION: The idea of this activity is to encourage prayer for everything we face. The goal is to surrender every part of our lives to God, and to expect Him to answer because He is sovereign. Discuss these questions to gain a better understanding of God's sovereignty.

• Why do you think it's important that we pray for what's going on in our lives?

• Have you ever wondered if something you wanted to ask God for was too small or insignificant?

YOUR FAMILY TIME WITH GOD

• Have you ever asked for anything even though you knew it was most likely against God's will? What kind of answer did you receive for that prayer?

• Are you certain that God will answer your prayers? Why?

• *Sovereign* is a big, unfamiliar word. What do you think it means?

God is sovereign because He really rules over the world. God is sovereign in each of our lives as well. He knows what we think, how we will act. He knows us very personally. His sovereignty extends to the far reaches of the universe, and to the innermost parts of our bodies. As **this week's memory verse** says:

"Not one sparrow . . . can fall to the ground without your Father knowing it. And the very hairs of your head are all numbered. So don't worry!" —Matthew 10:29-31

FAMILY BIBLE TIME: Remember the story of Job from a few weeks ago? Here is part of God's answer to Job about exactly Who is in charge. Read Job 38:12-15, 31-35. If Job can't do these things, who can?

FAMILY PRAYER TIME: As a family, begin to pray through the requests you've placed in your prayer box or bowl. Also, ask God to remind you to pray throughout the time your family has agreed upon for these requests. Finally, pray that God will reveal His sovereignty to each of you through this exercise of praying.

Family Worship Time (optional)

There's a story about a man who'd been stranded on an uncharted, desert island. He'd been sailing alone on the Pacific when a storm hit him that threw him off course. It almost killed him, but he'd made it to this island. After a whole day there— and no rescue ship in sight—he decided to build a shelter for himself and his only remaining possessions.

After a couple of days, he became bitter toward God. Why had God allowed this to happen? Was he going to starve to death? All he owned was stored in that small hut he'd built for himself. Maybe this was going to be a lesson in trusting God.

Then, the final tragedy struck. After hunting for food one

day, the man returned to his hut only to find it had caught on fire! It was going up in smoke. The man fell to his knees and cried, "God, how can I learn to trust You when things like this happen? I've lost all that I own!" As the man sulked and questioned God, an hour passed. Then, to his surprise, a rescue ship arrived. When the man asked how his rescuers had found him, they answered, "We saw your smoke signal."

When we study and understand the sovereignty of God, the common texts we look to are Romans 9:14-26 and 11:16-22. Both chapters are vivid discourses on God's ultimate rule and reign over the earth. Interestingly, chapter 9 illustrates God's role, and chapter 11, our role. Romans 9 teaches that God chooses as He wishes, controls what He wishes, and that His nature is consistent. He is just, good and loving. Romans 11 teaches how we should respond. We are to keep our heart cooperative, contrite and committed to God's purposes.

To gain a deeper understanding of God's sovereignty, spend some time going through these steps with your family. You may not completely understand how we relate to the sovereignty of God, but you'll make a beginning to apply it to your own lives.

PREPARATION TIME: Read Habakkuk 1:5. Then observe the various areas of your own lives. How is God moving sovereignly, performing His work in your personal lives, your family life, your life of service, your life at work or school?

WAITING TIME: During your waiting time, let God love you, search you and show each of you what He wants to instill in you about His sovereignty. Ask Him to give you phrases that complete these simple prayers:

"God, I feel Your love today, especially in the area of . . ."

"God, You have permission to reveal any control issue in my life, where I cling to control the situation . . .

"God, is there any area in which I need to trust You more, as I enter this day. . . ?"

CONFESSION TIME: Read Job 42:1-6. Confess to God and each other areas where you have not trusted God's sovereign hand, where you've spoken too quickly. Then, repent of your impatient, distrusting attitude.

BIBLE TIME: We can know that we are praying for God's will when we pray His Word back to Him. Read the above verses from Job again slowly a few times. Then close your eyes and ask God to bring a main truth to the surface in each of your hearts about His sovereignty. Now pray Job's words back to God and allow Him to minister to your family.

MEDITATION TIME: After praying the Scriptures, write down in a notebook any thoughts that God has impressed upon your minds about His sovereign will. Do you really believe in God's power and ability to do anything without anything stopping Him?

INTERCESSION TIME—PRAYING FOR OTHERS: Ask God to bring to your minds people who are unwilling to keep their hearts cooperative, contrite and committed to God's purposes (Romans 11). Then, pray that God would accomplish His purposes in their lives, and that they would be open to cooperate with Him.

PETITION TIME—PRAYING FOR YOURSELVES: How do you stack up in the attitude department? Individually check your own hearts. Do you have a spirit of cooperation? Are you open to God's purposes? Are you committed to them? Pray now that God will demonstrate through answered prayer in your lives that you can trust His purposes for your lives.

APPLICATION TIME: List in a notebook what steps your family can take toward obeying God in the area of trust. Note how being obedient is itself a step to help you trust God in the area of His sovereignty.

FAITH TIME: Faith is our positive response to what God has said. Spend a few moments praying through your eyes of faith. Tell God the positive things you see happening in your family because of His goodness!

PRAISE AND THANKSGIVING TIME: Read Romans 9:9-13. Praise God by recognizing who He is—an unchanging God. And thank Him by recognizing what He has done—kept His promises to us and every generation.

Family Time Throughout the Week

MONDAY—Do the Family Devotion Time, and get started on the Family Worship section.

TUESDAY—Read Job 40:1-9. Take some time and express to your family the concerns and questions you have about God. Then, confess God's wisdom, power and rule over each of them.

WEDNESDAY—Look at maps today. Pull out a map of your city and then go for a drive around town. Can God really rule over all of this? Talk about how God can see everything and be everywhere at once—kind of like how we get a bigger picture of things when we look at a map than we do when we drive down a single street. And it's neat to think about how God knows each of us better than we know ourselves, not just a picture or map of who we are.

THURSDAY—Today, simply review your memory verse together as a family. Sometimes, in the midst of what can become a very deep theological thought process, it helps to remember the simplicity of God's sovereignty as revealed in this verse. Thank God together for the way He knows and cares for us as part of His sovereign plan.

FRIDAY—Romans 11 ends with a beautiful benediction on God's sovereignty. Romans 12 then begins with our appropriate response to His sovereignty. Talk together with other family members about how our minds can be renewed to think like God thinks. How can we place our trust in Him in areas where it's not easy to trust at all? Thank God together for His sovereign reign over your world.

WEEK 40: SPIRITUAL DRYNESS

Family Devotion Time

ACTIVITY: YOU'RE NOT ALL WET! You've got a choice to make for your activity. It depends on how self-conscious your family is. Or you can try both.

Have family members take turns sitting in the tub—fully clothed. That's it, just sit there. No water, no soap, no washcloth, no bath toys!

> **Spiritual Dryness** *is when you don't feel close to God.*

Or if you have someone who feels that it's just too weird to sit in the tub with his clothes on, take turns holding your hands under the faucet in the sink. But again, that's it, just hold your hands there. No water, no soap, no washcloth—no need to dry either!

DISCUSSION: After you've spent some time not getting wet, gather together to discuss these questions:

• Why do we need water to take a bath or wash our hands?

• What do you think would happen if we didn't have water?

• Besides not being able to be clean, what would lack of water do to our bodies?

• Why do you think Jesus is sometimes called "living water" in the Bible?

• What happens to us if we don't stay close to God?

There are times when we might feel far away from God. We might be discouraged, depressed, lonely, hopeless. But God doesn't want us to stray far or to stay far from Him. Just as we would be thirsty (and dirty!) if we had to live without water, we are thirsty when we feel far from God. We're thirsty for God. That's why Jesus invited us to come to Him and "drink" of Him—in other words, not feel "thirsty" because we're closer to

Him. He can satisfy our thirst. In *this week's memory verse,*
Jesus says:

". . . If anyone is thirsty, let him come to me and drink."
—John 7:37

FAMILY BIBLE TIME: In a deep jungle, a traveler was making
a long trek. Local people had been hired to carry the loads of
supplies. The first day the party marched rapidly and made a lot
of progress, giving the traveler high hopes for a speedy journey.
But the second morning, the tribesmen refused to move. They
just sat and rested. When the traveler asked the reason for this
strange behavior, he was told that the people had gone too fast
the first day, and now they were waiting for their souls to catch
up with their bodies.

Spiritual dryness is the subject of Psalm 42. (Read it aloud.)
In this psalm we hear the heartfelt cry of the psalmist for God to
restore the life and passion he once knew. The writer was dry
spiritually. He had grown indifferent toward the sacred events
that once thrilled him; he was now needing time for his "soul to
catch up with his body," and to gain perspective again.

FAMILY PRAYER TIME: Before praying together, talk about
any emotions or feelings anyone in your family is having right
now. Is anyone feeling far from God? Why? Then spend some
time praying for each other. Claim Jesus' promise in John 8:37.
Ask Him to take away the thirst of family members who want for
His love. Ask that they will be drawn closer to God. Commit to
praying together several times this week, and to support anyone
who is feeling far from God with each others' love.

Family Worship Time (optional)

Read Psalm 42 again. Notice that the psalmist says his soul
pants for God like a running deer pants for water. The writer
can't seem to find God, even when he looks in places he's sensed
God's presence before. The psalmist says that he once led a
throng of people in procession to the Lord, yet now he can't find
God for himself! These are the thoughts of a dry man.

We've all had this feeling at some point. The psalmist finally closes his writing by posing some key questions to himself: Why is he in despair? Why is he disturbed?

Then, he ultimately tells himself the truth: he must hope in God, for the help of God.

We can make three general observations about spiritual dryness:

1. Every Christian experiences it at some time.

2. If you are heavily involved in ministry, it's an occupational hazard.

3. There are causes and cures for it.

Is it even possible that God might want us to have this feeling of dryness sometimes? Why would God want that? It's possible that when we feel dry, and we sense God's absence that:

1. God is demanding new growth and maturity from us.

2. He wants to introduce us to who He really is; more deeply reveal Himself to us.

3. We're on the edge of wanting Him for who He is, not what He gives.

Work through these familiar steps together to gain a deeper understanding of what causes spiritual dryness, and how it can be cured.

PREPARATION TIME: Read Psalm 42:2. Then think about the following areas of each of your lives, and ask yourselves, "Is there any area where I feel spiritually dry?" Examine your personal lives, your family life, your church and ministry life, and your school or business life.

WAITING TIME: During your waiting time, let God love you, search you and show each of you His desires in the area of your closeness to Him. Ask Him to provide the appropriate words to express answers to these simple prayers:

"God, I feel Your love today, especially in the area of . . ."

"God, You have permission to reveal any dry spot in my life . . ."

"God, show me if there are any causes for my dryness that I have initiated . . ."

CONFESSION TIME: Eight causes for spiritual dryness in our lives:

1. Physical exhaustion
2. A "cool" spiritual environment
3. Extensive spiritual output
4. Opposition from the Enemy
5. Cycles of life
6. TV and media
7. Extended temptation
8. Disobedience to God

Confess any of these areas that may be a source of "dryness" in your lives, praying silently.

BIBLE TIME: We can know that we are praying for God's will when we pray His Word back to Him. Read Psalm 42:1-5 slowly a few times. Then close your eyes and ask God to bring a main truth to the surface in each of your hearts about dryness spiritually. Now pray this Scripture back to God and allow Him to minister to you.

Your prayer might go something like this: "God, we do long for You. We think of running to the point of exhaustion, and yet at the end of the race there is nothing to quench our thirst. Sometimes, that's how we feel about our thirst for You! But we can't find You. Our thirst is so great, our exhaustion so terrible, that we do the only thing we can: We cry out for Your help. We ask You to find us. Our enemies—even the Enemy—tease us: 'Where is your God when you need Him?' But then we think of the other times when we've felt close to You, and we know that You are there, somewhere. And we keep asking for You and realize we have no reason to be down and out. We can hope in You! You will find us! You are not just there, somewhere. You are there, everywhere! All the time! And we can sense Your presence, Your quenching of our thirst, Your very indwelling of us. And we can praise You again—for Your help and for Your being. In Jesus' name, with thanksgiving *and* praise, Amen."

MEDITATION TIME: After praying the Scriptures, write down in a notebook any thoughts that God has impressed upon your minds about spiritual dryness. Think especially about what good can come out of feeling far from God.

INTERCESSION TIME—PRAYING FOR OTHERS: James 5:16

teaches that we experience healing as we pray for others. Ask God to bring to your minds people—including members of your family—who are feeling dry, thirsty, far from God. Pray for God to renew their spiritual passion.

PETITION TIME—PRAYING FOR YOURSELVES: God promises His help when we feel dry spiritually. Just as an oasis in the desert would provide relief from heat and dryness, God provides us with ways we can step out of the desert:

1. Praise and thanksgiving—sometimes it just takes a time of focusing on who God is and what He does for us to draw us closer to Him.

2. Extended time alone with God—it may take the removal of all the other distractions and influences in our lives to make us realize we need to lean on God alone for support.

3. Soul winning—this and other service to other people can draw us closer to God, and simply take our minds off our own feelings.

4. Cell group accountability—seek a group of people who will commit to pray for you and who will check on your growth regularly

5. Step of faith—there are times when we just have to say, "God, I believe in You, and in Your presence in my life," and accept it by faith, even patiently waiting for a sign of God's presence.

6. Rest and relaxation—stress is often like a powerful vacuum cleaner, sucking away our time with God, and our opportunities to feel close to Him.

7. Confession—is there any sin in your life that is an obstacle to sensing God's presence? Confess it and ask for forgiveness, and for strength to avoid further temptation.

Pray for yourselves, and ask God if you are to participate in any of these provisions.

APPLICATION TIME: List in a notebook what steps your family can take toward obeying God in the area of feeling closer to Him. How can lack of obedience keep you feeling distant from God? How can obeying God help you to feel His presence more keenly?

FAITH TIME: Faith is our positive response to what God has said. Spend a few moments praying through your eyes of faith. Tell God the positive things you see happening in your family because of His goodness!

PRAISE AND THANKSGIVING TIME: Read Revelation 22:17. Now praise God by recognizing who He is—the Living Water. And thank Him by recognizing what He has done—freely given Himself to those who will simply drink of Him.

Family Time Throughout the Week

MONDAY—Do the Family Devotion Time. Get started on the Family Worship section.

TUESDAY—Read Psalm 42 after a mealtime. Talk together as a family about what causes dry spells, spiritually speaking, in our lives. Are there things in our personalities that cause us to be downcast? What makes us feel discouraged and sad? If we know that God is present, why do we have periods of gloom and depression? Why do we sometimes even feel forsaken by God? Talk about why Christians might experience these emotions, and what can we do about them.

WEDNESDAY—Reread aloud this list of God's purposes for spiritual dryness under the Digging Deeper section. While God may not be the cause of our dry seasons, He certainly can use them to draw us to Himself. The key is, how will we respond? As a family, talk about what God may be up to when we feel the emotions described in Psalm 42. Talk about what He might be trying to teach us.

THURSDAY—Talk together about these signs that you might be spiritually "dried out":

• Do you get angry easily?
• Are you impatient with the rest of your family?
• Are you anxious to study God's Word or do you feel like staying away from it?
• Is it more important to be popular than to do what is right?
• Do other people see Jesus when they look at you?
• Are you jealous of what other people have?

Today, be honest with each other. Do any of the above statements describe you? Share them with the other members of your family. Even young children can feel far from God; they just might not know how to express it. Help them put their feeling into words they do understand and can express.

Finally, pray together as a family that God would cleanse you, speak truth into your life, and restore the joy of your salvation. God can't meet our needs if we don't admit that we have any.

FRIDAY—Review your memory verse together. This topic can be really difficult for children to grasp. But they will face spiritual dryness someday too, if they haven't already. Go through the verse, taking it apart phrase by phrase. You might also sing one of the praise songs your children already know, such as "As the Deer Panteth for the Water" or sing a hymn together, such as "Springs of Living Water."

WEEK 41: STEWARDSHIP

Family Devotion Time

ACTIVITY: CLIP AND SAVE. For several weeks, save the coupon sections from your Sunday newspaper, and from any other sources you have. This week's activity will be a family coupon-clipping party.

Not much to explain here, except to clip coupons to use for grocery purchases. The one

> ***Stewardship*** *is using the things I have—and myself—wisely for God.*

catch is that you will agree as a family to use as many coupons as possible for your purchases, and that you'll keep track of the money you save for a month. Then you will give that amount as a family to your church as a special offering, or to a needy family or organization that you agree upon.

DISCUSSION: You can have your discussion at the same time that you're clipping coupons. Sometimes, doing something with your hands will help open up a family member who is usually more quiet. He won't feel that all eyes are upon him.

• What do you think of when you think of the word steward?

• Why do you think God cares if we are good stewards, responsible users of what we have? After all, doesn't He really possess and have power over everything? Why does He even need us?

• Do you think that being a good steward and being a good servant are related? How and why?

• Do you think other people notice how well we handle our money? Do they notice how well we handle our time? Can you think of any examples?

• If you had as much money as you wanted, and you could spend it however you wanted, what would you do with it?

When we think of stewardship, we often think of giving an offering at church. God wants us to give what we really want to give. Of course, if our hearts are focused on God, we will want to give Him as much as we can. This week's memory verse says:

"Every one must make up his own mind as to how much he should give . . . cheerful givers are the ones God prizes."
—2 Corinthians 9:7

FAMILY BIBLE TIME: Read Luke 21:1-4. What did Jesus mean when He said the woman had given more than all the rest of the rich people? Do you think she was a cheerful giver? Why or why not?

FAMILY PRAYER TIME: The verse before this week's memory verse in 2 Corinthians expands the thought of stewardship to hit us where it counts: "If you give little, you will get little." Pray together as a family that your hearts will be cheerful in their giving to God—both of money and service. Pray that you will have desires that line up with God's. Ask God to bless you because of your faithfulness in giving, and yet to forgive you when you want His blessing more than you want to be a giver. Pray for stewardship in other areas too—in all of the resources God has given you, for the way you take care of things like creation or material blessings. Finally, pray for what you give, that God will use it to multiply His work and His glory, without any of the credit going to you.

Family Worship Time (optional)

Jesus talked much about money. Sixteen of the 38 parables were concerned with how to handle money and possessions. In the Gospels, an amazing one out of 10 verses (288 in all) deal directly with the subject of money. The Bible offers 500 verses on prayer, less than 500 verses on faith, but more than 2000 verses on money and possessions.

Martin Luther astutely observed, "There are three conversions necessary: the conversion of the heart, mind and the purse." Of these three, it may well be that we find the conversion of the purse most difficult.

A good steward is a mature Christian who has experienced that conversion. Stewardship is the proper management of my life in order to enhance God's Kingdom.

Just look at all the benefits God provides to people who practice good stewardship:

- Find their spiritual gifts—1 Corinthians 12
- Increase their faith—Malachi 3:10
- Become spiritually sensitive—Malachi 3:8-10
- Be fruitful in God's Kingdom—Matthew 25:14-30
- Receive blessings from God—Malachi 3:10-12
- Be a blessing to others—Galatians 6:10
- Make a lasting contribution to God—Matthew 6:20

As you seek to be better stewards in all areas of your lives, take some time to work through these steps:

PREPARATION TIME: Read Proverbs 3:9 and 1 Corinthians 16:2. Now ask yourselves these questions: Who is first in my life? If God is, doesn't He deserve the first of everything I have—including my finances?

WAITING TIME: During your waiting time, let God love you, search you and show each of you His desires in the area of stewardship.

Dr. Albert Schweitzer wrote: "Whatever you have received more than others—in health, in talents, in ability, in success, in a pleasant childhood, in harmonious condition of home life—all this you must not take to yourself as a matter of course. In gratitude for your good fortune, you must render some sacrifice of your own life for another life."

Our sacrifice should have three beneficiaries:

1. God
2. The last generation
3. The next generation

Think about these three areas. How are each of you indebted to each beneficiary?

CONFESSION TIME: Individually confess areas in which you have failed to place God first.

BIBLE TIME: We know that when we pray God's Word to

Him, we are praying in His will. Read 2 Corinthians 9:7, 8 slowly a few times. Then close your eyes and ask God to bring a main truth to the surface in each of your hearts about stewardship. Now pray this Scripture back to God and allow Him to minister to you. Your prayer might go something like this: "God, You say we can make up our minds about what to give to You. Remind us as we give—in every area of our lives—that You gave it all to us to begin with. Even with that in mind, help us not to give simply out of a sense of duty or obedience, though that is certainly a part of our giving. Help us to also desire to give cheerfully, happily, joyfully. To think that You would prize us for such a simple shift in our attitudes inspires us! And to think that You promise, on top of it all, that You will provide everything we need and more. We surely don't understand that. But help us to accept it by faith, and to allow You to prove it so in our family life. In Jesus' name, Amen."

MEDITATION TIME: After praying the Scriptures, write down in a notebook any thoughts that God has impressed upon your minds about stewardship. Think about these two things: How can God expect us to part with our resources "cheerfully"? How can God's economy possibly work—how can we give and still have everything we need and more?

INTERCESSION TIME—PRAYING FOR OTHERS: This week, pray for the people who will be served by your stewardship. You may be able to pray for some of them by name, but many may just be a general group of people. Think about the areas where you give, and ask God to bless those who are the recipients of your gifts.

PETITION TIME—PRAYING FOR YOURSELVES: Now thank God for the privilege and opportunity to participate in His work of serving others. Remember that as Creator and God, He could have devised a different way for His work to be carried out in the world. But because He cares so much for us, He wants us to experience the joy that can come through giving. Pray again that you would be cheerful, willing givers.

APPLICATION TIME: List in a notebook what steps your

family can take toward obeying God in the area of stewardship. Note how being obedient is itself a step to help you be a wise steward.

FAITH TIME: Faith is our positive response to what God has said. Spend a few moments praying through your eyes of faith. Tell God the positive things you see happening in your family because of His goodness!

PRAISE AND THANKSGIVING TIME: Read Malachi 3:7-12. Now praise God by recognizing who He is—a God of second chances. And thank Him by recognizing what He has done— promised His blessings to those who are faithful to Him.

Family Time Throughout the Week

MONDAY—Do the Family Devotion Time. Get started on the Family Worship section.

TUESDAY—For the next three days, ask your family to learn with you a new principle. While not everyone may understand exactly what each principle entails, talk through them and help younger members with the word pictures. Today, discuss the *river principle:* "Our life is to be like a river, not a reservoir. God will give to us what He knows will flow through us."

WEDNESDAY—Discuss as a family and agree to start living the *cheerful attitude principle:* "Stewardship begins with loving, not giving" (see 2 Corinthians 9:7).

THURSDAY—Discuss the *who has who principle:* "Until God is in control of my life, I'm out of control. Stewardship deals with the *person,* not just the *purse.*"

FRIDAY—Part of good stewardship is obedience to God's Word. Scripture establishes 10 percent as a tithe to be given to God. Out of obedience, figure out your tithe and place it in the offering this Sunday. Help your family members to figure their tithes as well—from allowances, income from doing jobs around the house, or from part-time jobs that older kids might have. Encourage them to begin a pattern of tithing to God. Reread 2 Corinthians 9:6-8. Be a model by giving your tithe, and encourage your children to follow you in their own obedience.

WEEK 42: STRESS

Family Devotion Time

ACTIVITY: WATER BALLOONS —in the house? Give each person a balloon. The object this week is not to get wet, but to see what happens if you stretch a balloon too far.

Head to the sink. If it's a warm time of year where you live, this activity can be done in your backyard. Whether you do this inside or out, raincoats and umbrellas are optional!

> ***Stress*** *is when everything that happens builds up inside me so much it hurts or makes me sick.*

Have each person take a turn making a water balloon. See how full you can fill your balloon with water before the balloon breaks. Wow! They can get pretty big, can't they? But half the fun is letting them pop.

Grab a mop and some sponges. Agree that everyone will help clean up any messes left over from doing this in the house.

By the way, if you want a little less fun but less messy activity, you can inflate the balloons with air. However, parents should always be careful when younger children have balloons— the water-balloon activity is messier, but it keeps balloons away from mouths and might help prevent a choking hazard.

DISCUSSION: Now, talk through these questions. The goal is to see what happens if pressure builds up inside us.

• Relive your water-balloon time. Was there a way you could tell when the balloon was ready to break?

• Did anyone in your family chicken out before his balloon broke?

• Do you think that there would be any way to keep filling the balloon without it breaking? What if you took the time to let some of the water out before you continued filling it?

• Do you think we're like balloons—can we end up with too much inside us? Too much pressure?

• What do you think happens when that pressure builds inside people?

God knows that our bodies can only stand so much. That's why He promises, as in **this week's memory verse:**

"We are pressed on every side by troubles, but not crushed and broken. . . . God never abandons us." —2 Corinthians 4:8, 9

FAMILY BIBLE TIME: Read Philippians 4:1-13 for God's idea of how to keep stress from becoming distress, then read through the outline below:

1. Know that you are loved—(verse 1).
2. Help others—(verses 2, 3).
3. Have a positive perspective—(verse 4).
4. Talk to God about everything—(verses 6, 7)
5. Think on the right things—(verse 8).
6. Draw strength from mature Christians—(verse 9)
7. Learn to be flexible—(verses 11, 12)
8. Receive strength from Christ—(verse 13)

FAMILY PRAYER TIME: Pray together for the pressures in your life. Make a list before you pray. Then use it as a request list to pray for each other. Encourage your family to pray for each other by name. Ask God to always be with you, to help you avoid pressure that could send you to the breaking point.

Family Worship Time (optional)

In the early 1900s, the top 10 killers of humankind in the U.S. were all infectious diseases. In the 1990s it is estimated that the top 10 killers of people are all stress-related diseases.

According to the National Association for Mental Health, here are eight ways to tell if the pressure inside you is becoming too great:

1. Do minor problems and disappointments get under your skin and rile you more than they should?

2. Are you finding it hard to get along with people? And are

people having trouble getting along with you?

3. Have you found that you're not getting much of a kick anymore from the things you used to enjoy—watching a basketball game, going fishing or camping, seeing a movie?

4. Do your anxieties haunt you? Are you unable to shut them out of your mind?

5. Are you now scared of people and situations that never used to bother you?

6. Have you noticed that you're becoming suspicious of people around you, even of your friends?

7. Does the feeling that you're being trapped come over you?

8. Do you feel inadequate, just not good enough to hack it?

Go through these familiar steps together as time permits the next couple of days. Your goal is not to add stress to your lives by following another program. It is to reduce stress by understanding God's prescription.

PREPARATION TIME: Think about this formula for knowing peace: Put God first in every area, and receive God's peace in every area.

Note the necessary relationship between these two statements. First you surrender to the Lordship of Christ, then you receive the peace. Do that now before you continue, spending a few minutes in silent prayer.

WAITING TIME: During your waiting time, let God love you, search you and show each of you His desires in the area of pressure within your life. Ask Him to help you complete the following simple prayers:

"God, I feel Your love today, especially in the area of . . ."

"God, You have permission to reveal any area that brings stress to my life . . ."

"God, is there anything that I need to know as I enter this day, any stress-filled situations You want to prepare me for now. . . ?"

CONFESSION TIME: Paul tells us to "pray about everything" (Philippians 4:6). Think about any areas that you fail to take to God, which are bringing you stress. Now confess these to God.

Remember, He knows your hearts, but wants you to exercise the relief that can come from confession to Him.

BIBLE TIME: We can know that we are praying for God's will when we pray His Word back to Him. Read Philippians 4:6-8 slowly a few times. Then close your eyes and ask God to bring a main truth to the surface in each of your hearts about stress in your own lives. Now pray this Scripture back to God and allow Him to minister to you. Your prayer might go something like this: "Dear God, we give it all up to You today. We're not sure we can take any more, and since You're telling us not to worry, we agree. Our needs are great, but we know You will answer our prayers in Your perfect timing. Help us to recognize Your answers and to thank You for them. Thank You for the peace You give for this simple, yet hard-to-do exercise in faith. Help us to trust in You, and to know that doing so will bring us peace, quiet and rest. Instead of our own worries, bring to our minds everything that is true and good and right. Help us to think about the pure and the lovely, the fine and the good in others, and the praise and gladness and thanksgiving we can offer back to You. In Jesus' name, Amen."

MEDITATION TIME: After praying the Scriptures, write down in a notebook any thoughts that God has impressed upon your minds about the relationship between your stress and God's peace.

INTERCESSION TIME—PRAYING FOR OTHERS: Pray for others God brings to your minds who are going through stressful times right now. Pray that they will be assured that God will not give them more than they can handle. Pray too that they will discover ways to release their stresses and experience God's perfect peace in their lives.

PETITION TIME—PRAYING FOR YOURSELVES: Each family member should have a private talk with God about the little things that are bothering you. Reread the list of eight signs of stress above. Are some of these things dragging you down? Ask God to remove stresses you can't handle right now, and to give you an additional measure of strength for those that remain. Ask

Him to help you focus on Him and to remember to cast your worries on Him. Thank Him in advance for the relief and peace that He provides.

APPLICATION TIME: List in a notebook steps your family can take toward obeying God in the area of stress relief. Is there a way that being obedient is a way to reduce your stress?

FAITH TIME: Faith is our positive response to what God has said. Spend a few moments praying through your eyes of faith. Tell God the positive things you see happening in your family because of His goodness!

PRAISE AND THANKSGIVING TIME: Read 1 Timothy 2:1-4. Now praise God by recognizing who He is—God, our Savior. And thank Him by recognizing what He has done—given us a direct line to Him, providing us with peaceful, quiet lives, and a measure of His goodness and holiness.

Family Time Throughout the Week

MONDAY—Do the Family Devotion Time. Get started on the Family Worship section.

TUESDAY—With your family, talk through the list at the beginning of the Family Worship section. Are there areas in your lives where stress is increasing? Again, make a list of stresses that individuals are facing. Pray for each other and the way you handle stress.

WEDNESDAY—Read Philippians 4:1-13 again after a mealtime. Talk together as a family about what areas each of you is the weakest. The strongest. Encourage each other in your areas of strength, and pray for areas of weakness. Agree to hold each other up in prayer, and to support others in areas where your strengths match their weaknesses.

THURSDAY—Take apart your memory verse. Work together on memorizing it, and on helping every member of the family to understand it. Discuss what good can possibly come out of facing pressures—there must be a reason God wants us to deal with some difficulties in our lives.

FRIDAY—Pair off as family members for prayer. Match parents with the youngest children and allow older siblings to pair off. Pray together concerning areas of stress in your lives. Also, pray that you will each understand and know God's peace in your lives.

WEEK 43: SUCCESS

Family Devotion Time

ACTIVITY: FAMILY AWARD NIGHT. Before your family's time together, think of simple prizes that relate to the personality of each person. Here are a couple of suggestions:
- A set of wind-up chattering teeth for the family jokester.
- A bookmark or new book for the family reader.
- A "Do Not Disturb" sign for the person who wants privacy.
- A spatula or other kitchen gadget for the best cook.

> ***Success*** *is achieving what I want—and especially what God wants.*

Try to reward positives, or at least to emphasize the positive aspects of a certain quality or personality trait.

If you have a personal computer, you could also print up certificates of award for family members. Don't be surprised if the prize and certificate end up in a prized place on a bedroom bookshelf.

DISCUSSION: Discuss these things together:
- How did it feel to be awarded your prize?
- How does it make you feel when other people—teachers, friends, co-workers, other family members—notice and mention positive things about you?
- Why do you think God created us with the feeling inside that we want to succeed?
- Without looking at the "Success is . . ." box on this page, how would you define success?
- If you are feeling more like a failure than a success, what do you think are some ways you can change your feelings?

God wants us to be successful. But He has His own definition of success. It's up to us to live within His will and desires—by obeying Him. Then He will prosper us, as *this week's memory verse* promises:

"Commit your work to the Lord, then it will succeed."
—Proverbs 16:3

FAMILY BIBLE TIME: Read Psalm 1:1-3. Describe a successful tree. How is the person who lives God's way a success, according to these verses?

FAMILY PRAYER TIME: Thank God together for success in your lives. Make a list, and pray them individually and specifically back to God. Make another list together, one of failures in your lives. Ask God to make His desires be your desires, and to help you succeed. Above all, commit your everything—your work, school, fun times—to God, and ask Him to help you succeed in these areas too.

Family Worship Time (optional)

Three men were trying to come up with a definition of "success." The first said, "I would consider myself successful if I could have a private, personal conversation with the President of the United States in the White House Oval Office."

The second man said, "I would consider myself successful if, while I am having a private, personal conversation with the President of the United States in the White House Oval Office, his hotline rings and he ignores it."

The third said, "For me to feel successful, I would be having a private, personal conversation with the President of the United States in the White House Oval Office, the hotline rings, he answers it and says, "It's for you.'"

A survey of 100 executives asked this question: "What does success mean to you?" These were their answers. See if you agree, discussing them with your family.

1. Possessing something specific and worthwhile.
2. Experiencing a special feeling.
3. The process of going from point A to point B.

4. Reaching my maximum potential at any given moment.
5. Overcoming obstacles.
6. Success is work.
7. Success is power.
8. Not looking back with regret.
9. Success is production.
10. Success is lasting.

Contrast that with this definition of success:

Knowing God and His desires for me;

Growing to my maximum potential;

Sowing seeds that benefit others.

Is success selfish or serving? The world and God might not agree on the answer to that question. Take some time going through these steps to affirm what God's answer would be.

PREPARATION TIME: Read Genesis 1:27, 28 together. Note that God expected Adam (man) to be successful—verse 28, and God equipped Adam (man) to be successful—verse 27.

God expected Adam to do that which was right and pleasing in His sight. God even gave him instructions so he could succeed. The only way Adam could fail was for him to disobey.

Remember . . . success is obedience to God!

WAITING TIME: During your waiting time, let God love you, search you and show each of you His desires in the area of success. Ask Him to provide phrases that complete these simple prayers:

"God, I feel Your love today, especially in the area of . . ."

"God, You have permission to reveal any wrong motive in my life . . ."

"God, is there anything that I need to know as I enter this day. . . ?"

CONFESSION TIME: If success is obedience to God, take a moment and silently confess to Him any areas of your lives where you've been disobedient to Him.

BIBLE TIME: We can know that we are praying for God's will when we pray His Word back to Him. Read Psalm 1:1-3 slowly a few times. Then close your eyes and ask God to bring a main truth to the surface in each of your hearts about success. Now pray this Scripture back to God and allow Him to minister to you. Your prayer might go something like this: "God, help us to know the joy that comes from focusing on You. Help us to delight in doing the things You want us to. Help us to always concentrate on following You more closely through our obedience to You. Thank You for Your wonderful promise, that our diligence will be rewarded. Make us like trees along a river or stream, with plenty of nourishment. Help us to bear fruit for You simply by the way we live our lives! Again, You amaze us with Your plans for us. Thank You for the success and prosperity that come when we focus on Your desires for our lives. In Jesus' name, Amen."

MEDITATION TIME: After praying the Scriptures, write down in a notebook any thoughts that God has impressed upon your minds about success. Keep trying to answer the question: Is success selfish or serving?

INTERCESSION TIME—PRAYING FOR OTHERS: Think of areas where each of you feels like a failure. Chances are that those around you experience many of the same feelings. Really. Failure is just something we seldom admit to each other, so you may not know that the people you love are experiencing it just as you are. Pray that God will work in the lives of those you love— friends, family members. Ask Him to help them discover exactly what will bring them God's success and prosperity to their lives.

PETITION TIME—PRAYING FOR YOURSELVES: Now that you've prayed for others, pray for yourselves. Privately confess again to God areas where you've failed because of your disobedience. Ask Him to help you understand areas where you aren't sure why you failed. Even ask God to show you what He wants you to learn from your failure; ask how your failures can become successes because of your victory (God's victory) over them.

APPLICATION TIME: List in a notebook what steps your family can take toward obeying God in the area of success. Note again how being obedient is itself a step to help you be successful.

FAITH TIME: Faith is our positive response to what God has said. Spend a few moments praying through your eyes of faith. Tell God the positive things you see happening in your family because of His goodness!

PRAISE AND THANKSGIVING TIME: Read Genesis 1:27, 28 again. Praise God by recognizing who He is—our Creator and Equipper. And thank Him by recognizing what He has done—given us the desire and means to be successful.

Family Time Throughout the Week

MONDAY—Do the Family Devotion Time. Get started on the Family Worship section.

TUESDAY—Read the Preparation Time section to your family. When Adam sinned, the nature of sin became a part of the human family. Our sinful nature causes us to:

1. Disobey God.
2. Keep a distance from Him.
3. Withhold affections from God.
4. Avoid responsibility for wrongdoing.

Talk as a family about examples from Scripture of people who did this. Can you think of examples from everyday life as well? Pray together that God would keep you from repeating sinful habits, and keep you close to Him.

WEDNESDAY—Memorize the "Knowing, Growing, Sowing" definition of success under the Family Worship section.

THURSDAY—Talk about the definitions of success, both the executive one and the one based on God's Word. Which would you choose? Which one seems to focus on self and which one on others? Discuss the questions, is success selfish or serving?

FRIDAY—This week's memory verse may not need much explanation, except to understand what "work" is. Talk as a family about what we should commit to God. Work on memorizing the verse together.

WEEK 44: TAMING THE TONGUE

Family Devotion Time

ACTIVITY: THE BALL TOSS. You may remember doing this activity a few months ago, but it's one worth repeating! It gives you a reason and a setting to do something that can be rather difficult—say nice things about other family members.

Taming the Tongue *means letting God guide the things I say.*

Use an air-filled soft ball or a Nerf® foam ball. Sit in a circle and toss the ball to another person. That person must then say something nice about you, to build you up. He then tosses the ball to another family member, who says something nice about him. Continue with the ball toss until everyone has heard several positive things about himself.

DISCUSSION: Our tongue—what the Bible calls the words we say—can be a deadly weapon or a tool for building each other up. Talk through these questions using the tool, not the weapon!

• Why is what we say about each other so important?
• Why is the way we feel about each other so important? Why is it important that we express our feelings for each other?
• Think about the worst thing you've ever said to someone. How do you think it made that person feel? Does anyone want to share that experience?
• Think about the kindest thing you've ever said to someone. How do you think it made that person feel? Anyone want to tell about this experience?
• Have you ever said something, and even as the words were coming out, you wished you could suck them back in? Why? What do you think that can teach you?

Why do we say the things we say? How can the things we

say either hurt or help others so much? All of us sometimes say hurting things. To stop that, it can help to concentrate on *this week's memory verse:*

"Help me, Lord, to keep my mouth shut and my lips sealed." —Psalm 141:3

FAMILY BIBLE TIME: It was James, the half-brother of Jesus, who first warned us about the tongue:

"So also the tongue is a small thing, but what enormous damage it can do. A great forest can be set on fire by one tiny spark. And the tongue is a flame of fire. It is full of wickedness, and poisons every part of the body. And the tongue is set on fire by hell itself, and can turn our whole lives into a blazing flame of destruction and disaster." —James 3:5, 6

One word can change the course of human history. Remember, the issue is control, not silence.

Consider these three biblical truths concerning the tongue:

1. The tongue contains an awesome power for good or evil.
2. We cannot control our tongues by our own power.
3. We must submit our tongue to the Holy Spirit.

FAMILY PRAYER TIME: Encourage everyone to think of one hurting thing he said to someone else in the past week. Now, have everyone, in their own minds, think of how he would feel if someone said the same thing to him. During a time of silent prayer, encourage each family member to confess this to God, and to ask for His forgiveness. Now pray aloud that God would help each of you to use your tongue—the words you say—as a positive tool to build others up.

Family Worship Time (optional)

Charles Swindoll, in his best-selling book *Growing Strong in the Seasons of Life,* has this to say about the tongue: "The tongue—what a study in contrasts! To the physician, it's merely a two-ounce slab of mucous membrane enclosing a complex array of muscles and nerves that enable our bodies to chew, taste and swallow. How helpful! Equally significant, it is the major organ of communication that enables us to articulate distinct sounds so we can understand each other. How essential!

"Without the tongue, no mother could sing her baby to sleep at night. No ambassador could adequately represent our nation. No teacher could stretch the minds of students. No officer could lead his fighting men in battle. No attorney could defend the truth in court. No pastor could comfort troubled souls. No complicated, controversial issue could ever be discussed and solved. Our entire world would be reduced to unintelligible grunts and shrugs. Seldom do we pause to realize just how valuable this strange muscle in our mouths really is.

"But the tongue is as volatile as it is vital. It was Washington Irving who first said, 'A tongue is the only edged tool that grows keener with constant use.'"

How are you doing with controlling your tongues? Take some time to work through these steps to evaluate your words, and to gain a sense of how you can "tame the tongue."

PREPARATION TIME: Read Psalm 39:1. Now think about the words you say to your family and friends, the words you've spoken in anger, words you've uttered without thinking, things you've said because of your own fear or insecurity, words spoken out of selfish interests. Are there areas where you must guard your tongue? (Since this study is about the tongue, be especially careful in your discussion this week to be constructive.)

WAITING TIME: During your waiting time, let God love you, search you and show each of you His desires in the area of your speech.

"God, help me to realize that You speak only truth and love to me . . ."

"God, You have permission to reveal any wrong use of my words, and especially my heart, the origin of my words . . ."

"God, is there anything that I need to know about use of my tongue as I enter this day. . . ?"

CONFESSION TIME: Reread James 3:5-8. In this passage, James isn't calling for silence as the answer to a tongue out of control, but he is suggesting discipline. Confess the areas of your hearts where your words have hurt God and people (be specific).

BIBLE TIME: We can know that we are praying for God's will when we pray His Word back to Him. Read Psalm 39:1-7 a few times. Then close your eyes and ask God to bring a main truth to the surface in each of your hearts about controlling your speech. Now pray this Scripture back to God and allow Him to minister to you. Your prayer might go something like this: "Dear God, forgive us for our complaining. Help us to hold our tongues in public, especially when those who don't know You are around. Even when we want to say something, when the words are just burning inside us to get out, we pray that You would help us to keep silent. And since You know our hearts anyway, let us speak to You. Let us plead with You, because You will help us put things into perspective: how short life is, how frail life is, how pointless it is to build up riches for ourselves. Help us realize that You are our hope—our only hope is in You. In fact, let our tongues be put to good use, and spread the good news of hoping only in You. In Jesus' name, Amen."

MEDITATION TIME: After praying the Scriptures, write down in a notebook any thoughts that God has impressed upon your minds about the use of your words. Especially reflect on the contrast of your ability to both bless and curse with your tongue.

INTERCESSION TIME—PRAYING FOR OTHERS: Can each of you think of someone who has a difficult time controlling his words? A hard time not letting divisive opinions or venomous anger come out? Pray that these people will be calmed down by God, that they will realize the harm they do to God's kingdom when they lash out with their tongues.

PETITION TIME—PRAYING FOR YOURSELVES: James also said, "If anyone can control his tongue, it proves that he has perfect control over himself in every other way" (James 3:2). Read the rest of James 3. Ask God to help you control your tongues so that you can claim, through God's strength and power, control over other areas of your lives.

APPLICATION TIME: List in a notebook what steps your family can take toward obeying God in the area of controlling your tongues. Ask God to help you see how being obedient is itself a step to taming this small yet powerful part of your body.

FAITH TIME: Faith is our positive response to what God has said. Spend a few moments praying through your eyes of faith. Tell God the positive things you see happening in your family because of His goodness!

PRAISE AND THANKSGIVING TIME: Read Psalm 34:1-4. Praise God by recognizing who He is—our exalted God. And thank Him by recognizing what He has done—given us a tongue that can praise His name.

Family Time Throughout the Week

MONDAY—Do the Family Devotion Time and work on the Family Worship section. Try to finish it in the next few days.

TUESDAY—Talk together as a family. Ask for an open and safe time together, and allow family members to tell if anyone has offended them with their words. Encourage family members to try to avoid reacting defensively. If necessary, let the offending family member ask for forgiveness. Encourage the offended family member to accept the apology. Pray together and ask God to help all of you be more sensitive with your words.

WEDNESDAY—With other members of the family, talk about people you know who might need you to speak a word of encouragement this week. Determine who in your family can best follow through—and then do it.

THURSDAY—Pray together today that God will use your family and their words to bring glory to Himself. Pray that you will all be careful when you speak around those who don't know God, that He will use your words to make unbelievers curious about Him.

FRIDAY—Review your memory verse. It's pretty simple and straightforward. But make sure that everyone in the family understands it as they memorize it. Talk about when you need to pray this verse to God. When do you need to ask God to make you bolder in your speech?

WEEK 45: TEMPTATION

Family Devotion Time

ACTIVITY: DON'T TOUCH! Put a big bowl of washed and ready-to-eat grapes in the middle of the table where you meet, or on a prominent end table or coffee table if you're meeting in your living room or family room.

Let everyone know that the grapes are for later— perhaps if someone is coming over later you can say the grapes are for company, or just say that you're saving them for

> **Temptation:** *giving in to things that come between me and God.*

something else, and you want them to be left alone in the bowl to look nice.

Now, have the adults—Mom and Dad—leave the room. Do this rather casually, as if there is just a delay in getting started. Maybe you can forget this book and ask your spouse to help you find it.

Once you're out of the room, peek back in without anyone knowing it, if possible. You're trying to see if anyone in the family gives in to the temptation of eating the fruit. Or, if you think you'll be seen watching, you can just leave for a while and ask later if anyone took any of the grapes. Give your family a few minutes before you come back in, and make sure they hear you coming!

Whether anyone took any grapes or not isn't important for the discussion time, because several family members were probably tempted to take some.

DISCUSSION: Spend some time talking through these questions with your family:

• Why do you think we have to deal with being tempted?

Why did God put things in the world that can get us in trouble or cause us harm?

• Do you remember the story of the first temptation? What happened? (It might be fun for a younger child to tell this familiar story. Others can join in, and you can ask questions to get the "whole story.")

• How do you think we can resist temptation, stay away or get away from things that are tempting? How could you have resisted/how did you resist taking any of the grapes?

• Can you think of any ways God provides help to resist temptation that comes our way? What are they?

God lets us be tempted so that we can learn to stay away from temptations! Because He knows us so well, He even will keep us away from any temptation that He knows we can't resist. If something is tempting you again and again, and you always give in, remember that God won't let you be tempted unless He knows that you can withstand or resist it. As *this week's memory verse* says:

"You can trust God to keep the temptation from becoming so strong that you can't stand up against it. . . . He will show you how to escape temptation's power. . . ." —1 Corinthians 10:13

FAMILY BIBLE AND PRAYER TIME: Pray the Lord's Prayer together. Though Jesus prayed many prayers we can read in Scripture, this is called the Lord's Prayer because Jesus is giving instruction on how to pray. If your family worships in a tradition where this prayer is not regularly a part of the worship service, you can read it together (Matthew 6:9-15). You can use the traditional *King James Version* of the words, or you can use the similar wording in the *New International Version.* If you do pray these words a lot, or if you want to use a paraphrase, *The Living Bible* offers nice wording. When you get to verse 13, regarding temptation, read the verse three times as your emphasis on prayer to God today.

Family Worship Time (optional)

The proof of God's love is His faithfulness in temptation. The proof of your love to God is your fleeing temptation.

God promises that we will never face a temptation that we can't flee or resist. Read this week's memory verse in its entirety (1 Corinthians 10:13), and look for these three biblical truths about temptation.

1. Temptation will never be more than we can handle for us to make a godly choice.

2. We need to be honest with God for Him to provide a way of escape.

3. Our responsibility is to continue to take the way of escape He provides.

Work through these familiar steps to gain a better understanding of what temptation is, and how you can resist it:

PREPARATION TIME: Read 1 John 2:15, 16. Now think about where and how each of you struggles in the following areas with temptation: Flesh? Eyes (coveting)? Ego?

WAITING TIME: During your waiting time, let God love you, search you and show each of you what He wants you to learn about fleeing temptation. Ask Him to help you complete these sentence prayers to Him:

"God, I feel Your love today, especially in the area of . . ."

"God, are there any "hidden" temptation areas in my life that You need to reveal . . . ?"

"God is there anything I need to know about a temptation I might face this day. . . ?"

CONFESSION TIME: The familiar verse, 1 John 1:9, reminds us how to deal with temptation we've given into. This is important because it clears our communication to God so He can help us flee the next tempting things we face. Individually confess to God any areas in your lives where you need His forgiveness and cleansing.

BIBLE TIME: We can know that we are praying for God's will when we pray His Word back to Him. Read Romans 12:1, 2 slowly a few times. Then close your eyes and ask God to bring a main truth to the surface in each of your hearts about temptation. Now pray this Scripture back to God and allow Him to minister to you. Your prayer might go something like this:

"Father, our bodies are Yours. We want them to be sacrifices to You, unblemished and holy. We know we can only offer them to You in this state because of the forgiveness You offer through Jesus Christ. Help us, strengthen us to focus on You, not copying what the world does, but being made new through You and for You. Then we can experience how who You are will satisfy us more than anything the world offers. Help us flee what the world offers, running away from it, and toward You and all that You are! In Jesus' name, Amen."

MEDITATION TIME: After praying the Scriptures, write down in a notebook any thoughts that God has impressed upon your minds about temptation and how you can resist it.

INTERCESSION TIME—PRAYING FOR OTHERS: Are there areas where you need to hold others accountable? Are you afraid to suggest to them that they might need you to be mutually accountable with them? Ask God to give each of you the courage to confront others lovingly, so that together you can learn from areas where you've been weak, and areas where you've been able to resist temptation.

PETITION TIME—PRAYING FOR YOURSELVES: Individually ask God if there are any areas of temptation where you need accountability from a mature Christian friend. Ask Him to provide an individual or a group of people you can ask to hold you accountable. Pray that your family would be sensitive to your areas of weakness, and that they would also hold you accountable.

APPLICATION TIME: List in a notebook what steps your family can take toward obeying God in the area of fleeing temptations. Is being obedient itself a step toward running from things that are tempting you?

FAITH TIME: Faith is our positive response to what God has said. Spend a few moments praying through your eyes of faith. Tell God the positive things you see happening in your family because of His goodness!

PRAISE AND THANKSGIVING TIME: Read 1 John 1:9 again. Praise God by recognizing who He is—our Savior! And thank Him by recognizing what He has done—forgiven our sins and cleansed us from the wrongs we have done.

Family Time Throughout the Week

MONDAY—Complete the Family Devotion Time together with your family. Work on the Family Worship section.

TUESDAY—Work on memorizing and understanding 1 Corinthians 10:13 together. Read the first part of the verse too, preferably from *The Living Bible.* Does knowing that others have faced temptations and been able to resist them encourage you? Some people find it discouraging, because it must mean that their faith is weak if they give in to temptation. How can we find encouragement, rather than discouragement, from other people's successes when it comes to fleeing temptation?

WEDNESDAY—Read Psalm 119:9-17 together as a family. Talk about what help these verses provide for fleeing temptation. What other ways are we able to resist temptation?

THURSDAY—Pray together as a family that each of you, no matter how old or young, would be able to find an accountability partner. For younger children, the partner may be a parent or an older brother or sister. For teens and parents, you might seek a peer or a group of peers to be accountable to. Discuss how and why being accountable to other Christians can help us be more accountable to God.

FRIDAY—Read the biblical truths about temptation under the first part of the Family Worship section. Discuss together times why we wouldn't want to be honest with God. Doesn't He know what we're thinking and doing anyway? If we are dishonest, aren't we only adding to the temptation and the resulting sin? Talk and pray about ways we can learn to be upfront and open and honest with God.

WEEK 46: THOUGHT LIFE

Family Devotion Time

ACTIVITY: SECRET MEMORY TRAY. When everyone gathers for this week's family time, have a tray sitting in the middle of the table, or on the coffee table if you sit on couches and chairs when you meet. On the tray, have a variety of items. Some suggestions: a button, a candle, a coin, a pen, a magnet. Try to have 15 or 20 small items on the tray. Have a list of the items as well.

> **Thought Life:** *No matter what I say or do, my thoughts tell who I really am.*

Don't mention anything about the tray, and if someone picks something up to look at it, that's OK. Just ask for it to be put back before the person sits down.

Make casual conversation, asking different family members about friends, school, their rooms, whatever. After about 10 minutes, slowly get up from where you are sitting, pick up the tray, and carry it out of the room.

Return to the room with sheets of paper and pencils, and ask everyone to write down as many items as they can remember that were on the tray. If you have children who are too young to write, they can either draw the objects simply, or they can whisper to you and you can make a list. Younger kids can also team up with older siblings to write their list together.

Set a time limit, four or five minutes. When time is up, have everyone listen as you read the list. See who remembers the most items. You might be surprised at how many some family members recall.

DISCUSSION: Now, spend some time thinking and talking about thinking:

• What do you think about more than anything?

• What is something you wish you could think about more, but don't seem to have time to?

• How much time in a day do you spend thinking about the rest of your family?

• How much time do you think you spend thinking about things that are wrong or bad?

• How much time do you spend thinking about God?

What we think about really makes us who we are. Instead of "you are what you eat," the truth is "you are what you think." Why? Because what is in our heads and hearts is going to come out in our words and actions. Think about what *this week's memory verse* says about how our thought lives affect our closeness to God:

". . . Who may stand before the Lord? Only those with pure hands and hearts, who do not practice dishonesty and lying." —Psalm 24:3, 4

FAMILY BIBLE TIME: Read Ephesians 4:8, 9 and talk about the good things we should focus our thoughts on.

FAMILY PRAYER TIME: Reread the discussion questions above, and use them as a guide to this prayer time. As you enter a time of prayer together as a family, ask others to answer these questions silently, and to pray for forgiveness when their thoughts are not on God or on things that bring honor to Him. In other words, it's not dishonoring to think positively and lovingly about another family member's act of kindness, because that isn't dishonoring to God. But holding a grudge because another family member hurt your feelings would be dishonoring to God because He wants us to forgive others. After family members have had time to pray silently, give them opportunity to pray out loud. Close your family time in prayer, asking God to guide all of your thoughts this day, week and in the future.

Family Worship Time (optional)

One of the most powerful and unforgettable stories of the Old Testament is about King David. It happened in the springtime, when kings go out to battle (2 Samuel 11). David got up from his bed and walked around on his roof. From this vantage point, he saw a beautiful woman, Bathsheba, bathing. Even though David learned that she was married to one of his military officers, Uriah the Hittite, he sent for her and slept with her. As a result, she became pregnant. David tried to set things right, but boy, did he mess up. He sent Uriah to an intense battle, where he was killed—actually murdered because of David's instructions. Then David married Bathsheba. But things still weren't right.

Just look at the results of one sin, David's sin of adultery:
• Immoral pregnancy—2 Samuel 11:5.
• Uriah murdered—2 Samuel 11:15-17.
• David and Bathsheba's obligatory marriage—2 Samuel 11:27.
• Conviction and guilt—2 Samuel 12:7.
• Poor witness to enemies of Israel—2 Samuel 12:14.
• Their child died—2 Samuel 12:14, 18.

David suffered all this from a wrong choice that began in his thought life. He could have obeyed God. Instead, he dwelled on his thoughts and acted them out.

Consider these biblical truths about our thoughts from 2 Corinthians 10:3-5.

1. A spiritual battle is being fought in our minds, between heaven and hell, seeking captivity of our thoughts.

2. We are unable to win this battle of the mind alone.

3. God wants us to surrender our thoughts to the purity of Christ by the power of the Holy Spirit.

But how? Spend some time together going through these steps to gain a better understanding of how we can "take our thoughts captive" through the Spirit's power.

PREPARATION TIME: Read Colossians 3:1, 2. Now, consider these possible areas we might face in our thoughts even before they become actions. Are there any you struggle with in your thought lives? Let family members think about each one as you read it.
• Lust
• Anger
• Bitterness
• Envy

- Covetousness
- Jealousy
- Greed
- Negativity

Think to yourselves of any specific examples where you've struggled in your thoughts with one or more of these areas.

WAITING TIME: During your waiting time, let God love you, search you and show each of you in the area of your thoughts. Ask Him to help you answer these simple phrases in prayer, even if your thoughts seem to be blocking your communication with Him now:

"God, I feel Your love today, especially in the area of . . ."

"God, You have permission to reveal any wrong thoughts in my life . . ."

"God, is there anything that I need to know or think on as I enter this day . . . ?"

CONFESSION TIME: Read Titus 1:15. Now look at the list under the Preparation Time and remember what came to your minds during that step. Individually take a few minutes to confess to God any thoughts that are not wholesome or pure.

BIBLE TIME: We can know that we are praying for God's will when we pray His Word back to Him. Read Philippians 4:8, 9 slowly a few times. Then close your eyes and ask God to bring a main truth to the surface in each of your hearts about your thought lives. Now pray this Scripture back to God and allow Him to minister to you. Your prayer might go something like this: "God, help us to focus on You. Even in this world, help us to concentrate our thoughts on things that are pure, lovely, true, good and right. Help us to see these qualities in other people and in our circumstances. For these are the things we can praise You for and rejoice in! Thank You for something so simple, that if we will just put it into practice, it will bring us unceasing joy and peace from You. In Jesus' name, Amen."

MEDITATION TIME: After praying the Scriptures, write down in a notebook what God has impressed upon your minds about your thought lives. Make a record to refer back to whenever you become concerned that your thoughts are not on God and the things He would like you to focus on.

INTERCESSION TIME—PRAYING FOR OTHERS: Spend this intercession time praying for family members and close friends who have admitted to you some of their struggles when it comes to their thoughts. (Be sure not to reveal any confidences to other family members.) Pray Philippians 4 for them—that they would be able to surrender their thoughts to God, and that He would bring them His peace and joy.

PETITION TIME—PRAYING FOR YOURSELVES: What thoughts came to mind that you confessed to God during the Confession Time? Ask God to remove those thoughts and the memories they create from your minds. Ask Him to help each of you forget the past when it comes to impure thoughts. If you've acted on any of these thoughts, consider how God would have you make it right. Remember not to take things into your own hands and make a worse mess like King David. Instead, ask God to direct and guide your actions so that through any necessary reconciliations, no matter how difficult, honor and glory would be brought to Him.

APPLICATION TIME: List in a notebook steps your family can take toward obeying God in the area of your thoughts. Is it true here that being obedient to God is itself a step to help you keep your thoughts pure and God-honoring?

FAITH TIME: Faith is our positive response to what God has said. Spend a few moments praying through your eyes of faith. Tell God about your new and revitalized thought lives because of the power of His Spirit.

PRAISE AND THANKSGIVING TIME: Praise God by recognizing who He is—a holy and pure God. And thank Him by recognizing what He has done—allowed us to share His purity and holiness if we allow His Spirit to direct and control our thoughts.

Family Time Throughout the Week

MONDAY—Do the Family Devotion Time together. Also get started on the Family Worship section.

TUESDAY—Read Titus 1:15 after a mealtime. Talk about what this verse means. Grab some sunglasses and have everyone try them on. How do sunglasses affect what we see? Do you see a relationship with this verse? How are impure thoughts like the dark glass in sunglasses?

WEDNESDAY—Give everyone a piece of paper and a pen. It's now been two days since you saw the memory tray from your family activity. But ask family members to list as many items from that tray as they can remember, or to team up again with younger family members to develop lists together. Talk about how even the most innocent of thoughts seems to stay with us. Is it possible that bad thoughts also stay with us longer than we realize?

THURSDAY—Talk through your memory verse as a family. Work on memorizing it, and also make sure that everyone understands the words. How do our thoughts affect our relationship with God?

FRIDAY—Try the list activity for the third time this week. See who can remember the most items on the tray. This time, reread Philippians 4:8, 9 and discuss why it's important to fill our minds with good thoughts, and to ask God to help us remember them and use them.

WEEK 47: THE TIME CRUNCH

Family Devotion Time

ACTIVITY: GO AHEAD AND YELL. The purpose of this week's activity is to get an idea of what one family—your family—goes through in a typical day. Ask someone to be the family's secretary, and then let everyone shout out the things they did today. These don't have to be outstanding, earth-shattering events. "Brushed my teeth" and "Fell asleep in study hall" count!

> **The Time Crunch:**
> *When we run out of time to do what we want to or should do.*

DISCUSSION: After you've compiled as large a list as you can, spend some time gathered around the tired secretary's notebook. Ponder all the things you do in a day as you discuss these questions:

• What's the most important thing you did today? How much time did it take?

• What's the least important thing you did today? How much time did that take?

• Do you think that all the things you did today were necessary? If not, what number was necessary—5 out of 10, 7 out of 10?

• Do you think the way you spend your time honors God? Do you use spare time as a time to relax, or do you feel that it's wasted?

• How do you look at time—as a tool, as hard to live by, as something that holds you back, as a gift from God?

Time is weird. God doesn't know it, meaning He isn't restricted by it. Yet He created it for us to use. Why? Wouldn't we better off if we didn't have to worry about time? Maybe the reason He created it is expressed in this week's memory verse: "There is a right time for everything." —Ecclesiastes 3:1

FAMILY BIBLE TIME: The memory verse is part of a whole chorus about time. Read Ecclesiastes 3:1-8. What examples can you think of for these times: a time to cry, a time to laugh; a time to be quiet, a time to speak up?

FAMILY PRAYER TIME: Ask as a family for God to bless your time, to guide your time, and to mark your time. Ask Him to help you spend your time wisely in every way—for work, for rest; for laughter, for crying; for pain, for healing. Ask Him to guide you through relationships that take time, to help you determine how best to spend your time in all the relationships you have— with each other in your family, with friends, with work or school, with church and ministry and service. Thank God for creating time, to keep us focused on Him and His work.

Family Worship Time (optional)

Everyone receives an equal supply of time. The only difference between us is the way we invest it. Each week brings us 168 golden hours. We use approximately 56 hours for sleep and recuperation. We spend approximately 24 hours for eating and personal duties. We spend approximately 50 hours earning a living.

We have approximately 38 hours left to spend just as we wish. But how do we spend them?
- Recreation
- Family
- God and church
- Education
- Physical fitness

The heart of time management is your willingness and ability to maximize God's gift of time, not to hyperventilate with calendars, clipboards and stopwatches.

God has given us the precious gift of time; we need to be good stewards of it. The management of time must be our number-one priority. Without some organization of our days, they will waste away without purpose, and drain away without accomplishment.

Consider these two foundational biblical principles:

Principle 1—You have enough time to do all that God wants you to do (Matthew 6:30-34).

Too much to do? Not enough time? Seek God's kingdom and righteousness first; that will set your priorities straight. If you really are unable to get everything done, perhaps you're doing some things that God doesn't need you to do! The key is to say yes to the right things, which is why we must always seek God first.

Principle 2—Come apart and rest or you'll come apart (Matthew 14:13, 23).

The best remedy for a schedule that is out of control is to get alone with God and practice principle number 1.

Now spend some time going through these steps to discern more clearly what God's principles of time management are.

PREPARATION TIME: Read Ecclesiastes 3:11, 12. Now think about the time each of you spends at work or school, the time you spend with family, with friends. What are the areas you struggle most with? Why?

WAITING TIME: During your waiting time, let God love you, search you and show each of you His desires in the area of how you spend your time. Ask Him to provide you with answers to the following simple prayers:

"God, I feel Your love today, and thank You for the gift of time . . ."

"God, You have permission to reveal any poor usage of time in my life . . ."

"God, is there anything that I need to know about time as I enter this day. . . ?"

CONFESSION TIME: Read Ecclesiastes 1:14. Now confess the areas in which each of you has wasted God's precious gift of time.

BIBLE TIME: We can know that we are praying for God's will when we pray His Word back to Him. Read Ecclesiastes 3:18 again slowly a few times. Then close your eyes and ask God to bring a main truth to the surface in each of your hearts about how you spend your time. Now pray this Scripture back to God and allow Him to minister to you.

MEDITATION TIME: After praying the Scriptures, write down in a notebook any thoughts that God has impressed upon your minds about time. Especially think about how you use your time—do you think it's wasted or well spent?

INTERCESSION TIME—PRAYING FOR OTHERS: Think of someone your family knows who never seems to have enough time. Pray that he will understand that time is a gift from God, and that He can help him learn how to spend his moments wisely. Now think of someone who seems to be a good manager of time. Pray that he will see if any of her energies are being used in improper directions or for things that detract from God's glory and kingdom work.

PETITION TIME—PRAYING FOR YOURSELVES: Of the two people described above—someone who never has enough time, and someone who is a good manager of time—which best describes you? Pray for yourselves, individually, asking God to teach you to use your time better, or to guide you in directing your well-managed time in proper ways.

APPLICATION TIME: List in a notebook what steps your family can take toward obeying God in the area of time. Is obedience a part of using time well in your own lives? How?

FAITH TIME: Faith is our positive response to what God has said. Spend a few moments praying through your eyes of faith. Tell God the positive things you see happening in your family because of His goodness!

PRAISE AND THANKSGIVING TIME: Read Ecclesiastes 3:14. Now praise God by recognizing who He is—all-powerful. And thank Him by recognizing what He has done—given us reason to be in awe of His mighty power.

Family Time Throughout the Week

MONDAY—Do the Family Devotion Time, and get started on the Family Worship section.

TUESDAY—Talk together about what the main causes of wasted time are in our lives. Discuss openly with each other about which ones each of you seem to fall victim to most often. Commit to pray for each other regarding your biggest time wasters.

WEDNESDAY—Spend some time praying together. Talk to God about His priorities for your life. Ask Him to reveal to each of you His purposes and timing. Ask Him to help you be patient as you wait for Him. And pray that He will guide each of you through the time you spend—both in terms of how you move through your life, and how you move through each day.

THURSDAY—Read and spend a few moments meditating on John 17:4. Then ask these questions of your family: How could Jesus have been finished? There were still the blind, the lame, the sick and the unconverted? How do you think He knew that His time on earth was nearly over? Can we have the same kind of insight into our "time"?

FRIDAY—Work together on memorizing your memory verse. Make sure all family members understand what it means.

WEEK 48: TRUTH

Family Devotion Time

ACTIVITY: GOSSIP, GOSSIP, GOSSIP. You get to play the gossip game, which you might remember. This is when one person whispers something in the next person's ear, and it continues to get whispered around the circle until it comes back to the person who spoke first. That person then tells what he originally said, and what the final version of it was.

> **Truth** *means being honest with others, myself and God—even if it hurts me.*

This might be fun to save for a week when you have extended family members visiting or your children have friends over. The more people who take part in this, the more twisted the original words become before they get back to the beginning.

DISCUSSION: With gossip on your mind, spend a few minutes talking through these questions:
- If you had to define the truth, what words would you use?
- If you had to say what lies are, how would you define them?
- Do you think lies are OK if they don't hurt anyone? Is that possible?
- Is lying ever OK?
- Do you think lies are ever better than the truth? Is it possible that lies might be more dramatic or thrilling than the truth? Why?

In a court, someone who committed a crime might try to lie in order to be set free. But an important question is, even if the criminal is set free, is he really free? With real truth comes freedom. As *this week's memory verse* says:

"Jesus said to them, '. . . you will know the truth, and the truth will set you free.'" —John 8:31, 32

FAMILY BIBLE TIME: Read Acts 5:1-11. Assure your children that usually the penalty for lying isn't instant death! Who does Peter say they lied to? When might a lie to another person also be a lie to God?

FAMILY PRAYER TIME: Pray this simple prayer together as a family: that God will help you tell the truth. No matter what telling the truth might cause—punishment or embarrassment— pray that God will help you tell the truth. Thank Him for the freedom that comes from not lying.

Family Worship Time (optional)

You remember the feelings that rushed through you a few years ago when you heard the news that the "Iron Curtain" was falling in Central Europe. The communist bloc, which had stood for decades in Russia, East Germany, Romania, Hungary, Poland, Yugoslavia and other countries was finally disintegrating as people demanded freedom from the control of themselves and their governments.

Those countries are a global illustration of the fact that knowing the truth will make us free. The power of truth is quite simple: Truth always liberates; lies always put us in bondage. One pastor in Romania said that communism was built upon two pillars: lies and intimidation. For years, the people in those nations had been fed lie after lie about life, their economy, their history, and the existence of God. Now they were free. When the shackles fell, the bondage was broken, simply because people were unafraid to confront and expose the lies of communism.

The lies we believe are very subtle. The Enemy is good at subtlety. He convinces us to believe lies like: "I'm only as good as what I do; I can't be happy unless things go my way; I must be perfect; I must meet the needs of everyone around me"—and the list goes on. Many of our lies begin in childhood, so we become oblivious to them. And the longer we tell ourselves a lie, the more rigidly we hold it to be true.

Lies put us in emotional bondage. They don't fit reality in the same way a bad road map doesn't give us a proper expectation of reality in a geographic location. Many of us have faulty roadmaps in life—that only produce misery for us. Jesus' desire is to set us free with the truth.

Here's the truth about the truth:

• The truth is needed for spiritual and emotional health.
• The truth often comes a piece at a time.
• The truth is not always easy.
• The truth is often painful to face.
• A "thrilling" lie can seem better than the truth.
• The truth may make you feel doubt.
• The truth will stand forever.

Go through the following steps together to discover more about the truth.

PREPARATION TIME: Read 2 Corinthians 13:5. Examine yourselves to see whether you are walking in faith. Look at the areas you know of where each of you has bought into lies regarding your personal lives, your family life, church life, your school or business life.

WAITING TIME: During your waiting time, let God love you, search you and show each of you His desires in the area of what truth really is.

"God, as I study what truth means, I feel Your love today, especially in the area of . . ."

"God, You have permission to reveal any lie I've believed in my life . . ."

"God, is there any truth You want to reveal to me as I enter this day. . . ?"

CONFESSION TIME: Read John 14:1-6. Here Jesus claims that He is the truth, He is the life—in fact, He is God. Silently confess to Him any areas where you've experienced bondage and are buying into a lie from the Enemy. These may be sins of thought or behavior.

BIBLE TIME: When we pray God's Word back to Him, we can know that we are praying for God's will. Read John 8:31-36, 43-

46 slowly a few times. Then close your eyes and ask God to bring a main truth to the surface in each of your hearts about truth. Following the example of the other sections of this book, honestly and openly pray this Scripture back to God and allow Him to minister to your family.

MEDITATION TIME: After praying the Scriptures, write down in a notebook any thoughts that God has impressed upon your minds about knowing the truth.

INTERCESSION TIME—PRAYING FOR OTHERS: Think of others who know God, but who seem to be temporarily misled by the Enemy. Or perhaps you know someone who is aware of the truth, yet refuses to let go of a lie about himself. Pray together that God would continually liberate these people, and that He would free them to walk in truth.

PETITION TIME—PRAYING FOR YOURSELVES: Pray this simple prayer to God: Ask Him to restore you and reveal to you those truths that will free you.

APPLICATION TIME: List in a notebook what steps your family can take toward obeying God in the area of truth. Is being obedient a step toward experiencing the truth?

FAITH TIME: Faith is our positive response to what God has said. Spend a few moments praying through your eyes of faith. Tell God the positive things you see happening in your family because of His liberating truth!

PRAISE AND THANKSGIVING TIME: Praise God by recognizing who He is—*the* God of truth. And thank Him by recognizing what He has done—freed you from the bondage of the Enemy.

Family Time Throughout the Week

MONDAY—Do the Family Devotion Time together. Get started on the Family Worship section.
TUESDAY—Read aloud the "truth" statements at the

beginning of the Family Worship section. Then ask these questions of the people in your family:

• What makes truth difficult for you to face in your life?

• Which truths about life are the toughest to deal with?

Pray that Jesus would reveal Himself to you as "the Truth" (John 14:6). Ask Him to open your eyes and to build a hunger for truth, above all else.

WEDNESDAY—Read 2 Corinthians 4:3, 4. Paul speaks of the Gospel being hid from those who are perishing. No doubt, Satan longs to blind people from the truth. But while all Christians have had their eyes open to the power of the Gospel to save them, it is possible for them to walk in blindness to other areas of God's Word, simply because a lie blinded them (John 8:43-46).

Take some time to openly talk with your family about some specific lies that you may have bought into in your past. Then pray together for each other, asking God to speak to you concerning the truth, and how you may walk in freedom from the lies.

THURSDAY—We are given a number of things to pray about in John 8:31-46. This is the text where Jesus teaches on the effects of truth and the effects of lies in our lives. Talk to your family about these questions:

• Jesus' concern in this passage is that we "fall in love" with truth. How are each of you doing in this area?

• The Jews were mistaken when they thought that belonging to God meant they would never believe in lies. Have you made this same assumption?

• Satan's primary objective seems to be to assault and attack the truth with lies. How has this been true in your life?

• We ultimately believe what we want to believe. Even when we know the truth, we often believe a lie. Has this ever happened to you?

Pray for yourself today.

FRIDAY—Review the Faith Time from the steps above. Now, talk with your family about what you see. What does your life look like when you picture yourself walking in truth and freedom? What specific steps will you need to take to realize this in real life? Talk about them and pray for each other that you will take them.

WEEK 49: VALUES

Family Devotion Time

ACTIVITY: VALUES BOARD. Buy an inexpensive bulletin board to put up in your kitchen or family room—preferably someplace where your family will see it often.

Bring some family photos to start the board with, and also any clippings you might have of sayings or Bible verses,

> **Values** *are the things in my life most important to me.*

especially ones that focus on values. This bulletin board is to become your family "values board." Any family members can add to it—their own creations, cartoons, sayings, verses, new photos, etc. But the goal should be to help your family see values or learn new values.

DISCUSSION:
- What is the most important thing in your life?
- What do you think values are?
- What do you want more—worldly or godly things?
- How do others know the things you value most?

Of course, not everything in the world is bad. A lot of times, it depends on how much we value something. For example, it's OK to value your bike or your room. But if you become selfish or if you want more and bigger and better things, that's when your values go bad. *This week's memory verse* warns:

"Stop loving this evil world and all that it offers you, for when you love these things you show that you do not really love God." —1 John 2:15

FAMILY BIBLE TIME: Read Colossians 3:1-4. What are some ways you can "let heaven fill your thoughts"?

FAMILY PRAYER TIME: Pray through the discussion questions above. As you read each one, ask your family members to pray short sentence prayers to God, admitting and confessing when their thoughts and desires are from the world; thanking and praising God when the desires and thoughts they have are from Him.

Family Worship Time (optional)

"All that is truly valuable in human society both honors God and develops man." What are your values—what is important to you?

Values are the things in life that are most important to us. They are the guideposts and convictions that shape our decisions, actions and everyday lifestyles.

In Matthew 6:19-21 Jesus addresses values. Ponder together these biblical insights about Christian values from this passage:

• There is a strong contrast between the temporary nature of the world and the eternal nature of God's Kingdom.

• Where you invest is where your rewards will be.

• Values are an issue of the heart. They begin there and express themselves in your actions.

Now spend some time going through the following steps to gain a better grasp on the values God wants you to have.

PREPARATION TIME: Reread Colossians 3:1-4, then list any areas in your lives where you have not settled in your personal value system. In other words, in what areas do you sometimes question or waver in your beliefs and actions? Ask this about the values each of you has in your family, your church and ministry, your relationships, your personal life, and your career or potential career.

WAITING TIME: During your waiting time, let God love you, search you and show each of you His desires in the area of beliefs and values. Ask Him to help you complete these simple sentences in prayer to Him:

"God, I feel Your love today, especially in the area of . . ."

"God, please reveal any wrong values in my life . . ."

"God, is there anything that I need to know or understand about my values as I enter this day. . . ?"

CONFESSION TIME: Read Joshua 24:14, 15. Then together or individually confess to God any areas where worldly values have crept into your lives.

BIBLE TIME: We can know that we are praying for God's will when we pray His Word back to Him. Read 1 John 2:15-17 slowly a few times. Then close your eyes and ask God to bring a main truth to the surface in each of your hearts about values. Now pray this Scripture back to God and allow Him to minister to each of you.

MEDITATION TIME: After praying the Scriptures, write down in a notebook any thoughts that God has impressed upon your minds about your beliefs and values.

INTERCESSION TIME—PRAYING FOR OTHERS: Ask God to bring to your minds friends and family members who are struggling with their values. Most likely, the values they are holding closest are the ones they are living by. Pray that God will help them not to "store up treasures here on earth," and instead "store them in heaven." Ask God to reveal to them the truth of Matthew 6:21: "If your profits are in heaven your heart will be there too."

PETITION TIME—PRAYING FOR YOURSELVES: Read this aloud, and then give family members silent time to pray. Now ask yourself honestly: What values are you living by? What values are you holding closest to yourself? Reread Matthew 6:19-21 and ask God to put into you a desire to values His treasures—those that will last for eternity.

APPLICATION TIME: List in a notebook what steps your family can take toward obeying God in the area of values. Note how being obedient, like it is with so many other godly qualities, is itself a step to help you hold eternal values.

FAITH TIME: Faith is our positive response to what God has

said. Spend a few moments praying through your eyes of faith. Tell God the positive things you see happening in your family because of His goodness!

PRAISE AND THANKSGIVING TIME: Praise God by recognizing who He is—Eternal God. And thank Him by recognizing what He has done—given us the ability to claim eternal values even while we remain in temporal bodies.

Family Time Throughout the Week

MONDAY—Do the Family Devotion Time. Work on the Family Worship section.

TUESDAY—Read Matthew 19:16-26 after a mealtime or some other time when your family is all together. Now ask these questions: The young man seemed to be obedient at first—why? But then Jesus mentioned an area of the young ruler's life where he wasn't obedient—what was it? Do you think God wants us to have His values so that we benefit from it? What kinds of benefits will we get? Or do you think He just wants us to obey Him? Will we have any benefits from doing so?

WEDNESDAY—Talk as a family about all of the things that influence you. Just look around the room: TV, music, magazines and newspapers, other people. Add to this list. Now, try to determine which of these things can teach us godly values and which will teach us worldly values. Do some things have the potential to do both? How can we know when to listen and when to run away?

THURSDAY—Talk about what values from yesterday's list that you would like to live by. Pray together today, committing your family to God, asking Him to help you to live by His values as you understand them from Scripture.

FRIDAY—Review your memory verse. Make sure, as always, that everyone in your family understands what it means. Go through the verse, talk about each word and each phrase, asking your family to help define its different parts so that everyone understands what the verse is saying.

WEEK 50: WISDOM

Family Devotion Time

ACTIVITY: KNOWLEDGE BOXES. Create study boxes together, and while the kids are making these, Mom and Dad can make boxes for storing their hobbies or their materials for paying bills. Younger kids can make boxes for crafts or playtimes.

> ***Wisdom*** *is knowing the right thing to do at the right time for the right reason.*

For the study boxes, use shoe boxes or collapsible storage boxes that can be purchased at discount or office supply stores. Bring a supply of markers, glue, wrapping or Contact® paper, and anything else that can be used to decorate and personalize each box.

Then, put in supplies you need for a productive study time: pens, pencils, notebooks, math tools, reference books, calculators, crayons, colored pencils. The items will vary depending on the purpose of the box and the age of the user.

DISCUSSION: You can hold your discussion while you work together on your boxes. After you talk through these questions and pray together, decide on a convenient place to store your knowledge boxes, make sure each is labeled, and put them away. But commit to using them as often as possible.

• Without peeking at the definition above, what do you think wisdom means?

• Do you think there's a difference between wisdom and knowledge? What does it mean to know something? What does it mean to be wise?

• Does wisdom come with age, or is it possible for someone young to be wise?

• Do you think wisdom comes from God? Why or why not?

Wisdom comes from God when we ask for it. But we can't let wisdom—or any other gift for that matter—go to our heads. As *this week's memory verse* says:

"God . . . is always ready to give a bountiful supply of wisdom to those who ask him." —James 1:5

FAMILY BIBLE TIME: One of the wisest people ever was King Solomon. Read how he became wise in 1 Kings 3:3-15.

FAMILY PRAYER TIME: Encourage your family members to pray in response to these simple phrases:

"God, give me Your wisdom as I go through each day. I need it in these areas . . ."

"God, help me to remember that wisdom is a gift from You. I tend to forget at these times . . ."

Then, close in prayer, or ask if another family member wants to.

Family Worship Time (optional)

A small factory in a small town had to stop operations when an essential piece of machinery broke down. No one could get the machine operating. An outside expert was finally called in at great expense. The pro looked over the situation for a moment, then took a hammer and gently tapped the machine at a certain spot. It began running again immediately and continued to run as if nothing had ever gone wrong.

When the expert submitted his bill for $100, the plant supervisor hit the ceiling and demanded an itemized bill. The bill the man submitted was as follows: For hitting machine, $1; for knowing where to hit, $99.

When James writes of "the wisdom that comes from heaven" (James 3:17), he uses the present tense to make his point. In essence, James is saying, "Wisdom from above is not available in one-time allotments, and you can't get it on the installment plan." Instead, James presents wisdom as a steady flow from the mind of God to His children. It just keeps on coming.

These three truths come from Scripture:

• The supply of God's wisdom never runs dry.

• Wisdom comes to us continually to meet the demands we face each hour.

• When we walk with God, He daily gives us the wisdom we need for our lives.

Now spend some time together going through these steps to gain a better understanding of God's wisdom.

PREPARATION TIME: Read Ecclesiastes 1:17. Now think about any issues each of you wrestles with in your personal life, your family life, your church or ministry life, and your school or business life.

WAITING TIME: During your waiting time, let God love you, search you and show each of you His desires in the area of experiencing and possessing the wisdom He gives. Ask God to help you complete these simple prayers:

"God, I feel Your love today, as You give Your wisdom. I sense Your love especially in the area of . . ."

"God, You have permission to reveal any wrong motive in my life when it comes to how I use the wisdom You provide . . ."

"God, is there anything that I need to know as I enter this day, any situation where I will need to be wise as You are wise. . . ?"

CONFESSION TIME: Reread Jeremiah 9:23, 24. Think to yourselves about areas where you boast. Are there some that have no eternal significance, that are not of God? Confess these to God, and ask for His forgiveness.

BIBLE TIME: We can know that we are praying for God's will when we pray His Word back to Him. Read James 3:13-17 slowly a few times. Then close your eyes and ask God to bring a main truth to the surface in each of your hearts about wisdom. Now pray this Scripture back to God and allow Him to minister to you. Your prayer might go something like this: "God, help us, empower us and strengthen us to live lives of goodness. Keep us steady. And let this lifestyle be an emblem of Your wisdom. As You help us to live this way, don't allow us to fall into the trap of bragging about our good deeds, because they're not coming from us—they're coming from You. Help us to know for sure that we are counting on and living by Your wisdom, not some cheap imitation of it that comes from the world instead. We can recognize Your wisdom because it is pure, quiet, gentle, peace-loving, courteous, selfless, merciful, good, wholehearted, straight-forward and sincere. Those sound like qualities about You, God. Your wisdom and You sound the same. Please help us to live that way, for then we will know we're growing ever closer to You! In Jesus' name, Amen."

MEDITATION TIME: After praying the Scriptures, write down in a notebook any thoughts that God has impressed upon your mind about wisdom. Think especially about how those around you will know your family is living by God's wisdom.

INTERCESSION TIME—PRAYING FOR OTHERS: Ask God to bring to your minds someone who is acting foolishly, who is boasting about their knowledge—someone who knows all the answers. Now pray that this person will recognize that *the* answer, true wisdom, comes from God and God alone. Pray for God to minister quietly to this person, to make him realize his own foolishness in boasting about the world's poor imitation of the wisdom of God.

PETITION TIME—PRAYING FOR YOURSELVES: Watch out! Read the above paragraph again. Does this sound like you? If so, silently pray the same thing for yourselves! If not, pray for God's protection and sustaining power to keep you focused on wisdom that He gives.

APPLICATION TIME: List in a notebook what steps your family can take toward following God in the area of wisdom. Think, as always, about obedience. How are wisdom and obedience to God related?

FAITH TIME: Faith is our positive response to what God has said. Spend a few moments praying through your eyes of faith. Tell God the positive things you see happening in your family because of His goodness!

PRAISE AND THANKSGIVING TIME: Praise God by recognizing who He is—a wise and powerful God. And thank Him by recognizing what He has done—given us His wisdom when we pray for it.

Family Time Throughout the Week

MONDAY—Do the Family Devotion Time. Get started on the Family Worship section.

TUESDAY—Together as a family, write a letter to God acknowledging the three truths from Scripture about wisdom under the first part of the Family Worship section. Incorporate each of these truths in your family letter.

WEDNESDAY—Ask others today: what do you brag about? Jeremiah 9:24 says that the only thing we should brag about is that we know God. Decide to start bragging about knowing God! Use your other family members as practice listeners, then listen to them.

THURSDAY AND FRIDAY—Read again James 3:13-17. Discuss as a family what kind of wisdom is from above. Spend these two days demonstrating to others both in your family and outside of it the qualities that are in your lives because of this heavenly wisdom. When you see other family members demonstrate these qualities to you, make sure you affirm them in it.

WEEK 51: WORK

Family Devotion Time

ACTIVITY: A JOB WELL DONE. Bring a large piece of white tagboard to your activity time. Or you can use a calendar that has room to write each day.

Schedule out this week together as a family, listing the activities and chores and duties that need to be done around the house. List specific

> **Work** *is not just a job, it's what we have to do to be obedient.*

cleaning duties, yardwork, homework (without complaining or being asked a hundred times), special chores (cleaning a closet or the garage), small spruce-up projects (painting a bathroom, changing around furniture in a room). Make sure these are things that can be accomplished this week.

Now next to each activity, list the names of volunteers for each project. Retain veto and assignment power! Make sure the activities are divided fairly, and that mom and dad get their share too.

Agree to complete these projects and to put a sticker or check mark or some other indication on the chart or calendar when the project has been done. Anyone who completes all of his individual projects will receive an evening meal of his choice sometime during the next month (the regular cook can decide which evening). And agree that when everyone in the family completes all of their tasks, the family will get a special night out for pizza!

DISCUSSION: Now talk through these questions about work and our attitudes toward it:
• Why do you think God created work? Couldn't He just provide what we need without us working for things?

• Is work just what we do to make money? If not, what else is it?

• Can work be fun? How?

• Do you think we should always be rewarded for work we do? Is there ever a time when we might do work and not get anything for it?

God values work. The word *work* (and related words like *worked* and *working*) occur more than 700 times in the Bible. Why work? **This week's memory verse** says, in just five words, exactly what God thinks of work:

"Whatever you do, do well. . . ." —Ecclesiastes 9:10

FAMILY BIBLE TIME: When God created the world, He worked for six days. Read Genesis 1:1—2:2. Did He do what our memory verse says? What are some examples that show this?

FAMILY PRAYER TIME: This week's prayer is simple, and you can encourage your family to pray it after you do, either silently, or in unison: "God, help us to do whatever we do for Your honor and glory. Amen."

Family Worship Time (optional)

For many days an old farmer had been plowing with an ox and a mule together and working them pretty hard. The ox said to the mule, "Let's play sick today and rest a little while." But the old mule said, "No, we need to get the work done for the season is short."

But the ox played sick and the farmer brought him fresh hay and corn and made him comfortable.

When the mule came in from plowing, the ox asked how he made out. The mule said, "We didn't get as much done but we made it all right, I guess."

The ox asked, "What did the old man say about me?"

"Nothing," said the mule.

The next day the ox, thinking he had a good thing going, played sick again. When the mule came in again very tired, the ox asked, "How did it go?"

The mule said, "All right, though we don't get much done."

The ox also asked, "What did the old man say about me?"

"Nothing to me," was the reply, "but he stopped and had a long talk with the butcher."

Again, Scripture has a lot to say about work. God Himself is not exempt from labor. In John 5:17, Jesus noted that His Father was still working. If you read the Old Testament accounts of Abraham, Isaac and Jacob, you'll see that God is a working God.

In the Old Testament, being lazy about work is condemned. Proverbs 18:9 says, "A lazy man is brother to the saboteur." Proverbs 6:6 points out that we can learn about work from some of God's tiniest creatures, noting that those who are lazy should observe the industrious ant and practice her diligent ways.

In the New Testament, Paul's letters contain many references to work. Paul warns the Thessalonians to "stay away from any Christian who spends his days in laziness." Paul also reminds the people in Thessalonica how his little band of missionaries "worked hard day and night" (2 Thessalonians 3:6-8). His cure for stealing is "honest work" (Ephesians 4:28).

What often has been referred to as the "Protestant Work Ethic" may better be described as the "Biblical Work Ethic." References to the value of honest labor recur over and over throughout the Bible. The Book of Ecclesiastes contains some of our most valuable insights about work. After surveying all the varied activities of people on the face of the earth, the writer concludes, "I saw that there is nothing better for men than that they should be happy in their work" (3:22).

This tribute to work in Ecclesiastes is reinforced by the ministry of Jesus, who says in John 9:4, "All of us must quickly carry out the tasks assigned us by the one who sent me, for there is little time left before the night falls and all work comes to an end." Jesus viewed work as important to the work of His ministry, saying in John 4:34, "My nourishment comes from doing the will of God who sent me, and from finishing his work."

To gain a deeper understanding of why God values work, and why He designed us to do it, go through the following steps together.

PREPARATION TIME: List any issues any of you are wrestling with regarding work in your personal lives, your family life, your church and ministry life, and your business or school life.

WAITING TIME: During your waiting time, let God love you, search you and show each of you His desires in the area of work. Ask Him to guide you during this time of simple prayer, giving you words to complete these sentences:

"God, when I think about work, I feel Your love today, especially in the area of . . ."

"God, You have permission to reveal any wrong motive in my life when it comes to my work . . ."

"God, is there anything that I need to know about my attitude toward work as I enter this day. . . ?"

CONFESSION TIME: Are you glorifying God in your jobs? Read each question that follows and let each person rate himself:

1. Does my work ever compete with Jesus for first place in my life?

2. Have I neglected the essential relationships of life among family or friends because of my work?

3. Am I tempted to compromise what I believe in order to give in or keep a position?

4. Do I overwork as an escape from other responsibilities?

5. Is my job one in which I can glorify Jesus Christ?

6. Do I give God 10 percent of the earnings from my job?

7. Do I live a wholesome life: a combination of work and recreation, enrichment and personal growth?

8. Do the people with whom I work know that I am a Christian?

9. Am I an attractive Christian—one whom others want to know because Christ is in my life?

10. Does my employer receive from me honesty and a willingness to work faithfully for my wages?

11. Have I claimed my place of employment for the Lord? Am I a communicator of grace there?

Now spend a few moments silently confessing to God your weak areas.

BIBLE TIME: We can know that we are praying for God's will when we pray His Word back to Him. Read Ecclesiastes 11:1-10 a few times. Then close your eyes and ask God to bring a main truth to the surface in each of your hearts about work. Now pray this Scripture back to God and allow Him to minister to you.

MEDITATION TIME: After praying the Scriptures, write down in a notebook any thoughts that God has impressed upon your minds about work

INTERCESSION TIME—PRAYING FOR OTHERS: Ask God to bring to your minds people who seem dissatisfied with their work. Look at the list under the Confession Time. Pray that God will help these people see the good qualities described here in their work. Pray that the negative aspects will be minimized so that each one will be able to see the reward and blessing of their work. Also, take some time to pray especially for those who are out of work. Ask God to remind them of other things they can do to have the fulfillment that comes from working and serving God.

PETITION TIME—PRAYING FOR YOURSELVES: Reread the 11 questions above. You've already confessed your weak areas to God. Now together thank Him for the areas where each of you finds your work is rewarding and brings you blessing. Ask Him to strengthen already strong areas, and to fill in the gaps in areas where you're failing and flailing.

APPLICATION TIME: List in a notebook what steps your family can take toward obeying God in the area of work. Is being obedient itself a step to helping you get the most out of your work?

FAITH TIME: Faith is our positive response to what God has said. Spend a few moments praying through your eyes of faith. Tell God the positive things you see happening in your family because of His goodness!

PRAISE AND THANKSGIVING TIME: Praise God by recognizing who He is—a working God, our Creator. And thank Him by recognizing what He has done—given us the ability to work and the desire to please Him through what we do.

Family Time Throughout the Week

MONDAY—Complete the Family Devotion Time. Then work on the Family Worship section.

TUESDAY—Talk together as a family about how you can each get a new job. Not a different one, but a different way of looking at the work each of you has to do. Before you get upset about completing any task—at work or at home—change your attitude.

WEDNESDAY—Encourage your family to go to work for a new boss. Same job but a different reason for working. The new boss is God and every day your desire is to please Him. Even if you don't have a job, you can still work for God—through what you do in school, through your relationships with friends and family, through the ministry you have for serving others.

THURSDAY—Think and talk about this question: Did God design us to work for a living? After you've discussed this for awhile, recall that the Apostle Paul said, "For me to live is Christ." He didn't say, "For me to live is to be a tentmaker." When Jesus Christ becomes the Lord of our lives, we become free to do our jobs and do them well, to the glory of God, but not as *the* purpose of our lives. A surrender of our lives to Christ gives us perspective on our work. It gives us power to work hard and gives us priorities in which to place work where it belongs as a part of a whole life.

FRIDAY—Did everyone make it through the tasks on the family job chart? Go out for pizza!

WEEK 52: WORSHIP

Family Devotion Time

ACTIVITY: WHAT'S GOD'S NAME? Appoint someone in the family to be the secretary for the day. Ask that person to list the letters of the alphabet. Now see how many of the letters you can write beside by calling out names for God. Remember that Jesus Christ and the Holy Spirit are God too, so names that they are given in Scripture count too.

> **Worship:** Giving God the place He deserves in my life.

Think through any verses you've committed to memory, and think through praise and worship songs and hymns that you know. Often, names of God are used in worship songs to focus our attention on God. Can you think of at least one name for every letter of the alphabet?

DISCUSSION: Now talk through these questions:

• What is your favorite name for God? Why?

• By just trying to remember the names of God, does it help you to think about who God is?

• Why do you think God wants us to think about Him, to worship Him?

• Do you think we can really worship God if our relationship with Him isn't healthy?

• Without looking at the definition given here, what do you think it means to worship?

• Do we need to be with other Christians to worship God, or can we do it on our own too? Give a reason for your answer.

Worship is listening to what God says to us—through music, through words, through fellowship. Worship is also how we respond to what He speaks. Worship occurs when we respond with an openness to how God might change our lives. As this week's memory verse says:

"Shout with joy before the Lord . . . come before him, singing with joy." —Psalm 100:1, 2

FAMILY BIBLE TIME: As a family act of worship, review the memory verses you've learned together while using this devotional book. Encourage each person to recite one or two verses and explain why these are important to him.

FAMILY PRAYER TIME: Pray together about your attitudes regarding worship. Do you pay attention during worship times? Do you focus on listening to God through worship? Are you open to new kinds of worship God might use to communicate to you? Talk through these attitudes together, and then pray for each other, that God will give you a new attitude about worshipping Him.

Family Worship Time (optional)

Once there was a small boy watching a parade come through his city. The only problem was that he was on the wrong side of a six-foot high fence. He could only see the parade through a tiny knothole in the fence. He saw only what was directly in front of him at any given time. So, when the lions came by, it was scary. When the clowns came by, it was funny. When the band came by it was exciting. Then, an adult friend walked up to the boy and hoisted him up onto his shoulder, so that he sat above the fence and could see the panorama of the parade. It was only at that point that the young boy understood what a parade was really all about.

Our worship experience should provide for us exactly what that man did for the boy. Through our worship, we can gain a new perspective; we can see the "big picture," the panorama of life through God's eyes. We are reminded of His sovereignty and control over all things, and in this process an eternal perspective and understanding come to us.

In Hebrews 13:10-15, we learn the centrality of praise and worship to our Christian experience. The sequence of verses covers the Old Testament sacrifice of animals (verse 11) and the New Testament sacrifice of Jesus Christ (verse 12). Then we are exhorted to offer up a new kind of sacrifice to God in this new day and age. It is referred to as the "sacrifice of praise." (If younger children are doing this section with you, skip to Preparation Time.)

The passage doesn't say we no longer need to prepare sacrifices for our church services or even for our own quiet times of worship. We are to continue to offer up a sacrifice constantly before God. However, the sacrifice has changed. The central act of a corporate church service is to offer up a sacrifice of praise. Further, the writer describes how our praise is to be offered:

1. Continually—not just weekly or monthly.
2. Sacrificially—not just when we feel like it.
3. Audibly—not just an internal, but an external act.

Now, consider these results of authentic worship:

1. We will sense the presence of God (Psalm 22:3).
2. God will use the time both to convict and direct us (Psalm 40:3, Acts 13:2, 3).
3. He will use the time to help us understand our deliverance from evil (Psalm 32:7, 2 Chronicles 20:18-22).
4. We will experience and understand the power of God (Acts 16:25, 26).
5. We will develop sensitivity to His voice (1 Samuel 3:1-11).
6. We will gain a different, eternal perspective on life (Psalm 73:16, 17).

Take some time to work through these steps to gain a deeper understanding of why worship is so central to our relationship to God.

PREPARATION TIME: Worship is not a text, but a context; it is not an isolated experience in life, but a series of life experiences. Think about how your worship experience affects (or doesn't affect) the different areas of your lives: your personal lives, your family life, your relationships and work in your church and ministry, your life at your job or school.

WAITING TIME: Keeping in mind that worship is listening to what God says to us and our response to what He says, use this waiting time to let God love you, search you and show each of you the areas of your lives where He is encouraging you to change. Ask Him to give you honest and meaningful answers to complete these simple sentence prayers:

"God, I feel Your presence and love today, especially in the area of . . ."

"God, You have permission to reveal any misdirected worship in my life . . ."

"God, is there anything You want to show me about Yourself to deepen my worship of You today. . . ?"

CONFESSION TIME: Harvey F. Ammerman writes: "The entire message of the Gospels is related to this attitude. I think the emphasis can be condensed into a single phrase: What we worship determines what we become. If we worship material possessions, we tend to grow more materialistic. If we worship self, we become more selfish still. That is why Christ continually endeavored to direct men's worship."

Spend a few minutes confessing the things that each of you have been prone to worship that displaces God from His rightful position in your life and ministry.

BIBLE TIME: Read Isaiah 6:1-8 together. We can know that we are praying for God's will when we pray His Word back to Him. After you've read these verses slowly a few times, close your eyes and ask God to bring a main truth to the surface in each of your hearts about worship. Now pray this Scripture back to God and allow Him to minister to you. Your prayer might focus on these key words: "saw the Lord," "sitting on a lofty throne," "filled with glory," "Holy is the Lord," "Your sins are forgiven," "Lord, I'll go! Send me."

MEDITATION TIME: After praying the Scriptures, write down in a notebook any thoughts that God has impressed upon your minds about worship. Think especially about not just "going" to worship, but having the attitude that worshiping God has the potential to change you.

INTERCESSION TIME—PRAYING FOR OTHERS: Think of elderly or sick people you know who are not able to join others for a time of worshiping together. Though they may spend a lot of time worshiping God on their own, they miss out the act of worshiping with others. Pray that God will grant them a special time of worship whenever they focus on Him. Also, pray for a group of people—your family included—who might be able to take a time of worship to these people since they can't come to worship.

PETITION TIME—PRAYING FOR YOURSELVES: Do this section individually:

1. Begin by taking time to adore God. Read through Psalm 103 and declare the qualities God possesses.

2. Be personal and intimate in your worship.

3. Pray "Thy will be done," in those areas where you need to allow God to assume His Lordship in your life.

APPLICATION TIME: List in a notebook what steps your family can take toward obeying God in the area of worshiping Him. Note how being obedient is itself a step to helping you deepen your times of worship.

FAITH TIME: Faith is our positive response to what God has said. Spend a few moments praying through your eyes of faith. Tell God the positive things you see happening because of His rulership and your acknowledgment of that rulership. Ask each person to visualize himself as a child of God, seated on His lap, loving Him intimately with your words and thoughts. Embrace Him. How does He respond? Someone once said: "Those who are wise consider how God responds to their worship."

PRAISE AND THANKSGIVING TIME: Praise God by recognizing who He is—an awesome God. And thank Him by recognizing what He has done—allowed us to enter into His presence, to give Him our praise and worship.

Family Time Throughout the Week

MONDAY—Do the Family Devotion Time. If possible, get started on the Family Worship section.

TUESDAY—Talk honestly together about these questions:

Think about your own experience of worship. Be honest. Don't say what it ought to be, but what it is right now. Is it consistent? Is it a routine, cold or sterile? Do you sing? Are you intimate with God? Are you good at expressing your love to Him?

How has worship affected your perspective on life? On your difficult days? On your view of God?

Now, talk about how you'd each like your worship experience to look in the future. Talk about your beliefs about its place in your family life. Your workplace. Your ministry. How central of an act is it to you?

WEDNESDAY—The Family Worship section includes a list of the divine results of authentic worship. For the purpose of meditation and application, talk together with your family about how each of you have (or have not) experienced these results in your own personal worship experience.

THURSDAY—Reread Isaiah 6:1-8, this time aloud to your family. What an incredible worship experience Isaiah had! This passage includes stages we go through as we grow in worship. It's a step-by-step process that deepens us, from one phase to another, leading up to an obedient response to God in the end. The process of worship looks like this:

1. God is revealed to us. We get to know Him better (verses 1, 2).

2. We realize that He is holy (verses 3, 4).

3. We recognize that in this holy God's presence, we are sinners (verse 5).

4. But the way we see things changes. We begin to see things as God sees them (verses 6, 7).

5. Finally, we respond by asking God to change our lives (verse 8).

Talk about each of these stages of worship together. Which of them has God brought you through? Which of them are you experiencing now?

Now pray about taking a step forward. Ask God to reveal Himself to you in fresh ways and in new dimensions of His character, so that your life will be a response to your worship of Him. Pray together as a family for this. The next few weeks, ask each other if you are sensing changes because of your desire to move forward.

FRIDAY—Read Psalm 103 together. This psalm declares several qualities of God in a worshipful manner. It is a hymn that expresses adoration for the Lord. Take a moment and meditate on those qualities of God's character you see in Psalm 103. Then, pray these back to the Lord in corporate worship as a family, adding any other qualities of God's character to your time of worship and prayer. Be sure to praise God for His qualities, and for the way they affect and change your lives.

A FAMILY TIME CELEBRATION!

You made it! Wow! This is a huge accomplishment. And how neat to end your family's time of study with the subject of worship.

Worship is also a celebration. A celebration of God. A celebration of how He relates to us and how we relate to Him. You've grown a lot closer to God through this study, and your family's relationship with God has changed.

Plan a special time of family worship—a celebration—to take place during the next two weeks. Head out of the house if you can. Go to a park or a beach. Or if the weather doesn't allow, give your home a different feel by dimming the lights and worshiping by candlelight.

Announce today that you will be gathering to hold this worship and celebration time. Pick a date that works for everyone. Between now and then, every member of the family should decide how he wants to take part in your family worship service. Someone may want to bring a favorite item that was made during the family activity time. Someone else may just want to talk about how doing this study has changed him. Someone may want to recite a favorite memory verse, or a prayer written during one of the daily activities of Family Time Throughout the Week.

Encourage creativity. Remember that God wants our worship to include new and fresh ways that He can use to communicate to us. Be open and have fun as you celebrate God, and the things He has taught you throughout this year of study together.